Carsten Ihlemann

Reasoning in Combinations of Theories

Carsten Ihlemann

Reasoning in Combinations of Theories

A Study of Locality

Südwestdeutscher Verlag für Hochschulschriften

Impressum/Imprint (nur für Deutschland/ only for Germany)
Bibliografische Information der Deutschen Nationalbibliothek: Die Deutsche Nationalbibliothek verzeichnet diese Publikation in der Deutschen Nationalbibliografie; detaillierte bibliografische Daten sind im Internet über http://dnb.d-nb.de abrufbar.

Alle in diesem Buch genannten Marken und Produktnamen unterliegen warenzeichen-, marken- oder patentrechtlichem Schutz bzw. sind Warenzeichen oder eingetragene Warenzeichen der jeweiligen Inhaber. Die Wiedergabe von Marken, Produktnamen, Gebrauchsnamen, Handelsnamen, Warenbezeichnungen u.s.w. in diesem Werk berechtigt auch ohne besondere Kennzeichnung nicht zu der Annahme, dass solche Namen im Sinne der Warenzeichen- und Markenschutzgesetzgebung als frei zu betrachten wären und daher von jedermann benutzt werden dürften.

Verlag: Südwestdeutscher Verlag für Hochschulschriften GmbH & Co. KG
Dudweiler Landstr. 99, 66123 Saarbrücken, Deutschland
Telefon +49 681 37 20 271-1, Telefax +49 681 37 20 271-0
Email: info@svh-verlag.de
Zugl.: Saarbrücken, Universität des Saarlandes, Diss., 2010

Herstellung in Deutschland:
Schaltungsdienst Lange o.H.G., Berlin
Books on Demand GmbH, Norderstedt
Reha GmbH, Saarbrücken
Amazon Distribution GmbH, Leipzig
ISBN: 978-3-8381-2465-0

Imprint (only for USA, GB)
Bibliographic information published by the Deutsche Nationalbibliothek: The Deutsche Nationalbibliothek lists this publication in the Deutsche Nationalbibliografie; detailed bibliographic data are available in the Internet at http://dnb.d-nb.de.

Any brand names and product names mentioned in this book are subject to trademark, brand or patent protection and are trademarks or registered trademarks of their respective holders. The use of brand names, product names, common names, trade names, product descriptions etc. even without a particular marking in this works is in no way to be construed to mean that such names may be regarded as unrestricted in respect of trademark and brand protection legislation and could thus be used by anyone.

Publisher: Südwestdeutscher Verlag für Hochschulschriften GmbH & Co. KG
Dudweiler Landstr. 99, 66123 Saarbrücken, Germany
Phone +49 681 37 20 271-1, Fax +49 681 37 20 271-0
Email: info@svh-verlag.de

Printed in the U.S.A.
Printed in the U.K. by (see last page)
ISBN: 978-3-8381-2465-0

Copyright © 2011 by the author and Südwestdeutscher Verlag für Hochschulschriften GmbH & Co. KG and licensors
All rights reserved. Saarbrücken 2011

Meinen Eltern gewidmet

Acknowledgements

I am grateful to a number of people for their contribution to this dissertation.

First of all I would like to thank my advisor Viorica Sofronie-Stokkermans for her scientific and personal support. Without her unstinting encouragement and advice this thesis would not have been possible. Over the years I have become a better mathematician under her guidance.

Many thanks also to Christoph Weidenbach for creating an environment conducive to research, to Bernd Finkbeiner and Silvio Ghilardi for agreeing to be on the reading committee and to my colleagues Thomas Hillenbrand and Swen Jacobs for fruitful discussions.

My personal thanks go foremost to my parents for everything they have done for me.

Many thanks also to my friends Annette Soelter, Frank Quante, Keith Becker (in order of appearance) and my sister Caren for sustaining me through the process.

Zusammenfassung

Weil die Komplexität von Systemen und Programmen in der Informatik stetig zunimmt, ist einerseits das Wissen, inwieweit diese Systeme korrekt sind, immer wichtiger, und andererseits ist diese Korrektheit immer schwieriger zu zeigen.

Ein naheliegender Ansatz, mit Komplexität umzugehen, ist das Teile-und-Herrsche-Prinzip: Hat man effiziente Techniken zur Verifikation von Teilen des Systems zur Verfügung, so möchte man möglichst viele dieser Techniken zur Verifikation des gesamten Systems verwenden.

Mathematisch gesehen stellt sich daher die Frage, ob und wie man aus zwei Entscheidungsverfahren für (Fragmente von) Theorien der Logik erster Stufe T_1 und T_2 ein Entscheidungsverfahren für (ein Fragment) ihre(r) Vereinigung $T_1 \cup T_2$ bekommt. Selbst im einfachsten Fall, in dem T_1 und T_2 keinerlei Symbole gemein haben, man sich auf das universelle (quantorenfreie) Fragment beschränkt und Entscheidungsverfahren für die universellen Fragmente beider Theorien bekannt sind, ist es im allgemeinen nicht möglich, ein Entscheidungsverfahren für das universelle Fragment der Vereinigung beider Theorien zu finden, wohl aber, wenn man zusätzliche Anforderungen an diese Theorien stellt, die in der Praxis oft erfüllt sind ([NO79]).

Es ist jedoch für die Praxis nicht ausreichend, nur Kombinationen von disjunkten Theorien zu betrachten. Diese Arbeit befaßt sich daher mit der Kombination von Theorien, die nicht disjunkt sind, d. h. Symbole oder sogar eine Untertheorie teilen. Dabei unterscheiden wir zwei Fälle: Theorieerweiterungen und Theoriekombinationen. Im Fall der Theorieerweiterung ist eine Hintergrundtheorie gegeben, die um neue Funktionen und deren Axiomen erweitert wird. Theoriekombinationen sind eine Verallgemeinerung dieses Falles. Hier betrachtet man zwei oder mehr Erweiterungen derselben Hintergrundtheorie.

Sowohl bei Theorieerweiterung als auch bei Theoriekombinationen, ist der gewählte Ansatz derjenige der *Lokalität*. Hierbei ist der Suchraum für Gegenbeispiele einer Beweisanfrage auf diejenigen Instanzen der Theorieerweiterung beschränkt, in denen die Terme so instanziiert werden, daß sie nicht nur variablenfrei, sondern auch Terme der Beweisanfrage sind. Ist eine Theorieerweiterung lokal, so ist eine hierarchische Reduzierung stets möglich: Für eine Beweisanfrage in der erweiterten Sprache läßt sich eine gleichwertige Beweisanfrage in der Hintergrundsprache angeben. Diese Reduzierung geschieht ohne Verlust der Vollständigkeit – die neue Beweisanfrage ist unerfüllbar (hinsichtlich der Hintergrundtheorie) genau dann, wenn die ursprüngliche Beweisanfrage unerfüllbar ist (hinsichtlich der erweiterten Theorie). Des weiteren läßt sich diese Beweisanfrage der Hintergrundtheorie konstruktiv angeben, und zwar in polynomieller Zeit. Dies und die Tatsache, daß viele der Verifikationsprobleme, die in der Praxis auftreten, als Beweisanfragen einer lokalen Theorieerweiterung aufgefaßt werden können, machen den Ansatz der Lokalität höchst relevant für die Praxis.

In dieser Arbeit wird zunächst die Theorie der lokalen Theorieerweiterungen dargelegt; und es werden einige Anwendungsbeispiele gegeben, nämlich monotone und quasi-monotone Funktionen als lokale Erweiterung. Danach werden *Datenstrukturen* betrachtet, die Lokalitätseigenschaften aufweisen.

Es zeigt sich, daß ein großes Teilstück der Theorie der Arrays lokal ist. Allerdings lokal im erweiterten Sinne: Nur wenn man mehr Instanzen zuläßt, als bei der Standardlokalität vorgesehen, läßt sich die Reduzierung von Beweisanfragen durchführen. Dies führt zum Begriff der *minimalen Lokalität*, der diesen erweiterten Anforderungen Rechnung trägt.

In einem Abstraktionsschritt wird daraufhin der Begriff der Ψ-Lokalität entwickelt, wobei Ψ hier ein Hüllenoperator auf Grundtermen ist. Es wird gezeigt, daß Ψ-Lokalität den Begriff der minimalen Lokalität verallgemeinert.

Die zweite zentrale Datenstruktur, die ein wichtiges lokales Teilstück enthält, ist die Theorie der Zeiger, welche die Grundlage aller dynamischen Datenstrukturen bildet. Auch für die Theorie der Zeiger ist ein etwas anderer Begriff der Lokalität vonnöten, derjenige der *stabilen Lokalität*. Zwar läßt sich dieser Begriff nicht unter den der Ψ-Lokalität subsumieren, was daran liegt, daß in diesem Falle auch eine andere Semantik zugrundegelegt werden muß, aber die Ψ-Lokalität stellt dennoch das Muster bereit, welches es erlaubt, auch diesen Fall zu handhaben.

Danach wenden wir uns dem Fall der Theoriekombinationen zu. Zunächst wird die nötige Modelltheorie entwickelt. Es zeigt sich, daß der Begriff der Modellvollständigkeit und derjenige der Amalgamierung von Modellen von zentraler Bedeutung sind. Wir betrachten zunächst den Fall der Kombination zweier Theorien, deren Schnitt eine universelle Theorie ist, die eine Modellvervollständigung besitzt, mit der Eigenschaft, daß jedes Modell einer der beiden Theorien sich stets erweitern läßt zu einem Modell dieser Theorie und der Modellvervollständigung des Schnittes. Schließlich betrachten wir den Fall der Kombinationen von lokalen und Ψ-lokalen Theorien.

Zum Schluß dieser Arbeit stellen wir eine Implementierung des hierarchischen Schließens für lokale Theorieerweiterungen vor: das Programm H-PILoT. Die hierarchische Reduzierung von Beweisaufgaben ist in jüngster Zeit besonders relevant geworden, weil leistungsfähige Beweiser für gängige Hintergrundtheorien entwickelt worden sind. Diese sogenannten SMT-Beweiser erlauben die effiziente Behandlung von Theorien wie z. B. der linearen Arithmetik der ganzen oder der reellen Zahlen. H-PILoT ist unter anderem an mehrere dieser SMT-Beweiser gekoppelt, um ein effizientes Werkzeug für Theorieerweiterungen über einer dieser Hintergrundtheorien zur Verfügung zu stellen. H-PILoT hat Anwendungen in der Mathematik, bei mehrwertigen Logiken, bei der Verifikation von Datenstrukturen und in der Verifikation komplexer Systeme gefunden.

Kurzzusammenfassung

Verifikationsaufgaben kombinieren oft verschiedene Theorien. Eine naheliegende Frage ist, ob man Entscheidungsverfahren für die Einzeltheorien auf die gesamte Theorie übertragen kann. In den Fällen, wo das möglich ist, hat man eine mächtige Technik zur Hand, um mit komplexen Theorien effizient umgehen zu können.

Der Ansatz, der in dieser Arbeit betrachtet wird, ist stets der einer Hintergrundtheorie, die durch eine oder mehrere Theorien erweitert wird. Die Frage ist dann, ob und wann sich eine gegebene Beweisanfrage bezüglich der Theorieerweiterung effektiv auf eine äquivalente Beweisanfrage bezüglich der Hintergrundtheorie reduzieren läßt. Ein Fall, in dem diese Reduzierung immer möglich ist, ist derjenige der *lokalen Theorieerweiterungen*.

Die Theorie der lokalen Erweiterungen wird entwickelt, und es werden einige Anwendungen für monotone Funktionen gegeben. Danach wird die Theorie der lokalen Erweiterungen verallgemeinert, um mit Datenstrukturen umgehen zu können, die Lokalitätseigenschaften aufweisen. Es wird gezeigt, daß sowohl ein geeignetes Fragment der Theorie der Arrays wie auch der Theorie der Zeiger lokal im erweiterten Sinne sind. Schließlich wird der Fall mehrerer Theorieerweiterungen betrachtet. Insbesondere wird ein *Modularitätsresultat* gezeigt, das besagt, daß unter gewissen Umständen die Lokalität der einzelnen Erweiterungen hinreichend ist, um die Lokalität der gesamten Erweiterung zu gewährleisten.

Die oben erwähnte Reduzierung von Beweisaufgaben ist in jüngster Zeit besonders relevant geworden, weil leistungsfähige Beweiser für gängige Hintergrundtheorien entwickelt worden sind. Diese sogenannten SMT-Beweiser behandeln Theorien wie z. B. lineare Arithmetik der ganzen oder der reellen Zahlen effektiv. Als Teil der vorgelegten Arbeit wurde ein Programm namens *H-PILoT* entwickelt, welches die Reduzierung von Beweisaufgaben für lokale Theorien durchführt. H-PILoT hat Anwendungen in der Mathematik, bei mehrwertigen Logiken, bei der Verifikation von Datenstrukturen und in der Verifikation komplexer Systeme gefunden.

Abstract

Verification problems are often expressed in a language which mixes several theories. A natural question to ask is whether one can use decision procedures for individual theories to construct a decision procedure for the union theory. In the cases where this is possible one has a powerful method at hand to handle complex theories effectively.

The setup considered in this thesis is that of one base theory which is extended by one or more theories. The question is if and when a given ground satisfiability problem in the extended setting can be effectively reduced to an equi-satisfiable problem over the base theory. A case where this reductive approach is always possible is that of so-called *local theory extensions*.

The theory of local extensions is developed and some applications concerning monotone functions are given. Then the theory of local theory extensions is generalized in order to deal with data structures that exhibit local behavior. It will be shown that a suitable fragment of both the theory of arrays and the theory of pointers is local in this broader sense. Finally, the case of more than one theory extension is discussed. In particular, a *modularity* result is given that under certain circumstances the locality of each of the extensions lifts to locality of the entire extension.

The reductive approach outlined above has become particularly relevant in recent years due to the rise of powerful solvers for background theories common in verification tasks. These so-called SMT-solvers effectively handle theories such as real linear or integer arithmetic. As part of this thesis, a program called *H-PILoT* was implemented which carries out reductive reasoning for local theory extensions. H-PILoT found applications in mathematics, multiple-valued logics, data-structures and reasoning in complex systems.

Contents

1 Introduction   1
     1.1 Hierarchical Reasoning 2
     1.2 Locality in Data Structures 3
     1.3 Contributions of the Thesis 3
     1.4 Related Work 6
     1.5 Structure of the Thesis 8

2 Preliminaries   9
     2.1 First-order Logic 9
     2.2 Partial Algebras and Partial Semantics 16
     2.3 Term Abstraction 24
     2.4 Extensions of Theories 25
     2.5 Purification, Reduction and Flattening 27

3 Local Theory Extensions   31
     3.1 Locality Implies Embeddability 32
     3.2 Embeddability Implies Locality 33
     3.3 Stable Locality 35
     3.4 Embeddability and Stable Locality 36
     3.5 Decidability and Complexity 37
     3.6 Applications 38
         3.6.1 Definitional Extensions 38
         3.6.2 Monotone Functions 40
         3.6.3 Bounded Functions 46

4 Generalized Locality   49
     4.1 Minimal Locality 49
     4.2 The Array Property Fragment 51
     4.3 Example 55
     4.4 The Λ-Array Property Fragment 58
     4.5 Example 60
     4.6 Ψ-Locality 63
     4.7 Arrays Revisited 70
     4.8 Pointers Directly 71

5 Combinations of Theories — 75

- 5.1 Model Completeness and Quantifier Elimination 75
- 5.2 Combinations of Theories 80
- 5.3 Elementary Amalgamation 81
- 5.4 Combinations of Local Theories 85
- 5.5 Combinations of Ψ-Local Theories 88

6 Implementation: H-PILoT — 93

- 6.1 Structure of the Program 95
- 6.2 Modules of H-PILoT 96
- 6.3 Application Areas 98
- 6.4 Examples 99
- 6.5 Arrays 105
- 6.6 Global Constraints 108
- 6.7 Types 109
- 6.8 Pointers 110
- 6.9 Extended Locality 113
- 6.10 Clausification 115
- 6.11 System Evaluation 116
- 6.12 A Case Study 119
- 6.13 Parameters of H-PILoT 120
- 6.14 Error Handling 121
- 6.15 A Run Example of H-PILoT 121
- 6.16 Model Generation and Visualization 126
- 6.17 The Input Grammar 129

7 Conclusion — 133

Bibliography — 135

Index — 144

Chapter 1

Introduction

As the complexity of systems and programs in computer science steadily increases, establishing the correctness of these systems becomes ever more important yet more difficult to show. Verification problems in computer science often mix several theories. For example, there could be a type of abstract data structure such as lists, arrays or queues and the type of elements stored in this data structure; or one could have heterogeneous constraints over data whose joint consistency needs to be checked.

A natural approach to take here is a building-block or modular one. Provided one has tools or methods available that allow one to effectively handle the theories separately, when and how is it possible to use these tools for the union of these different theories? In the cases where this is possible one has a powerful method at hand for handling complex theories effectively.

From a logical point of view, the question, then, is if and how one can get a decision procedure for (a fragment of) a union of first-order theories $T_1 \cup T_2$ from decision procedures for (fragments of) the theories T_1 and T_2. Many real-life verification tasks in computer science can be considered as a validity problem over such a union of theories, i.e., does $T_1 \cup T_2 \models \varphi$ hold, for some formula φ in the combined language? Often we may additionally assume that the above formula φ is universal or, equivalently, quantifier-free and that T_1 and T_2 are themselves universal theories.

Hence, it would already be quite useful to obtain a decision procedure for the universal fragment of the union theory from decision procedures for the universal fragments of T_1 and T_2. However, even in the restricted case where the theories T_1 and T_2 have no symbols in common, the universal fragment of the union $T_1 \cup T_2$ is in general not decidable (cf. [BGN+06a]). One has to impose additional restrictions on T_1 and T_1 in order to get a decision procedure for the universal fragment of their union. In practice, one can often meet these restrictions ([NO79], [Opp80a]).

Even so, it is not enough for real-life verification problems to only consider theory combinations over disjoint signatures. This thesis will consider the case where the theories T_1 and T_2 are not disjoint: they may share symbols or even have a common subtheory. We distinguish two cases, *theory extensions* and *theory combinations*. In the case of a theory extension we have a base theory T_0 which is extended by some new function symbols together with their axioms. Theory combinations generalize this setup. There we consider two or more theory extensions over a common base theory.

The approach taken in this thesis towards theory extensions and theory combinations is that of *locality*. In local extensions the reduction of a proof task to the underlying theory is always possible. This makes the approach relevant to real life verification problems because off-the-shelf provers can be used as decision procedures.

The theory of *locality* was introduced by Givan and McAllester ([GM92], [McA93]). It was generalized to equational theories and related to a semantical approach towards the uniform word problem going back to Skolem ([Sko20]), Evans ([Eva51]) and Burris ([Bur95]) by Harald Ganzinger in [Gan01]. The theory of *local theory extensions* was developed by Viorica Sofronie-Stokkermans in a series of papers [SS05, SS10, SS06a, SS07].

The main idea in locality is to limit the search space for counterexamples (hence the name). It is expedient to reformulate the above validity problem for a universal formula φ to an equivalent satisfiability problem. We may assume that φ is in disjunctive normal form. The validity problem $T_1 \cup T_2 \models \varphi$ is equivalent to the satisfiability problem $T_1 \cup T_2, \neg \varphi \models \bot$. Using Skolemization for the existential variables and introducing new constants for the free ones, we obtain a set of ground clauses G and a satisfiability problem $T_1 \cup T_2 \cup G \models \bot$, such that $T_1 \cup T_2 \cup G$ is satisfiable if and only if $T_1 \cup T_2, \neg \varphi$ is.

Suppose now, in particular, that we have a theory extension $T_0 \subseteq T_0 \cup \mathcal{K}$, where $\mathcal{K}$ is a set of (universally closed) clauses axiomatizing some new function symbols and we want to know whether $T_0 \cup \mathcal{K} \cup G$ is satisfiable for a given set G of ground clauses (in the extended signature plus additional constants). If it is the case that $\mathcal{K}$ extends our background theory in a local manner, we can answer this question by considering only those instances of $\mathcal{K}$ in which each extension term already appeared as ground term of $\mathcal{K}$ or G.

1.1 Hierarchical Reasoning

Not only does the locality of a theory extension $T_0 \subseteq T_0 \cup \mathcal{K}$ allow one to shed universal quantifiers of the clauses in $\mathcal{K}$, while answering a given satisfiability problem[1] $T_0 \cup \mathcal{K} \cup G$, but it also makes *hierarchical reasoning* possible: we may carry out a full-fledged reduction to the base theory without loss of completeness. Provided that an extension $T_0 \subseteq T_0 \cup \mathcal{K}$ is local, we may reduce a satisfiability problem of the above form $T_0 \cup \mathcal{K} \cup G \models \bot$ to a satisfiability problem $T_0 \cup \mathcal{K}_0 \cup G' \models \bot$, where neither $\mathcal{K}_0$ nor G' contains any new function symbols, G' is a set of ground clauses (with additional constants) and it holds that $T_0 \cup \mathcal{K} \cup G$ is satisfiable if and only $T_0 \cup \mathcal{K}_0 \cup G'$ is. Further, this reduction can always be carried out in polynomial time. This gives us decidability results for local theory extensions ([SS05]). If all variables in the extension clauses appear below new function symbols and the universal fragment of the underlying theory is decidable, then the universal fragment of the extension is. (Otherwise the $\forall\exists$-fragment of the underlying theory must be decidable in order to decide the universal fragment of the extension.)

Hierarchical reasoning has become particularly relevant in recent years due to the availability of powerful provers for common background theories. These so-called SMT-solvers, such as Yices ([DdM06]), CVC3 ([BT07]) and Z3 ([dMB08]), are able to handle theories prevalent in verification, e.g., real or integer linear arithmetic, very efficiently. Their power notwithstanding, it is one-sided: SMT solvers are very efficient for testing the satisfiability of ground formulas over standard theories, but use heuristics in the presence of universally quantified formulas, hence cannot

---
[1]If all variables appear below a new function symbol we even get ground instances of $\mathcal{K}$.

detect satisfiability of all such formulas. Aside from its general usefulness, hierarchical reasoning is therefore crucial for satisfiable problems ([ISS09]).

1.2 Locality in Data Structures

In two recent papers, locality properties of two ubiquitous data structures have been discovered and studied. The data structures are lists and arrays. Necula and McPeak ([MN05]) study local equality axioms for dynamic data structures such as linked lists in order to gain a decision procedure for some global properties of these data structures. They consider shape properties which they call *local* that have the property that any counterexample will be local in nature, that is in the neighborhood of the counterexample.

In a similar vein, Bradley, Manna and Sipma ([BMS06]) study a decidable fragment of the theory of arrays, the so-called *array property fragment*. They show how the satisfiability of an array property fragment formula can be reduced to satisfiability of a quantifier-free formula of the underlying theory of elements and indices. They do this by finding a sufficient set of instances for the universally quantified parts of the problem.

These locality results for data structures can be subsumed, and thereby unified, under the notion of locality.

1.3 Contributions of the Thesis

This thesis contributes to the theory and practice of local reasoning in the following ways.

1. It relaxes and demarcates more precisely the criteria for showing locality.

2. It gives generalizations of locality, viz. minimal and Ψ-locality.

3. It gives locality results for extensions of theories with monotone or antitone functions.

4. It shows how to subsume a decidable fragment of the theory of arrays under this extended notion of locality.

5. It gives a direct proof for an information exchange lemma of Ghilardi ([Ghi03a, Ghi04]): Two theories which are compatible with their mutual intersection have $\exists$-$\forall$-Interpolation.

6. It gives new criteria for the combination of local theories.

7. It gives a combination result for Ψ-local theories.

8. It gives an implementation for hierarchical reasoning in local theory extensions.

We describe the contributions in more detail, combining some of them under a single heading for ease of exposition.

Variants of locality and criteria for showing locality (1–2). The main technique for showing the locality of a theory extension is the embeddability of partial models of the extension into total ones ([SS05], extending [Gan01]). For this criterion to be applicable, technical requirements have to be met: the extension clauses $\mathcal{K}$ must be *flat* and *linear*. Flatness of the extension clauses means that only variables may appear below new function symbols. We were able to relax this constraint. It is sufficient that the extension clauses are *quasi-flat*: variable and ground terms not containing new function symbols may now appear below a new function symbol.

The theory extensions we consider as candidates for locality are of a certain form. Theories are to be extended by (universally closed) clauses which axiomatize new function symbols. Our initial conjecture was that this syntactical restriction to universally closed clauses could be relaxed while embeddability of partial models of the extended theory into total models of the extended theory would still imply locality. This turned out to be not the case. Even relaxing the syntactical requirements of the extending formulas from universally closed clauses to universal formulas in negation normal form vitiates this implication as we will show. We will give an example of a theory extension by universal formulas in negation normal form with the property that its partial models can always be embedded into total ones but which fails to be local.

Locality for monotone functions (3). An important application of local reasoning are monotone functions ([SSI07a, SSI07b]), not least due to its connection to sortedness in data structures. Here we extend a base theory containing a partial order $\leq$ with new functions. These functions all comply with some monotonicity axiom of the form $\forall x, \forall y.\ x \leq y \to f(x) \leq f(y)$. We consider these axiom types in full generality: A function f can also be antitone as in $\forall x, \forall y.\ x \geq y \to f(x) \leq f(y)$ or monotone in some components, antitone in others and free in yet others as in

$$\forall x, \forall x', \forall y, \forall z, \forall z'.\ x \leq x' \land z \geq z' \to f(x, y, z) \leq f(x', y, z').$$

We will show that all extensions of a base theory containing a partially ordered set with functions that are monotone in this general sense are local.

Generalized locality and locality in data structures (4). For some applications more instances of the extension clauses $\mathcal{K}$ are needed than those used in standard locality, in order to eliminate universal quantifiers of $\mathcal{K}$. An example is a fragment of the theory of arrays, the so-called *array property fragment* ([BMS06]) mentioned above. To handle this locality phenomenon in arrays, we developed the notion of *minimal locality*. It also lead to the development of a general treatment of this and similar cases, viz. Ψ-locality, here Ψ is a closure operator on ground terms ([IJSS08]), which generates all the instances of $\mathcal{K}$ needed. We develop the theory of Ψ-locality and show how this subsumes the notion of minimal locality. The pointer fragment of Necula and McPeak ([MN05]) referred to above also exhibits a sort of Ψ-locality but with a different underlying semantics, rendering the use of a term closure operator inherently more complicated. However Ψ-locality can still be used as a template for solving practical verification tasks involving dynamic data structures as we will illustrate.

Information exchange (5). Another way of viewing the joint unsatisfiability of two theories is as an *interpolation* problem. Recall our setup. We have two theories T_1 and T_2 over respective signatures Σ_1 and Σ_2, sharing some signature Σ_0 and maybe also a Σ_0-theory T_0. We wanted to answer the question whether $T_1 \cup T_2, \varphi(\bar{a}) \models \bot$, where φ is a quantifier-free ground sentence in the combined signature $\Sigma_1 \cup \Sigma_2$ with some fresh constants $\bar{a}$. By using yet more fresh constants, we can split up

φ into a Σ_1-part and a Σ_2-part, giving us an equi-satisfiable problem $T_1 \cup T_2, \varphi_1(\bar{a}, \bar{b}), \varphi_2(\bar{a}, \bar{c}) \models \bot$, where $\varphi_i(\bar{x}, \bar{y})$ is a Σ_i-formula for $i = 1, 2$. By Craig's Interpolation theorem, we know that there is a Σ_0-formula $\chi(\bar{x})$ such that $T_1, \varphi_1(\bar{a}, \bar{b}) \models \chi(\bar{a})$ and $T_2, \varphi_2(\bar{a}, \bar{b}) \models \neg \chi(\bar{a})$. For verification purposes this is not quite good enough, because we want χ to be quantifier-free at the least (cf. [Tin03]), which in general it will not be. Seen as an interpolation problem, we therefore want to solve the existential-universal interpolation problem with respect to $T_1 \cup T_2$ (cf. [Bac75]): finding an open (= quantifier-free) formula to interpolate between the existential formula φ_1 and the universal formula $\neg \varphi_2$ (w.r.t. $T_1 \cup T_2$). Recently, this problem has gotten fresh impetus from the work of Ghilardi ([Ghi03a, Ghi04]). We will present a direct proof for one of his theorems, viz. that the combined theory has existential-universal interpolation given that both theories are compatible with their joint subtheory.

Combining local theories (6–7). Considering the setting where we have two local theory extensions $T_1 \supseteq T_0, T_2 \supseteq T_0$ over a common base theory T_0, we examine criteria which would establish the locality of the union extension $T_1 \cup T_2 \supseteq T_0$. In particular, we would like to lift the above criterion for locality (embeddability of partial models implies locality) to this setup. This requires us to extrapolate the embeddability of the separate models T_i ($i = 1, 2$) to the embeddability of models of the union $T_1 \cup T_2$.

Pioneering work in this area was done by Viorica Sofronie-Stokkermans ([SS10, SS07]). Assuming that T_0 is extended with clauses that are flat and linear in both cases and that T_1 and T_2 do not share any more symbols except those in T_0, it was shown there that embeddability of partial models of T_1 and of T_2 into total ones is enough to ensure the locality of the extension $T_0 \subseteq T_1 \cup T_2$ provided that one of the following conditions holds.

(1) Partial models of T_1 and T_2 can be embedded into total ones such that the reducts of the partial and the total model of T_i to the base language are isomorphic ($i = 1, 2$).

(2) Partial models of T_1 and T_2 can be embedded into total ones such that the (reducts of the) partial and the total model of T_1 are isomorphic and all variables in T_1 appear below extension function symbols.

(3) Partial models of T_1 and T_2 can be embedded into total ones and all variables in both T_1 and T_2 appear below extension function symbols and T_0 is an $\forall\exists$-theory.

We were able to add to this list in the following way (these results are published in [ISS10a]). Under the same assumptions as above, the extension $T_0 \subseteq T_1 \cup T_2$ is local provided that one of the following conditions holds.

(4) Partial models of T_1 and T_2 can be embedded into total ones such that the embeddings restricted to the base language are elementary.

(5) Partial models of T_1 and T_2 can be embedded into total ones and T_0 is model complete.

(6) Partial models of T_1 and T_2 can be embedded into total ones such that the embedding of the partial model of T_1 restricted to the base language is elementary and all variables in T_1 appear below extension function symbols.

A natural generalization is the question when the combination of Ψ-local theories is Ψ-local again. We were able to establish the following positive result. Suppose we have Ψ_i-local theory extensions $T_0 \supseteq T_i$, $i = 1, 2$ and we again assume that all the extension clauses are flat and linear. Let Ψ_3 be any closure operator on ground terms with $\Psi_3 \supseteq \Psi_1 \cup \Psi_2$. Suppose that partial models (in which certain additional terms are defined) of both T_1 and T_2 can be embedded into total ones, all variables in both extension theories appear below extension function symbols and that T_0 is an $\forall\exists$-theory, then $T_0 \subseteq T_1 \cup T_2$ is Ψ_3-local.

Implementation (8). We present the program H-PILoT (Hierarchical Proving by Instantiation in Local theory Extensions)[2] which was developed as part of this thesis ([ISS09]). As the name indicates, H-PILoT implements the hierarchical reduction described above for local theory extensions. It also fully incorporates local reasoning for data structures (arrays and pointers). It automatically checks whether a given problem is in the fragment of those data structures which are known to be local. By this means, H-PILoT provides a decision procedure for these fragments (it also detects satisfiability of a given problem).

Recently, H-PILoT has proven its practical usefulness in a large case study involving a train controller ([FIJSS10]). In the case study, an entire hierarchy of local extensions was employed together with reasoning about pointers. In particular, H-PILoT's ability to provide a model for satisfiable problems was useful for refining the axiomatization.

1.4 Related Work

Besides the work already cited we would like to indicate other related works regarding the combination of theories.

Extending Nelson-Oppen. In their seminal papers, Nelson and Oppen [NO79, Opp80a] showed how decision procedures for the universal fragment of theories can be lifted to a decision procedure for the universal fragment of their union provided that a) the signature of the theories are disjoint and b) both theories are stably infinite, i.e., have an infinite model property for universal formulas. Considerable effort has been expended to relax either requirement.

In [Gan02], Ganzinger lifted the requirement of stable infinity for both theories by allowing arbitrary theories to be combined with the theory of equality. This result was extended by Tinelli, Ranise and Zarba ([TZ05, RRZ05]) to the extension of arbitrary theories with so called *shiny* or *polite* theories.

Regarding the other requirement, in [TR03] Tinelli and Ringeissen allow for the combination of non-disjoint theories sharing so-called constructors.

When using a modular approach towards a satisfiability problem, the question is of how much information needs to be exchanged between the different modules. This question has been studied by Silvio Ghilardi in his work on information exchange in [Ghi03a, Ghi04] (cf. Section 1.3.(5)). Information exchange between (non-disjoint) theories can be restricted to syntactically simple formulas provided the shared theory admits a model completion (cf. Section 5.2).

In [GSSW04, GSSW06] superposition is used as a modular approach to combinations of theories

---

[2] The name was suggested to us by Viorica Sofronie-Stokkermans.

over a common base theory. Function (symbols) which are not shared between the theories are considered to be partial. The superposition calculus presented only requires pure inferences, i.e., inferences in which only one type of extension functions occur.

This gives rise to an interesting result for the case of theory extensions where only one extension over a base theory is considered. The variant of the calculus presented (constraint superposition) is shown to be complete for *shallow theory extensions*, such as extensions by tail-recursive functions. This is due to the fact that in this case a partial model can always be completed to a total one.

In [Hil04] the Nelson-Oppen combination procedure is recast into a superposition framework. This angle could be employed together with a chaining calculus for transitive relations in order to cope with ordered data types. In [ARR03] the authors show that superposition-based modular reasoning is possible in a special case of combinations of theories (lists and arrays), and amounts to propagating equalities between constants as in the Nelson-Oppen combination method. More general results are given in [ABRS05] where a modularity theorem (based also on rewriting) for combinations of theories with no shared function symbols is proved.

Application to data structures. Decision procedures for data structures employing a combination framework have been much researched in recent years. Already in [Opp80b] a decision procedure for the universal fragment of recursively defined data structures such as lists was given.

In [FRZ04], the validity of universal sentences in the combination of (flat) lists with an element theory T was shown to be decidable. This extends the combination method of Nelson and Oppen ([NO79], [Opp80a]) but drops the requirement of stable infiniteness for the element theory and relaxes the disjointness requirement in the sense that there might be a length function for lists in the combined signature of lists and integers, say.

Inspired by the work of Bradley, Manna and Sipma ([BMS06]) which gives a decision procedure for a fragment of the theory of arrays, Ghilardi, Nicolini, Ranise and Zucchelli also consider decision procedures for arrays ([GNRZ06]). Their approach mainly differs form Bradley, Manna and Sipma's and ours in that they only consider deciding the satisfiability of quantifier-free formulas over the combined theory. On the other hand, they were able to solve an open problem in [BMS06] (injective arrays). Their angle is also different in that they use more a modular than a reductive approach: their main thrust is to combine decision procedures for arrays with a decision procedure for their indices (such as Presburger arithmetic).

In [GNRZ08] the same authors use decision procedures for arrays for the model checking of properties of array-based systems. Array-based systems serve there as an abstraction of infinite state systems. States and transitions of those systems are presented as quantified first-order formulas of a restricted form. The satisfiability of those formulas can be decided by augmenting SMT-provers by suitable instantiation strategies. To be able to handle restricted universal quantification is essential in this context.

In [ZSM05, ZSM06] decision procedures for the quantifier-free and the first-order theory of recursive data structures with length function and integer constraints, such as lists with length function, are presented. From a different angle - using a rewriting approach - there have also been decidability results for the satisfiability problem for data structures, such as lists, established recently ([ARR01, ARR03, ABRS05, BGN+06b, BE07a, BE07b, ABRS09]).

Instantiation strategies. In [GdM09] Ge and de Moura try to overcome the inherent weakness of SMT-solvers concerning satisfiable proof tasks for a restricted class of problems. They consider complete instantiation strategies for universal clauses in the language of arithmetic plus free functions, where variables may only appear below those free functions. That is, they look at a set of instances F^* for a set of universally closed clauses F such that F and F^* are equi-satisfiable. The motivation here is to enable SMT-solvers to handle universal quantifiers for this fragment, which is very important for real-life verification problems. They build the set of instances needed incrementally until they reach closure. This is similar to our notion of Ψ-locality where we consider closure operator Ψ that gives us enough instances to eliminate quantifiers (which we can always do when all variables appear below extension functions).

Differences to our approach. Our own approach differs from the above work in several respects. In contrast to the (extended) Nelson-Oppen framework, we consider the case where one or more theories share a common theory (with non-disjoint) signature from the outset. Local extensions and combinations impose no a priori restrictions on the shared theory, whereby circumventing the severe restrictions on the common theory of the Nelson-Oppen approach. For this reason, local extensions and combinations provide orthogonal criteria for the transfer of decidability results to the combinations of theories.

We use the same hierarchical/reductive approach for data structures. This again allows us to consider the case where the data structure and the underlying element theory share more than one bridging function (e.g. length).

Our framework not only allows us to offer a general, unifying treatment of locality phenomena in common data structures by developing our notion of Ψ-locality but also allows us to subsume the instantiation strategies developed by Ge and de Moura.

1.5 Structure of the Thesis

The thesis is structured as follows. In Chapter 2 we fix our notation and present some common facts about first-order logic, theories and partial algebras which we will need. In Chapter 3 we develop the theory of locality and give some applications. In Chapter 4 we present generalizations of standard locality, in particular minimal and Ψ-locality, and treat local data structures. Chapter 5 focuses on combinations of theories sharing a common base theory. First we introduce the necessary model-theoretic machinery which we then use on information exchange and the combination of local and Ψ-local theories. Finally, Chapter 6 presents our implementation of local reasoning: H-PILoT.

Chapter 2

Preliminaries

2.1 First-order Logic

We assume known common notions from first-order logic. We will give a brief synopsis of the notions that will be needed for the thesis. For background information we refer the reader to [Dal04, Hod97, CK90]. We write $\bar{x}, \bar{a}$ for sequences $(x_0, x_1, \ldots), (a_0, a_1, \ldots)$. Finite sequences are called *tuples*. If $\bar{x} = (x_0, x_1, \ldots)$ is a sequence and h a map, we write $h\bar{x}$ for the sequence $(h(x_0), h(x_1), \ldots)$. We will start with the syntax and semantics of a first-order language.

Syntax. A *first-order language* $\mathcal{L}$ is characterized by its *signature* $\Pi = (\Sigma, \text{Pred})$ which contains function symbols Σ and relation symbols Pred together with their arity. Constants are 0-ary function symbols. We will exclusively consider first-order logic with equality, that is equality is always built-in and need not be included in the signature. We will write the built-in, object-language equality as $\approx$. We will consider a countably infinite sets of *variables* X to be fixed. We define terms and formulas (w.r.t. a signature Π) inductively.

A *(Π)-term* is a variable, a constant in Π or a string $f(t_1, \ldots, t_n)$ such that f is a function symbol in Π of arity n and t_i are Π-terms, $i = 1, \ldots, n$. We recursively define the *depth* of a term t as follows. If t is a variable or a constant its depth is 0, if $t = f(t_1, \ldots, t_n)$ its depth is defined as $1 + \max_i(\text{depth}(t_i))$.

The *root* of a term $t = f(t_1 \ldots, t_n)$ is the function symbol f or the term itself if t is a constant or a variable. We write root(t) for the root of t. We will sometimes consider the set of Π-terms generated from a set of terms Γ (possibly from another signature) and denote this set by $\text{Term}_\Pi(\Gamma)$. This will also be inductively defined, i.e $\text{Term}_\Pi(\Gamma)$ is the smallest set S containing Γ and each string $f(t_1 \ldots, t_n)$ for $t_i \in S, f \in \Pi$ and the arity of f is n. If Π is clear from the context we will often drop it and simply write $\text{Term}(\Gamma)$ for $\text{Term}_\Pi(\Gamma)$. A *subterm* t of u is a substring of u which is a term in its own right. We will write $t \trianglelefteq u$ if t is a subterm of u.

A *(Π)-atom* is an equation between Π-terms $t \approx u$ or the application of a predicate symbol to Π-terms $P(t_1, \ldots, t_n)$ where P is n-ary. The set of Π-*formulas* is the smallest set S containing the Π-atoms which is closed under the rules

(1) if $\varphi \in S$ then $\neg \varphi \in S$,

(2) if $\varphi, \psi \in S$ then $\varphi \wedge \psi, \varphi \vee \psi$ and $\varphi \rightarrow \psi$ are in S and

(3) if $\varphi \in S$, $x \in X$ then $(\forall x). \varphi \in S$ and $(\exists x). \varphi \in S$.

We identify a first order language $\mathcal{L}$ in the signature Π with the set of Π-formulas and will from now on also talk of $\mathcal{L}$-formulas, $\mathcal{L}$-atoms etc. We are also interested in formulas of a certain structure. A *(Π)-literal* is an atom or the negation of an atom. A *(Π)-clause* is a finite disjunction of (Π)-literals $\lambda_1 \vee \ldots \vee \lambda_n$. A formula is in *conjunctive normal form* if it is a conjunction of clauses. We write $t \leq \cdot \varphi$ if the term t appears in the formula φ.

The *free variables* $FV(t)$ of a term t are the variables occurring in t. The free variables $FV(\varphi)$ of a formula φ are defined by recursion on the structure of formulas:

(0) $FV(t \approx u) := FV(t) \cup FV(u)$
and $FV(P(t_1, \ldots, t_n)) := FV(t_1) \cup \ldots \cup FV(t_n)$ for atoms,

(1) $FV(\neg \varphi) := FV(\varphi)$,

(2) $FV(\varphi \square \psi) := FV(\varphi) \cup FV(\psi)$, for $\square \in \{\wedge, \vee, \rightarrow\}$,

(3) $FV((\forall x). \varphi) := FV((\exists x). \varphi) := FV(\varphi) \setminus \{x\}$.

The *bound variables* of a formula φ are those that appear quantified in φ and are defined dually. Note that a variable can appear both bound and free in a formula. We call a term or formula *ground* if it does not contain any variables. We will denote the set of ground terms of signature Π by GTerm_Π.

We write $\varphi(x_1, \ldots, x_n)$ if the free variables of a formula φ are contained in the set $\{x_1, \ldots, x_n\}$. We will also abbreviate formulas like $(\forall x_1).(\forall x_2).(\forall x_3).(\forall y_1).(\forall y_2).\varphi$ by writing $\forall \bar{x}, \forall \bar{y}.\varphi$.

A formula which has no free variables but only bound variables or none at all is called *closed* or a *sentence*. A formula not containing any quantifiers is called *quantifier-free* or *open*. By a *universal formula* we mean a formula of the form $\forall \bar{x}.\varphi(\bar{x}, \bar{y})$ where $\varphi(\bar{x}, \bar{y})$ is open; by the *universal closure* of a formula $\varphi(\bar{x})$ we mean the formula $\forall \bar{x}. \varphi(\bar{x})$. We will denote the universal closure of φ by $\forall \varphi$.

By an *existential formula* we mean a formula of the form $\exists \bar{x}.\varphi(\bar{x}, \bar{y})$ where $\varphi(\bar{x}, \bar{y})$ is open; by an $\forall\exists$-*formula* we mean a formula of the form $\forall \bar{x} \exists \bar{y}.\varphi(\bar{x}, \bar{y}, \bar{z})$ where $\varphi(\bar{x}, \bar{y}, \bar{z})$ is an open formula. By a *universal clause* we mean a universal formula of the form $\forall \bar{x}.\varphi$ where φ is a clause; by a *universally closed clause* we mean the universal closure of a clause. A formula in *negation normal form* is a universal formula of the form $\forall \bar{x}. \varphi$ where φ is built from literals with the connectives $\{\wedge, \vee\}$. We will speak of universal/existential/$\forall\exists$-sentences if the corresponding formula does not contain any free variables.

Following [Hod97] and [CK90], we define a *(Π)-theory* simply as a set of Π-sentences. We write $T \vdash \varphi$ if the Π-sentence φ can be formally deduced from the Π-theory T in a first-order calculus such as a sequent calculus. We will also talk of an $\mathcal{L}$-*theory*, where $\mathcal{L}$ is the first-order language determined by the signature Π. The *deductive closure* of a Π-theory T is the set of all Π-sentences that can be deduced from T (Notation: $T^\vdash$).

A *substitution* σ is a map $\sigma : X \rightarrow \text{Term}_\Pi(X)$ from the variables into the terms of the signature. We will write $\varphi \sigma$ for the formula which results from φ when we replace simultaneously every free variable x by $\sigma(x)$. There is one technical complication with substitution, viz. we need to avoid that a variable in $\sigma(x)$ becomes bound as a result of the substitution lest we change the semantics of the formula. In order to avoid this we will always implicitly assume that bound variables are renamed when necessary.[1] We call a substitution σ *ground* if $\sigma(x)$ is always a ground term. By the notation $\varphi(t)$ we mean the substitution of t for the variable x in $\varphi(x)$.

Semantics. A Π-*structure* for a signature Π is a tuple $\mathcal{A} = (A, \Sigma^{\mathcal{A}}, \mathrm{Pred}^{\mathcal{A}})$, consisting of a non-empty set A, called the *carrier* of $\mathcal{A}$, together with a set of functions and relations interpreting each symbol of Π. That is for each function symbol $f \in \Sigma$ of arity n, $\Sigma^{\mathcal{A}}$ contains a function $f^{\mathcal{A}} : A^n \to A$ and for each relation symbol $R \in \mathrm{Pred}$ of arity k, $\mathrm{Pred}^{\mathcal{A}}$ contains a relation $R^{\mathcal{A}} \subseteq A^k$. We will denote first-order structures by $\mathcal{A}, \mathcal{B}, \ldots$ and their respective carriers by $A, B, \ldots$. We will also call a Π-structure $\mathcal{A}$ an $\mathcal{L}$-*structure*, where $\mathcal{L}$ is the first order-language with the signature Π.

A *valuation* β for a structure $\mathcal{A}$ is a map $\beta : X \to A$ from the set of variables into the carrier A. A structure together with a valuation induces a truth value for all Π-formulas. A valuation extends canonically to terms. The value of a term t under β (w.r.t. $\mathcal{A}$) is again an element of A. We write $(\mathcal{A}, \beta)(t)$ for the value of the term t w.r.t. $\mathcal{A}$ and β, or simply $\beta(t)$ if the structure is clear from the context. We will write $\beta[x \mapsto a]$ for the valuation that maps x to a and every other value y to $\beta(y)$. The value $(\mathcal{A}, \beta)(\varphi)$ of a formula φ w.r.t. $(\mathcal{A}, \beta)$ is either 1 (which stands for 'true') or 0 ('false'). It is sufficient to define the value for the connectives $\{\neg, \wedge\}$ and the quantifier '$\exists$' because the other connectives and the other quantifier can be thought of as defined in terms of these.

Definition 2.1.1 (Truth value in a model) $(\mathcal{A}, \beta)(\varphi)$ *is defined recursively on the structure of formulas as follows.*

0) $(\mathcal{A}, \beta)(t \approx u) := \begin{cases} 1 & \text{if } (\mathcal{A}, \beta)(t) = (\mathcal{A}, \beta)(u), \\ 0 & \text{otherwise.} \end{cases}$

and

$(\mathcal{A}, \beta)(P(t_1, \ldots, t_n)) := \begin{cases} 1 & \text{if } ((\mathcal{A}, \beta)(t_1), \ldots, (\mathcal{A}, \beta)(t_n)) \in P^{\mathcal{A}}, \\ 0 & \text{otherwise.} \end{cases}$

1) $(\mathcal{A}, \beta)(\neg\varphi) := 1 - (\mathcal{A}, \beta)(\varphi)$,
2) $(\mathcal{A}, \beta)(\varphi \wedge \psi) := \min((\mathcal{A}, \beta)(\varphi), (\mathcal{A}, \beta)(\psi))$,
3) $(\mathcal{A}, \beta)((\exists x). \varphi) := \max_{a \in A}(\mathcal{A}, \beta[x \mapsto a])(\varphi)$.

Instead of $(\mathcal{A}, \beta)(\varphi) = 1$ we will commonly write $\mathcal{A}, \beta \models \varphi$ and say that $(\mathcal{A}, \beta)$ *satisfies* φ or that $(\mathcal{A}, \beta)$ is a *model* of φ. Dually, if $(\mathcal{A}, \beta)(\varphi) = 0$ we will say that $(\mathcal{A}, \beta)$ *does not satisfy* φ and write $\mathcal{A}, \beta \not\models \varphi$. For a set of formulas Γ, we say that $(\mathcal{A}, \beta)$ *satisfies* Γ if $(\mathcal{A}, \beta)$ satisfies each $\varphi \in \Gamma$.

The value $(\mathcal{A}, \beta)(\varphi)$ of a formula $\varphi(\bar{x})$ under $\mathcal{A}$ depends only on the free variables $\bar{x}$ of φ: If β and β' are two valuations which do not differ on $\bar{x}$, then the values $(\mathcal{A}, \beta)(\varphi)$ and $(\mathcal{A}, \beta')(\varphi)$ are the same. In particular, if φ is a sentence a valuation is irrelevant. In that case we will simply write $\mathcal{A}(\varphi)$ for the value of φ and $\mathcal{A} \models \varphi$ if the value is true and call φ *true in* $\mathcal{A}$. For the same reason, we will also write $\mathcal{A} \models \varphi[\bar{a}]$ if $\mathcal{A}, \beta \models \varphi(\bar{x})$, for any β with $\beta\bar{x} = \bar{a}$ and $t^{\mathcal{A}}[\bar{a}]$ for the value of a term $t(\bar{x})$ under any valuation β with $\beta\bar{x} = \bar{a}$. For ground terms, valuations are as idle as in sentences. We will write $t^{\mathcal{A}}$ for the value of a ground term t in $\mathcal{A}$.

We say that a Π-structure $\mathcal{A}$ *satisfies* an open formula $\varphi(\bar{x})$ if $\mathcal{A} \models \forall\varphi$. Equivalently, $\mathcal{A} \models \varphi(\bar{x})$ if it holds for all valuations β, that $\mathcal{A}, \beta \models \varphi(\bar{x})$. We call a formula *satisfiable in* $\mathcal{A}$ if there is some

---
[1] cf. [EFT96], ch. III, §8 and [Dal04], ch. 2.5.

valuation β such that $(\mathcal{A}, \beta)$ satisfies φ and *unsatisfiable in* $\mathcal{A}$ otherwise. We call a Π-formula *satisfiable* if there is a Π-structure $\mathcal{A}$ such that φ is satisfiable in $\mathcal{A}$ and *unsatisfiable* otherwise. Similarly, we say that a set of formulas Γ is *satisfiable* if there is a structure $\mathcal{A}$ such that Γ is satisfiable in $\mathcal{A}$ and *unsatisfiable* otherwise. Two formulas are *equivalent* if they have exactly the same models. We will need the fact later that every quantifier-free formula is equivalent to a formula in conjunctive normal form.

The notion of satisfaction of a formula in a model allows us to define *semantic consequence*. Overloading notation as is customary, we write $\Gamma \models \Delta$ for sets of formulas Γ, Δ to mean that every model $(\mathcal{A}, \beta)$ which satisfies Γ also satisfies at least one formula in Δ. In particular if Γ and Δ are both finite, $\Gamma \models \Delta$ is equivalent to $\bigwedge \Gamma \models \bigvee \Delta$. If Γ or Δ is a singleton we will drop the curly brackets. We should also note the simple but significant fact that semantic consequence is *monotone*, that is if it holds that $\Gamma \models \Delta$ we also have $\Gamma^+ \models \Delta^+$ for any sets Γ^+, Δ^+ with $\Gamma^+ \supseteq \Gamma$ and $\Delta^+ \supseteq \Delta$.

The following theorem is one of the most significant in first-order logic.

Theorem 2.1.2 (Compactness) *Let $\mathcal{L}$ be a first-order language and Γ, Δ sets of $\mathcal{L}$-formulas. Then $\Gamma \models \Delta$ if and only if there are finite subsets $\Gamma_0 \subseteq_{fin} \Gamma$ and $\Delta_0 \subseteq_{fin} \Delta$ such that $\Gamma_0 \models \Delta_0$.*

Many-Sorted logic. On one occasion (Section 4.8) we will consider many-sorted first-order logic. Many-sorted first-order logic distinguishes different *types* or *sorts* s_i, $i = 1, \ldots, n$. Syntactically, variables, quantifiers and the equality symbol must now be relativized to a type. The same holds for a signature. We must now not only indicate the arity of function or predicate symbols but also their types. For example, we say that a function symbol f has arity $s_1 \times s_2 \to s_3$. This means that for a term $t = f(u_1, u_2)$ to be well-defined, u_i must be of type s_i, for $i = 1, 2$, while t itself will be of type s_3. Similarly for predicate symbols and atoms.

Semantically, a many-sorted structure $\mathcal{A}$ must now assign to each sort s_i a set A_{s_i}. These sets can be supposed to be mutually disjoint because there is no equality symbol "across sorts". For each function or predicate symbol, a many-sorted structure must assign a sort-compliant function or predicate. In our example, the symbol f must be assigned some function $f^{\mathcal{A}} : A_{s_1} \times A_{s_2} \to A_{s_3}$ in a many-sorted structure $\mathcal{A}$. The definition of truth and satisfaction lifts effortlessly to a many-sorted structure.

Many-sorted logics are convenient in theoretical computer science but logically they offer nothing new. We can always reduce many-sorted logic to one-sorted logic by using predicates instead of sorts (cf. [End02], 4.3).

Homomorphisms and embeddings. Given a signature $\Pi = (\Sigma, \mathrm{Pred})$ and map $h : A \to B$ between the carriers of two Π-structures $\mathcal{A}$ and $\mathcal{B}$ we say that h *preserves* $\varphi(\bar{x})$ if for any $\bar{a} \in A$ it holds that

$$\mathcal{A} \models \varphi[\bar{a}] \text{ implies } \mathcal{B} \models \varphi[h\bar{a}].$$

Definition 2.1.3 *A homomorphism between two Π-structures $\mathcal{A}$ and $\mathcal{B}$ is a map $h : A \to B$ such that for all function symbols $f \in \Sigma$ it holds that*

$$h(f^{\mathcal{A}}(a_1, \ldots, a_n)) = f^{\mathcal{B}}(h(a_1), \ldots, h(a_n)),$$

and for all relation symbols $R \in \text{Pred}$ it holds that

$$R^{\mathcal{A}}(a_1, \ldots, a_n) \text{ implies } R^{\mathcal{B}}(h(a_1), \ldots, h(a_n)).$$

An embedding $h : \mathcal{A} \to \mathcal{B}$ of $\mathcal{A}$ into $\mathcal{B}$ is an *injective homomorphism* with the property that for all relation symbols $R \in \text{Pred}$ it holds that

$$R^{\mathcal{A}}(a_1, \ldots, a_n) \text{ if and only if } R^{\mathcal{B}}(h(a_1), \ldots, h(a_n)).$$

We will write $h : \mathcal{A} \hookrightarrow \mathcal{B}$ if h embeds $\mathcal{A}$ into $\mathcal{B}$.

An *isomorphism* is a surjective embedding. A map is a homomorphism if and only if it preserves every atom, a map is an embedding if and only if it preserves every literal (cf. [Hod97], 1.3.1).

An embedding preserves any existential formula ([CK90], 3.2.2; [Hod97], 2.4.1). A *substructure* $\mathcal{A}$ of $\mathcal{B}$ (notation: $\mathcal{A} \subseteq \mathcal{B}$) is a structure such that the identity is an embedding from $\mathcal{A}$ into $\mathcal{B}$. In particular, any universal sentence true in a structure will be true in any of its substructures. If $\mathcal{A} \subseteq \mathcal{B}$ we call $\mathcal{B}$ an *extension* of $\mathcal{A}$. Given an $\mathcal{L}$-structure $\mathcal{A}$ and some subset Y of A we will call the smallest substructure of $\mathcal{A}$ which contains Y the *substructure generated by* Y and write $<Y>_{\mathcal{A}}$ for that structure.

Definition 2.1.4 *A map $f : A \to B$ which preserves all formulas is called an* **elementary embedding** *(Notation: $f : \mathcal{A} \preccurlyeq \mathcal{B}$). A structure $\mathcal{A}$ is called an* **elementary substructure** *of another structure $\mathcal{B}$ (and $\mathcal{B}$ an* **elementary extension** *of $\mathcal{A}$) if $\mathcal{A} \subseteq \mathcal{B}$ and the inclusion is an elementary embedding (Notation: $\mathcal{A} \preccurlyeq \mathcal{B}$).*

Language extensions. We sometimes want to extend a first-order language $\mathcal{L}$ of signature Π by new constant symbols which do not occur in $\mathcal{L}$ already. Let $C = \{c_0, c_1, \ldots\}$ a set of constant symbols such that $c_i \notin \Pi$, for all i, we call $C = \bar{c}$ a set of *fresh constants*. We will write $\mathcal{L}_C$, or more suggestively $\mathcal{L}(\bar{c})$, for the extended language. Given an $\mathcal{L}$-structure $\mathcal{A}$ we write $(\mathcal{A}, \bar{a})$ for the $\mathcal{L}(\bar{c})$-structure which is exactly like $\mathcal{A}$ except that $c_i^{\mathcal{A}} = a_i$ for all i. In general, if we have two signatures $\Pi \subseteq \Pi'$ and a Π'-structure $\mathcal{A}'$ we call the corresponding Π-structure $\mathcal{A}$ the Π-*reduct* of $\mathcal{A}'$ (notation $\mathcal{A}'\restriction_\Pi$). Dually, we call $\mathcal{A}'$ a Π'-*expansion* of $\mathcal{A}$.

If $\mathcal{A}$ is an $\mathcal{L}$-structure, we often expand the language and the structure by introducing new constant symbols $\underline{a}$ for each $a \in A$ and interpret these constants by the respective element. We denote the extended language by $\mathcal{L}_A$, the extended signature by Π_A and the expanded Π_A-structure by $(\mathcal{A}, A)$. It holds that $(\mathcal{A}, A) \models \varphi(\underline{a}) \Leftrightarrow \mathcal{A} \models \varphi[a]$. For this reason, we will not distinguish between the name for an element and the element itself. This is due to the following lemma which states that substitutions are the syntactical counterparts of valuations (cf. [Dal04], Theorem 2.5.8 and Corollary; [EFT96], Lemma 8.3).

Lemma 2.1.5 (Substitution lemma) *Let $\mathcal{A}$ be a Π-algebra, $\beta : X \to A$ a valuation for $\mathcal{A}$ and $\sigma : X \to \text{Term}(X)$ a substitution. Define the valuation $\beta \circ \sigma : X \to A$ by $x \mapsto (\mathcal{A}, \beta)(\sigma(x))$. It holds that*

(1) $(\mathcal{A}, \beta \circ \sigma)(t) = (\mathcal{A}, \beta)(t\sigma)$ for any term t.

(2) $(\mathcal{A}, \beta \circ \sigma)(\varphi) = (\mathcal{A}, \beta)(\varphi\sigma)$.

(3) $\mathcal{A}, \beta \circ \sigma \models \varphi \Leftrightarrow \mathcal{A}, \beta \models \varphi\sigma$.

The set of ground $\mathcal{L}_A$-atoms which are true in $(\mathcal{A}, A)$ is called the *positive diagram* of $\mathcal{A}$. The positive diagram of $\mathcal{A}$ is denoted by $\Delta_\mathcal{A}^+$. The set of ground $\mathcal{L}_A$-literals which are true in $(\mathcal{A}, A)$ is called the *diagram* of $\mathcal{A}$. and denoted by $\Delta_\mathcal{A}$. The *elementary diagram* of $\mathcal{A}$, written as $\Delta_\mathcal{A}^{el}$, is the set of $\mathcal{L}_A$-sentences true in $(\mathcal{A}, A)$. Additionally, we also allow expansions for subsets of $\mathcal{A}$. If $X \subseteq A$ and f is a mapping from X into the carrier of an $\mathcal{L}$-structure $\mathcal{B}$, we get an $\mathcal{L}_X$ structure $(\mathcal{B}, fa)_{a \in X}$ in the obvious way. Diagrams are an important tool for model constructions due to the following lemma.

Lemma 2.1.6 ([Hod97], 1.4.2) *Let $\mathcal{A}$ and $\mathcal{B}$ be $\mathcal{L}$-structures, $\bar{c}$ a sequence of new constants and $(\mathcal{A}, \bar{a})$ and $(\mathcal{B}, \bar{b})$ be $\mathcal{L}(\bar{c})$-structures. Then (1) and (2) are equivalent.*

(1) For every atomic sentence φ of $\mathcal{L}(\bar{c})$, if $(\mathcal{A}, \bar{a}) \models \varphi$ then $(\mathcal{B}, \bar{b}) \models \varphi$.

(2) There is a homomorphism $f : <\bar{a}>_\mathcal{A} \to \mathcal{B}$ such that $f(a_i) = b_i$, for all i.

The homomorphism f in (2) is unique if it exists; it is an embedding if and only if

(3) For every atomic sentence φ of $\mathcal{L}(\bar{c})$, $(\mathcal{A}, \bar{a}) \models \varphi \Leftrightarrow (\mathcal{B}, \bar{b}) \models \varphi$.

In particular if $\bar{a}$ generates $\mathcal{A}$, the implication (1) $\Rightarrow$ (2) in the above lemma tells us that $\mathcal{A}$ can be mapped homomorphically to a reduct of $\mathcal{B}$ whenever $\mathcal{B}$ is a model of the positive diagram of $\mathcal{A}$; and (3) tells us that any model of the diagram of $\mathcal{A}$ has a reduct into which $\mathcal{A}$ can be embedded (cf. [CK90], 2.1.8; [Hod97], Ibid.).

Corollary 2.1.7 (Lemma on diagrams) *Let $\mathcal{A}$ and $\mathcal{B}$ be $\mathcal{L}$-structures.*

(1) $\mathcal{A}$ can be mapped homomorphically to a reduct of $\mathcal{B}$ whenever $\mathcal{B} \models \Delta_\mathcal{A}^+$.

(2) If $\mathcal{B} \models \Delta_\mathcal{A}$ then $\mathcal{A}$ can be embedded into a reduct of $\mathcal{B}$.

Something similar holds for elementary diagrams. Recall that an elementary embedding is a map $f : \mathcal{A} \to \mathcal{B}$ between $\mathcal{L}$-structures such that for all formulas $\varphi(x_1, \ldots, x_n)$ and all elements $a_1, \ldots, a_n$ we have $\mathcal{A} \models \varphi[a_1, \ldots, a_n]$ if and only if $\mathcal{B} \models \varphi[fa_1, \ldots, fa_n]$. Note also that every isomorphism is an elementary embedding.

Lemma 2.1.8 ([Hod97], 2.5.3) *Let $\mathcal{A}$ and $\mathcal{B}$ be $\mathcal{L}$-structures and $\bar{c}$ a tuple of new constants not in $\mathcal{L}$. Suppose $(\mathcal{A}, \bar{a})$ and $(\mathcal{B}, \bar{b})$ are $\mathcal{L}(\bar{c})$-structures and $\bar{a}$ generates $\mathcal{A}$. Then the following are equivalent.*

(1) For every formula $\varphi(\bar{x})$ of $\mathcal{L}$, if $(\mathcal{A}, \bar{a}) \models \varphi(\bar{c})$ then $(\mathcal{B}, \bar{b}) \models \varphi(\bar{c})$.

(2) There is an elementary embedding $f : \mathcal{A} \to \mathcal{B}$ with $f(a_i) = f(b_i)$, for all i.

From this we get the *elementary diagram lemma*, (cf. [CK90], 3.1.3; [Hod97], Ibid.).

Corollary 2.1.9 *If $\mathcal{D}$ is a model of the elementary diagram of an $\mathcal{L}$-structure $\mathcal{A}$, then there is an elementary embedding of $\mathcal{A}$ into the reduct $\mathcal{D}\restriction\mathcal{L}$.*

The standard usage of these lemmas on diagrams always goes like this. We want to extend a model $\mathcal{A}$ to a model of some theory T. If we can show that $T \cup \Delta_\mathcal{A}$ is consistent we can use the lemma on diagrams to establish the claim.

They are two more often-employed techniques we want to mention. Both techniques are concerned with 'fresh' terms, i.e terms that occur nowhere else (cf. [Dal04], Theorem 2.8.3 and Lemma 2.9.1). The first deals with 'fresh' variables. Its slogan is: Free variable means '$\exists$' left of the turnstile and '$\forall$' right of it The second deals with fresh constants. Its slogan is: Fresh constants behave exactly as 'fresh' variables. The first two assertions of the following lemma are also know as $\forall$-*elimination* and $\forall$-*introduction*.

Lemma 2.1.10 *Let Γ be a set of $\mathcal{L}$-formulas and let φ, ψ be $\mathcal{L}$-formulas. Let x be a variable which does not occur freely in either Γ or ψ. Then it holds that*

(1) $\Gamma \models \varphi(x) \Leftrightarrow \Gamma \models \forall x.\varphi(x)$

(2) $\Gamma, \varphi(x) \models \psi \Rightarrow \Gamma, \forall x.\varphi(x) \models \psi$

(3) $\Gamma, \varphi(x) \models \psi \Leftrightarrow \Gamma, \exists x.\varphi(x) \models \psi$

The second technique does the same for constants that do not appear anywhere else.

Lemma 2.1.11 (Lemma on constants) *Let $\mathcal{L}$ be a first-order language, Γ a set of $\mathcal{L}$-formulas and φ an $\mathcal{L}$-formula. Let c be an $\mathcal{L}$-constant not occurring in Γ. Then it holds that $\Gamma \models \varphi(c) \Leftrightarrow \Gamma \models \forall x.\varphi(x)$*

Here are two more golden classics.

Lemma 2.1.12 (Craig's Interpolation Theorem, [Cra57]) *Let $\mathcal{L}$ be a first-order language, φ, ψ be $\mathcal{L}$-sentences such that $\varphi \models \psi$. Then there is a $\mathcal{L}$-sentence δ which contains only function and predicate symbols that occur in both φ and ψ with $\varphi \models \delta \models \psi$.*

In isomorphic structures the same sentences are valid ([Hod97],2.4.3.(c)). In general

Definition 2.1.13 (Elementary equivalence) *Let Π be a first-order signature and $\mathcal{A}, \mathcal{B}$ be two Π-structures. $\mathcal{A}$ and $\mathcal{B}$ are called elementarily equivalent (Notation: $\mathcal{A} \equiv \mathcal{B}$) if it holds for all Π-sentences φ that*

$$\mathcal{A} \models \varphi \Leftrightarrow \mathcal{B} \models \varphi.$$

Not all elementarily equivalent structures are isomorphic. In fact, every infinite structure will have an elementarily equivalent structure in every infinite cardinality bigger or equal to the size of the language due to the *Löwenheim-Skolem theorems* (cf. [Hod97], 3.1.4 and 5.1.4). For finite structures, however, the two notions coincide ([CK90], 1.3.19.).

Definition 2.1.14 (Complete theory) *Let T be a satisfiable $\mathcal{L}$-theory. T is called complete if it holds that $T \models \varphi$ or $T \models \neg\varphi$, for every $\mathcal{L}$-sentence φ.*

In other words, a theory is complete if it has at least one model and all its models are elementarily equivalent.

Corollary 2.1.15 (Robinson Consistency Theorem; [CK90], 2.2.23) *Let T_1, T_2 be satisfiable theories in the language $\mathcal{L}_1, \mathcal{L}_2$ respectively and let $\mathcal{L} := \mathcal{L}_1 \cap \mathcal{L}_2$. If there is a complete $\mathcal{L}$-theory T with $T \subseteq T_1, T_2$ then $T_1 \cup T_2$ is satisfiable as well.*

Because it gives us a lot of control, we often want to build up a model of a theory inductively, i.e., step by step, by repeatedly adding elements and then considering the limit (cf. [Hod97], 6.1). By a *chain of models* we mean an increasing sequence of models

$$\mathcal{A}_0 \subseteq \mathcal{A}_1 \subseteq \mathcal{A}_2 \subseteq \ldots \subseteq \mathcal{A}_\beta \subseteq \ldots, \qquad \beta < \alpha,$$

whose length is some ordinal α.

The *union of the chain* is the model $\mathcal{A} = \bigcup_{\beta < \alpha} \mathcal{A}_\beta$ which is defined as follows. Its carrier is the union $A = \bigcup_{\beta < \alpha} A_\beta$ of the carriers, each relation $R^\mathcal{A}$ is the union of the corresponding relations $\bigcup_{\beta < \alpha} R^{\mathcal{A}_\beta}$. Similarly, each function $f^\mathcal{A}$ is the union of the corresponding functions $\bigcup_{\beta < \alpha} f^{\mathcal{A}_\beta}$. The models $\mathcal{A}_\beta$ all agree on constants, so take $c^\mathcal{A} := c^{\mathcal{A}_0}$.

We say that a formula $\varphi(\bar{x})$ is *preserved in union of chains* if whenever $(\mathcal{A}_\beta \mid \beta < \alpha)$ is a chain of models, $\bar{a}$ is a sequence of elements of $\mathcal{A}_0$ and $\mathcal{A}_\beta \models \varphi(\bar{a})$ for all $\beta < \alpha$ then $\bigcup_{\beta < \alpha} \mathcal{A}_\beta \models \varphi(\bar{a})$.

Theorem 2.1.16 (Chang-Łos-Susko; [Hod97], 5.4.9) *A formula φ is preserved in union of chains if and only if φ is equivalent to an $\forall\exists$-formula.*

Another interesting application of chains is when all inclusions are elementary, i.e., $\mathcal{A}_\beta \preccurlyeq \mathcal{A}_\gamma$ for all $\beta < \gamma < \alpha$.

Theorem 2.1.17 (Elementary chain theorem; [CK90], 3.1.9) *Let $(\mathcal{A}_\beta \mid \beta < \alpha)$ be an elementary chain of models. Then $\mathcal{A}_\gamma \preccurlyeq \bigcup_{\beta < \alpha} \mathcal{A}_\beta$, for all $\gamma < \alpha$.*

Definition 2.1.18 (Model completeness) *Let T be an $\mathcal{L}$-theory. T is called* model complete *if every embedding between its models is elementary.*

Definition 2.1.19 (Elimination of quantifiers) *An $\mathcal{L}$-theory T is said to admit elimination of quantifiers if for every $\mathcal{L}$-formula $\varphi(x_1, \ldots, x_n)$ there is an open (i.e., quantifier-free) $\mathcal{L}$-formula $\varphi'(x_1, \ldots, x_n)$ such that*
$$T \models \varphi(x_1, \ldots, x_n) \leftrightarrow \varphi'(x_1, \ldots, x_n).$$

2.2 Partial Algebras and Partial Semantics

Partial algebras and partial semantics play a crucial role in the theory of locality. This goes back all the way to Skolem ([Sko20]). In order to show that the uniform word problem for lattices is decidable in polynomial time, he considered relational encodings of the lattice operations. The operations were replaced by relations representing their graphs: $\vee$ and $\wedge$ were replaced by ternary relations $r_\vee$ and $r_\wedge$ and lattice axioms $x \vee y \approx z$ were rewritten as $r_\vee(x, y, z)$ (similar for $\wedge$-equations). Additionally, $r_\wedge$ and $r_\vee$ are required to be functional, i.e., axioms of the form

$r_\vee(x,y,z) \wedge r_\vee(x,y,z') \to z = z'$ were added. What gets lost, however, in the translation is the totality of the lattice operations. The relational encoding resulted in function-free Horn clauses which were then used to decide the uniform word problem in polynomial time.

Independently, similar ideas were used by Evans in the study of algebras with a PTIME decidable word problem ([Eva51]). These approaches were rediscovered and extended by Burris ([Bur95]). He showed that if a quasi-variety, i.e., a class of algebras axiomatized by a set of Horn clauses $\mathcal{H}$, has the property that every finite partial model of $\mathcal{H}$ can be extended to a total one, then the uniform word problem for the quasi-variety is decidable in polynomial time.

In [Gan01] Ganzinger established a connection between locality (for Horn clauses) and the embeddability of partial models of Horn clauses into total ones.

Definition 2.2.1 (Partial function) *Let $f : A \to B$ be some function with arity bigger than 0 and $A' \supseteq A$. Then $f : A' \to B$ is called a partial function. For $a \in A' \setminus A$ we say that $f(a)$ is undefined and write $f(a)\uparrow$, for $a \in A$ we say that $f(a)$ is defined and write $f(a)\downarrow$. We call A the* domain *of the partial function $f : A' \to B$. The* image $f(U)$ *of a set $U \subseteq A'$ under f is the set $\{f(u) \mid u \in U, f(u) \text{ defined.}\}$. Let $\Pi = (\Sigma, \text{Pred})$ be a signature. A* partial Π-algebra *is a tuple $(A, \{f^\mathcal{A}\}_{f \in \Sigma}, \{c^\mathcal{A}\}_{c \in \Sigma}, \text{Pred}^\mathcal{A})$, where A is a non-empty set and for every function symbol $f \in \Pi$ with arity n, $f^\mathcal{A}$ is a partial function from A^n to A, every constant symbol $c \in \Sigma$ is defined in $\mathcal{A}$ and for every k-ary predicate symbol $P \in \text{Pred}$, $P^\mathcal{A}$ is a subset of A^k. The structure is a* (total) algebra *if all functions $f^\mathcal{A}$ are total.*

Note that we will always consider constants to be defined. There is no canonical way to define partial semantics. We certainly want partial semantics to be *conservative*, i.e., if all terms in a formula or term are defined, partial semantics should give the same value as the total one. This still leaves us a lot of leeway in the case where we have some undefined terms.

Consider an equation $f(s) \approx t$ and suppose the term t is defined in some model while $f(s)$ is not. Should we say that the equation is true in the model or not? How about when s is also defined? There is no prevailing answer. It is a matter of expediency[2].

For local extensions, two different partial semantics are used: *weak* and *strong* partial semantics. Strong partial semantics is sometimes also called Evans semantics (cf. [Bur95, Gan01, GSSW04, GSSW06, SS05]). Weak and strong partial semantics would answer the above question differently. In weak semantics, any equation is true in some model provided at least one side is undefined in the model. In strong semantics, the equation $f(s) \approx t$ would be false in any model where both s and t are defined but $f(s)$ is undefined.

Following [GSSW04, GSSW06], we will distinguish two ways in which a term can be undefined in a partial model for which we reserve two special values $\bot_u$ ("undefined") and $\bot_i$ ("irrelevant"). In a nutshell, $\bot_i$ means that a subterm was already undefined, while $\bot_u$ indicates that all subterms are defined but are not in the domain of the function at the root of the term.

Definition 2.2.2 (Value of a term in a partial model) *Let $\mathcal{A}$ be a partial Π-algebra and $\beta : X \to A$ a valuation for its variables. The value $(\mathcal{A}, \beta)(t)$ of a term t is recursively defined as follows.*

---

[2]cf. the discussion in [Bur86], particularly Section 0.4.

(1) $(\mathcal{A}, \beta)(x) = \beta(x)$ for a variable x.

(2) $(\mathcal{A}, \beta)(c) = c^{\mathcal{A}}$ for a constant c.

(3) $(\mathcal{A}, \beta)(t) = \bot_u$ if $t = f(t_1, \ldots, t_n)$, $(\mathcal{A}, \beta)(t_i) \notin \{\bot_u, \bot_i\}$
for all i, $1 \leq i \leq n$, but $f^{\mathcal{A}}(\beta(t_1), \ldots, \beta(t_1))$ is undefined.

(4) $(\mathcal{A}, \beta)(t) = \bot_i$ if $t = f(t_1, \ldots, t_n)$ and there is an i, $1 \leq i \leq n$ with $(\mathcal{A}, \beta)(t_i) \in \{\bot_u, \bot_i\}$.

(5) $(\mathcal{A}, \beta)(t) = a$ if $t = f(t_1, \ldots, t_n)$, $(\mathcal{A}, \beta)(t_i) \notin \{\bot_u, \bot_i\}$
for all i, $1 \leq i \leq n$ and $f^{\mathcal{A}}(\beta(t_1), \ldots, \beta(t_1)) = a$.

If $(\mathcal{A}, \beta)(t) \in \{\bot_u, \bot_i\}$ we call t undefined in $\mathcal{A}$ w.r.t. β, otherwise we call t defined in $\mathcal{A}$ w.r.t. β,

For the value of a formula φ in $(\mathcal{A}, \beta)$ we will similarly distinguish three truth values: 1 ("true"), 0 ("false") and $\frac{1}{2}$ ("undefined"), with $0 < \frac{1}{2} < 1$. Since the difference between weak and strong partial semantics concerns only equational atoms, we will define the notions simultaneously.

Definition 2.2.3 (Partial semantics) *Let $\mathcal{A}$ be a partial Π-algebra and $\beta : X \to A$ a valuation for its variables. The weak value $(\mathcal{A}, \beta)_w(\alpha)$ of a Π-atom α is defined as follows.*

(1) $(\mathcal{A}, \beta)_w(\alpha) = \frac{1}{2}$ *if a)* $\alpha = t \approx u$ *and one of the terms t, u is undefined in $(\mathcal{A}, \beta)$ or b)* $\alpha = P(t_1, \ldots, t_n)$ *and one t_i, $1 \leq i \leq n$ is undefined in $(\mathcal{A}, \beta)$.*

(2) $(\mathcal{A}, \beta)_w(\alpha) = 1$ *if a)* $\alpha = t \approx u$ *and both terms t, u are defined and equal in $(\mathcal{A}, \beta)$ or b)* $\alpha = P(t_1, \ldots, t_n)$ *and all terms t_i, $1 \leq i \leq n$ are defined in $(\mathcal{A}, \beta)$ and it holds that $P^{\mathcal{A}}(\beta(t_1), \ldots, \beta(t_n))$.*

(3) $(\mathcal{A}, \beta)_w(\alpha) = 0$ *if a)* $\alpha = t \approx u$ *and both terms t, u are defined but not equal in $(\mathcal{A}, \beta)$ or b)* $\alpha = P(t_1, \ldots, t_n)$ *and all terms t_i, $1 \leq i \leq n$ are defined in $(\mathcal{A}, \beta)$ but it does not hold that $P^{\mathcal{A}}(\beta(t_1), \ldots, \beta(t_n))$.*

The strong value $(\mathcal{A}, \beta)_s(\alpha)$ of a Π-atom α is defined as follows.

(1) $(\mathcal{A}, \beta)_s(\alpha) = \frac{1}{2}$ *if a)* $\alpha = t \approx u$ *and (at least) one value $\beta(t)$ or $\beta(u)$ is $\bot_i$, $\alpha = t \approx u$ and both values $\beta(t)$ and $\beta(u)$ are $\bot_u$; b)* $\alpha = P(t_1, \ldots, t_n)$ *and one t_i, $1 \leq i \leq n$ is undefined in $(\mathcal{A}, \beta)$.*

(2) $(\mathcal{A}, \beta)_s(\alpha) = 1$ *if a)* $\alpha = t \approx u$ *and both terms t, u are defined and equal in $(\mathcal{A}, \beta)$ or b)* $\alpha = P(t_1, \ldots, t_n)$ *and all terms t_i, $1 \leq i \leq n$ are defined in $(\mathcal{A}, \beta)$ and it holds that $P^{\mathcal{A}}(\beta(t_1), \ldots, \beta(t_n))$.*

(3) $(\mathcal{A}, \beta)_s(\alpha) = 0$ *if a)* $\alpha = t \approx u$ *and both terms t, u are defined but not equal in $(\mathcal{A}, \beta)$, b)* $\alpha = t \approx u$ *and one of the terms t, u is defined in $(\mathcal{A}, \beta)$ while the other is of the form $f(s_1, \ldots, s_n)$ where $\beta(s_i)$ is defined for $1 \leq i \leq n$ but $(\beta(s_1), \ldots, \beta(s_n))$ is not in the domain of $f^{\mathcal{A}}$ or
c)* $\alpha = P(t_1, \ldots, t_n)$ *and all terms t_i, $1 \leq i \leq n$ are defined in $(\mathcal{A}, \beta)$ but it does not hold that $P^{\mathcal{A}}(\beta(t_1), \ldots, \beta(t_n))$.*

Note that weak and strong partial semantics differ only on how they treat equality atoms. The definition for composed formulas are also the same for weak and strong partial semantics. We will write $(\mathcal{A}, \beta)_p$ for either.

(1) $(\mathcal{A},\beta)_p(\neg\varphi) := 1 - (\mathcal{A},\beta)_p$.
(2) $(\mathcal{A},\beta)_p(\varphi \wedge \psi) := \min((\mathcal{A},\beta)_p(\varphi),(\mathcal{A},\beta)_p(\psi))$.
(3) $(\mathcal{A},\beta)_p(\varphi \vee \psi) := \max((\mathcal{A},\beta)_p(\varphi),(\mathcal{A},\beta)_p(\psi))$.
(4) $(\mathcal{A},\beta)_p(\forall x.\varphi(x)) := \min(\{(\mathcal{A},\beta[x \mapsto a])_p(\varphi) \mid a \in A\})$.
(5) $(\mathcal{A},\beta)_p(\exists x.\varphi(x)) := \max(\{(\mathcal{A},\beta[x \mapsto a])_p(\varphi) \mid a \in A\})$.

Definition 2.2.4 (Partial model) Let $\mathcal{A}$ be a partial Π-algebra and $\beta : X \to A$ a valuation for its variables. We will write $\mathcal{A}, \beta \models_w \varphi$ ($\mathcal{A}, \beta \models_s \varphi$) if $(\mathcal{A},\beta)_w(\varphi) \geq \frac{1}{2}$ ($(\mathcal{A},\beta)_s(\varphi) \geq \frac{1}{2}$) and $\mathcal{A},\beta \not\models_w \varphi$ ($\mathcal{A},\beta \not\models_s \varphi$) otherwise. We call $(\mathcal{A},\beta)$ a weak (strong) partial model of φ if $\mathcal{A},\beta \models_w \varphi$ ($\mathcal{A},\beta \models_s \varphi$). For a set of formulas Γ, we write $\mathcal{A},\beta \models_w \Gamma$ ($\mathcal{A},\beta \models_s \Gamma$) if it hold that $\mathcal{A},\beta \models_w \varphi$ ($\mathcal{A},\beta \models_s \varphi$) for every formula $\varphi \in \Gamma$. For sets of formulas Γ, Δ we write $\Gamma \models_w \Delta$ ($\Gamma \models_s \Delta$) if every weak (strong) model of Γ weakly (strongly) satisfies at least one formula in Δ.

Example 2.2.5 *[GSSW04]* Let $\mathcal{A}$ be a partial Π-algebra, where $\Pi = \{\mathsf{car}, \mathsf{nil}\}$. Assume that $\mathsf{nil}^\mathcal{A}$ is defined and $\mathsf{car}^\mathcal{A}(\mathsf{nil}^\mathcal{A})$ is not defined. Then $A \models_w \mathsf{car}(\mathsf{nil}) \approx \mathsf{nil}$ and $A \models_w \mathsf{car}(\mathsf{nil}) \not\approx \mathsf{nil}$ (because one term is not defined in $\mathcal{A}$) but $A \not\models_s \mathsf{car}(\mathsf{nil}) \approx \mathsf{nil}$ because the immediate subterm of $\mathsf{car}(\mathsf{nil})$ is defined but not in the domain of $\mathsf{car}^\mathcal{A}$.

We gather some simple but useful facts about partial semantics.

Observation 2.2.6

(1) $\mathcal{A},\beta \not\models_w t \approx s$ if and only if both terms t, u are defined but different in $(\mathcal{A},\beta)$.
(2) $\mathcal{A},\beta \models_w t \not\approx s$ unless both terms t, u are defined and equal in $(\mathcal{A},\beta)$.
(3) $\mathcal{A},\beta \models_p P(t_1,\ldots,t_n)$ for $\models_p \in \{\models_w, \models_s\}$ unless all terms t_i are defined in $(\mathcal{A},\beta)$ and $(\beta(t_1),\ldots,\beta(t_n)) \notin P^\mathcal{A}$.
(4) $\mathcal{A},\beta \models_p \neg P(t_1,\ldots,t_n)$ for $\models_p \in \{\models_w, \models_s\}$ unless all terms t_i are defined in $(\mathcal{A},\beta)$ and $(\beta(t_1),\ldots,\beta(t_n)) \in P^\mathcal{A}$.
(5) $\mathcal{A},\beta \not\models_s t \approx s$ if and only if $\beta(t)$ and $\beta(s)$ are both defined but not equal or if one of $\beta(t)$ and $\beta(s)$ is defined while the other is not although all of its subterms are.
(6) $\mathcal{A},\beta \models_s t \not\approx s$ unless $\beta(t)$ and $\beta(s)$ are both defined and equal.
(7) $(\mathcal{A},\beta)$ weakly (strongly) satisfies a clause C if and only if it weakly (strongly) satisfies one of its literals.
(8) If there is some term t in a clause $C(\bar{x})$ which is undefined in a partial model $(\mathcal{A},\beta)$, then $\mathcal{A},\beta \models_w C(\bar{x})$.
(9) Let $t = t(\bar{x})$ be a term appearing in a universal clause $\forall \bar{y}. C(\bar{x}, \bar{y}, \bar{z})$ such that $\bar{x}$ and $\bar{y}$ are pairwise distinct, i.e., there is no variable that appears in both $\bar{x}$ and $\bar{y}$. If t is undefined in a partial model $(\mathcal{A},\beta)$ then $\mathcal{A},\beta \models_w \forall \bar{y}. C(\bar{x},\bar{y},\bar{z})$.
(10) Let t be a non-maximal term of a clause C, i.e., t always appears as $f(\ldots,t,\ldots)$ in C for some function f. If t is undefined in a partial model $(\mathcal{A},\beta)$ then $\mathcal{A},\beta \models_s C$.

(11) Let $t = t(\bar{x})$ be a term and $\forall \bar{y}. C(\bar{x}, \bar{y}, \bar{z})$ a universal clause such that $\bar{x}$ and $\bar{y}$ have no variables in common and t always appears as $f(\ldots, t, \ldots)$ in C for some function f. If t is undefined in a partial model $(\mathcal{A}, \beta)$ then $\mathcal{A}, \beta \models_s \forall \bar{y}. C(\bar{x}, \bar{y}, \bar{z})$.

Proof. (1) – (7) are immediate from the definitions.
(8) follows from (7) by (1) and (2).
For (9), let $\bar{y} = (y_1, \ldots, y_n)$ and β' be an arbitrary but fixed valuation that is exactly like β except (possibly) for the values for the $\bar{y}'s$, i.e., $\beta'(v) = \beta(v)$, for all $v \notin \{y_1, \ldots, y_n\}$. We need to show that $\mathcal{A}, \beta' \models_w C(\bar{x}, \bar{y}, \bar{z})$. But since $\bar{x}$ and $\bar{y}$ do not have any variables in common, we know in particular that $\beta'(t)$ is undefined and the claim follows from (8).
For (10), note that if t is undefined then the value w.r.t. $(\mathcal{A}, \beta)$ of any term in which t appears will be $\perp_i$. It follows from the definition that the strong truth value of any atom in which t appears will be $\frac{1}{2}$. Hence, the strong truth value of clause in which t appears will be at least $\frac{1}{2}$.
For (11), let β' be an arbitrary but fixed valuation that is exactly like β except for the values for the $\bar{y}'s$, i.e., $\beta'(v) = \beta(v)$, for all $v \notin \{y_1, \ldots, y_n\}$. We need to show that $\mathcal{A}, \beta' \models_s C(\bar{x}, \bar{y}, \bar{z})$. Since $\bar{x}$ and y do not overlap we have in particular that $\beta'(t)$ is undefined as well and the claim now follows from (10). $\square$

Remark 2.2.7 *In partial semantics we no longer have equivalence between $\mathcal{A}, \beta \models_p \neg \varphi$ and $\mathcal{A}, \beta \not\models_p \varphi$. As a consequence $\varphi \wedge \neg \varphi$ can be partially satisfiable; modus ponens, i.e., $\varphi, \varphi \to \psi \models_p \psi$, does not hold; nor does the deduction theorem $\Gamma, \varphi \models_p \psi \Leftrightarrow \Gamma \models_p \varphi \to \psi$.*

It follows that for clauses strong partial semantics really is stronger than weak partial semantics.

Lemma 2.2.8 *Let $\mathcal{A}$ be a partial Π-structure, C a universal clause. If $\mathcal{A} \models_s C$ then $\mathcal{A} \models_w C$.*

Proof. Let $C = \forall \bar{x}. D(\bar{x}, \bar{y})$ and β be arbitrary but fixed. We need to show that $\mathcal{A}, \beta \models_w D$. If there is a term t occurring in D which is undefined in $(\mathcal{A}, \beta)$ there is nothing to show by Observation 2.2.6.(8). Otherwise, if all terms that occur in D are defined then weak and strong partial semantics do not differ on D. $\square$

The substitution lemma does hold for partial algebras provided all the relevant terms are defined.

Lemma 2.2.9 (Substitution Lemma for partial algebras)
Let t be a Π-term, φ a Π-formula, $\mathcal{A}$ a partial Π-algebra, $\beta : X \to A$ a valuation for $\mathcal{A}$ and $\sigma : X \to \mathrm{Term}(X)$ a substitution. Define the valuation $\beta \circ \sigma : X \to A$ by

$$(\beta \circ \sigma)(x) := \begin{cases} \beta(\sigma(x)) & \text{if this is defined,} \\ \beta(x) & \text{otherwise.} \end{cases}$$

It holds that

(1) $(\mathcal{A}, \beta \circ \sigma)(t) = (\mathcal{A}, \beta)(t\sigma)$ if $\sigma(x)$ is defined in $(\mathcal{A}, \beta)$, for all variables x occurring in t.

(2) $(\mathcal{A}, \beta \circ \sigma)_w(\varphi) = (\mathcal{A}, \beta)_w(\varphi \sigma)$ if for all free variables x of φ, $\sigma(x)$ is defined in $(\mathcal{A}, \beta)$.

(3) $(\mathcal{A}, \beta \circ \sigma)_s(\varphi) = (\mathcal{A}, \beta)_s(\varphi\sigma)$ if for all free variables x of φ, $\sigma(x)$ is defined in $(\mathcal{A}, \beta)$.

(4) $\mathcal{A}, \beta \circ \sigma \models_w \varphi \Leftrightarrow \mathcal{A}, \beta \models_w \varphi\sigma$ if for all free variables x of φ, $\sigma(x)$ is defined in $(\mathcal{A}, \beta)$.

(5) $\mathcal{A}, \beta \circ \sigma \models_s \varphi \Leftrightarrow \mathcal{A}, \beta \models_s \varphi\sigma$ if for all free variables x of φ, $\sigma(x)$ is defined in $(\mathcal{A}, \beta)$.

Proof. (1) We use induction on terms. If t is a constant there is nothing to show. If t is a variable the claim is immediate from the definition of $(\beta \circ \sigma)$. For the induction step, let $t = f(u_1, \ldots, u_n)$. We have

$$\begin{aligned}
(\mathcal{A}, \beta \circ \sigma)(t) &= (\mathcal{A}, \beta \circ \sigma)(f(u_1, \ldots, u_n)) \\
&= f^{\mathcal{A}}((\mathcal{A}, \beta \circ \sigma)(u_1), \ldots, (\mathcal{A}, \beta \circ \sigma)(u_n)) \\
&= f^{\mathcal{A}}((\mathcal{A}, \beta)(u_1\sigma), \ldots, (\mathcal{A}, \beta)(u_n\sigma)) \qquad \text{(By hypothesis)} \\
&= (\mathcal{A}, \beta)(f(u_1\sigma, \ldots, u_n\sigma)) \\
&= (\mathcal{A}, \beta)(t\sigma).
\end{aligned}$$

(2) We use induction on formulas. The base case is a direct consequence of (1). Suppose φ is an equality atom, say $\varphi = t \approx u$. If $(\mathcal{A}, \beta \circ \sigma)(\varphi) = \frac{1}{2}$ this means that (at least) one of t, u is undefined in $(\mathcal{A}, \beta \circ \sigma)$, say t. By hypothesis, $t\sigma$ is then undefined in $(\mathcal{A}, \beta)$ too. Hence, $(\mathcal{A}, \beta)(t\sigma \approx u\sigma) = \frac{1}{2}$. Next suppose that $(\mathcal{A}, \beta \circ \sigma)(\varphi) = 1$. This means that both t, u are defined and equal in $(\mathcal{A}, \beta \circ \sigma)$. By hypothesis, it follows that $t\sigma, u\sigma$ are defined and equal in $(\mathcal{A}, \beta)$. Hence, $(\mathcal{A}, \beta)(t\sigma \approx u\sigma) = 1$. If $(\mathcal{A}, \beta \circ \sigma)(\varphi) = 0$ then t, u are defined but not equal in $(\mathcal{A}, \beta \circ \sigma)$ and therefore $t\sigma, u\sigma$ are defined but not equal in $(\mathcal{A}, \beta)$. The case where φ is a predicate atom is similar. This covers the base case.

The connectives step is trivial as usual. For the quantifier step, let $\varphi(\bar{x}) = \forall y.\psi(\bar{x}, y)$. Since substitutions are blocked from changing bound variables we might assume that $\sigma(y) = y$ in $\varphi(\bar{x})\sigma$. Thus,

$$\begin{aligned}
(\mathcal{A}, \beta)(\varphi\sigma) &= (\mathcal{A}, \beta)((\forall y.\psi(\bar{x}, y))\sigma) \\
&= (\mathcal{A}, \beta)(\forall y.(\psi(\bar{x}, y)\sigma)) \\
&= \min\{(\mathcal{A}, \beta)[y \mapsto a](\psi(\bar{x}, y)\sigma) \mid a \in A\} \\
&= \min\{(\mathcal{A}, \beta[y \mapsto a] \circ \sigma)(\psi(\bar{x}, y)) \mid a \in A\} \qquad \text{(By hypothesis)} \\
&= \min\{(\mathcal{A}, (\beta \circ \sigma)[y \mapsto a])(\psi(\bar{x}, y)) \mid a \in A\} \qquad (\sigma(y) = y) \\
&= (\mathcal{A}, \beta \circ \sigma)(\forall y.\psi(\bar{x}, y)) \\
&= (\mathcal{A}, \beta \circ \sigma)(\varphi)
\end{aligned}$$

(3) By induction on formulas again. The base case is an immediate consequence of (1) and the induction step is as in (2).

(4) and (5) are a trivial consequence of (2) and (3) respectively. $\square$

Corollary 2.2.10 ($\forall$-Elimination for partial algebras) *Let $\varphi(x, \bar{y})$ be a Π-formula, $\mathcal{A}$ a partial Π-algebra, $\beta : X \to A$ a valuation for $\mathcal{A}$ and t be a Π-term such that $(\mathcal{A}, \beta)(t)$ is defined. Suppose $\mathcal{A}, \beta \models_p \forall x.\varphi(x, \bar{y})$, then $\mathcal{A}, \beta \models_p \varphi(t, \bar{y})$.*

Proof. Let σ the substitution that maps x to t and leaves the other variables unchanged, let $b := (\mathcal{A}, \beta)(t)$. $\mathcal{A}, \beta \models_p \forall x.\varphi(x, \bar{y})$ is equivalent to $\mathcal{A}, \beta[x \mapsto a] \models_p \varphi(x, \bar{y})$, for all $a \in A$. In particular, $\mathcal{A}, \beta[x \mapsto b] \models_p \varphi(x, \bar{y})$. Note that $\beta[x \mapsto b]$ is the same as $\beta \circ \sigma$. By the Substitution Lemma for partial algebras it holds that $\mathcal{A}, \beta \circ \sigma \models_p \varphi(x, \bar{y}) \Leftrightarrow \mathcal{A}, \beta \models_p \varphi(t, \bar{y})$. □

The lemma on constants does also hold for partial algebras. The only difference to Lemma 2.1.11 is that we use the substitution lemma in lieu of $\forall$-elimination.

Corollary 2.2.11 *Let Γ be a set of $\mathcal{L}$-formulas and let φ be an $\mathcal{L}$-formula. Let c be an $\mathcal{L}$-constant not occurring in Γ and x be a variable which is not among the free variables of Γ. Then it holds that $\Gamma \models_p \varphi(c) \Leftrightarrow \Gamma \models_p \forall x.\varphi(x)$ for $\models_p \in \{\models_w, \models_s\}$.*

Proof. The direction from right to left is just an instantiation of a universal quantifier because constants are always defined in partial algebras. For the direction from left to right, let $(\mathcal{A}, \beta)$ be a partial model of Γ. We want to show that $\mathcal{A}, \beta \models_p \forall x.\varphi(x)$. Let β' be a valuation with $\beta'(y) = \beta(y)$, for all $y \neq x$. We have to show that $\mathcal{A}, \beta' \models_p \varphi(x)$. Let $a := \beta'(x)$ and let $\mathcal{A}'$ be exactly as $\mathcal{A}$ but with $c^{\mathcal{A}'} := a$. By assumption c did not appear in Γ, thus, $\mathcal{A}', \beta' \models_p \Gamma$. It follows that $\mathcal{A}', \beta' \models_p \varphi(c)$. Let σ be a substitution with $\sigma(x) = c$ and $\sigma(y) = y$, for $y \neq x$. By Lemma 2.2.9.(4) and Lemma 2.2.9.(5) respectively, we have $\mathcal{A}', \beta' \models_p \varphi\sigma \Leftrightarrow \mathcal{A}, \beta' \circ \sigma \models_p \varphi(x)$. Since $\beta' \circ \sigma = \beta'$ by construction, this implies $\mathcal{A}, \beta' \models_p \varphi(x)$ and this is what we wanted. □

We also want to lift the notion of homomorphisms to partial algebras. If our partial algebras happen to be total, a homomorphism for partial algebras should boil down to the usual notion of a homomorphism.

Definition 2.2.12 (Weak embedding) *Let $\mathcal{A}, \mathcal{B}$ be Π-algebras. A (total) map $h : A \to B$ between partial Π-algebras $\mathcal{A}$ and $\mathcal{B}$ is called a* weak Π-homomorphism *if whenever $f^{\mathcal{A}}(a_1, \ldots, a_n)$ is defined (in $\mathcal{A}$), then $f^{\mathcal{B}}(h(a_1), \ldots, h(a_n))$ is defined (in $\mathcal{B}$) and*

$$h(f^{\mathcal{A}}(a_1, \ldots, a_n)) = f^{\mathcal{B}}(h(a_1), \ldots, h(a_n)).$$

A weak homomorphism $h : \mathcal{A} \to \mathcal{B}$ is called a weak Π-embedding *of $\mathcal{A}$ into $\mathcal{B}$ if it is injective and if we have for all predicate symbols $P \in \Pi$ with arity n and every $a_1, \ldots, a_n \in \mathcal{A}$,*

$$P^{\mathcal{A}}(a_1, \ldots, a_n) \Leftrightarrow P^{\mathcal{B}}(h(a_1), \ldots, h(a_n)).$$

Note that if $\mathcal{A}$ and $\mathcal{B}$ are total then a weak homomorphism is the same as a homomorphism between the algebras. If the inclusion map is a weak embedding from $\mathcal{A}$ into $\mathcal{B}$ we say that $\mathcal{A}$ is a *weak substructure* of B. Similarly as with total algebras, we can identify weak embeddings with weak substructures.

Lemma 2.2.13 *Every weak embedding $\varphi : \mathcal{A} \to \mathcal{C}$ can be factored into a weak embedding ι, where ι is the inclusion map, and a weak isomorphism ψ such that $\varphi = \iota \circ \psi$*

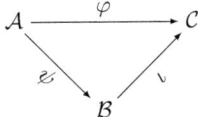

Similarly to Lemma 2.1.8, we can lift a partial homomorphism to a language extension.

Lemma 2.2.14 *Let $\mathcal{A}$ and $\mathcal{B}$ be partial Π-structures, $\bar{c}$ a sequence of fresh constants and $\varphi : \mathcal{A} \to \mathcal{B}$ a weak embedding. Then there is a unique weak embedding $\varphi^+ : (\mathcal{A}, \bar{a}) \to (\mathcal{B}, \varphi\bar{a})$ with $\varphi^+(a) = \varphi(a)$, for $a \in A$.*

However, existential sentences are not in general preserved under weak embeddings. This is due to the partial semantics. As an easy example, consider the sentence $\exists x. f(x) \approx d$ and the weak embedding $\varphi : \mathcal{A} \to \mathcal{B}$ and suppose that the domain of $f^\mathcal{A}$ is empty and $f^\mathcal{B}(b)$ is always defined but never equal to $d^\mathcal{B}$.

We have to demand definedness of certain terms to arrive at preservation results for weak embeddings.

Lemma 2.2.15 *Let $\mathcal{A}$ and $\mathcal{B}$ be partial Π-structures, $\varphi : \mathcal{A} \to \mathcal{B}$ a weak embedding, β a valuation for $\mathcal{A}$ and F a quantifier-free Π-formula. Suppose that all terms which occur in F are defined in $(\mathcal{A}, \beta)$. Then it holds that $(\mathcal{A}, \beta)_w(F) = (\mathcal{B}, \varphi \circ \beta)_w(F)$ and $(\mathcal{A}, \beta)_s(F) = (\mathcal{B}, \varphi \circ \beta)_s(F)$*

Proof. The claim follows from the fact that if all terms under consideration are defined, then partial semantics behaves just like total semantics and the fact that embeddings preserve all literals and, therefore, all quantifier-free formulas. □

Even though existential formulas are not automatically preserved in weak superstructures, the dual - universal formulas are reflected in weak substructures - is true for weak partial semantics.

Corollary 2.2.16 *Let $\mathcal{A}$ and $\mathcal{B}$ be partial Π-structures, $\varphi : \mathcal{A} \to \mathcal{B}$ a weak embedding, β a valuation for $\mathcal{A}$ and F a universal Π-formula. Then $\mathcal{B}, (\varphi \circ \beta) \models_w F$ implies $\mathcal{A}, \beta \models_w F$.*

Proof. We first show by induction that $\mathcal{A}, \beta \not\models_w F$ implies $\mathcal{B}, (\varphi \circ \beta) \not\models_w F$ for any quantifier-free formula F. If F is a literal, $(\mathcal{A}, \beta)_w(F) = 0$ can only happen if all terms in F are defined and then the above lemma applies. The induction step is clear. Now consider a universal formula $\forall \bar{x}.F$ and assume towards a contradiction that $\mathcal{A}, \beta \not\models_w \forall \bar{x}.F$. This means that for some $\bar{a} \in A$ we have $\mathcal{A}, \beta[x_i \mapsto a_i] \not\models_w F$. It follows from the claim that $\mathcal{B}, \varphi \circ \beta[x_i \mapsto a_i] \not\models_w F$. Contradiction. □

Universal formulas are not reflected in substructures w.r.t. strong partial semantics. For example, take $\mathcal{A} \subseteq_w \mathcal{B}$, the formula $F = \forall x. f(x) \approx d$ and suppose that $f^\mathcal{B}$ is always defined and equal to $d^\mathcal{B}$ whereas the domain of $f^\mathcal{A}$ is empty, then the formula F is true in $\mathcal{B}$ but false in $\mathcal{A}$ according to strong partial semantics.

2.3 Term Abstraction

We will often want to transform theory clauses and proof tasks over that theory. Theory clauses and proof tasks (= ground clauses) are treated differently as they are thought of as being left respectively right of '$\models$'. This implies that a fresh variable (= fresh constant) is quantified existentially in the former and universally in the latter case, cf. Lemmas 2.1.10 and 2.1.11. Accordingly we use two different yet similar notions of *term abstraction* depending on whether we want to transform a universal or a ground clause.

Definition 2.3.1 (Variable abstraction) *Let $\mathcal{L}$ be a first-order language. Let $t_1, ..., t_k$ be $\mathcal{L}$-terms and $\varphi(t_1, ..., t_k, x_1, ..., x_n)$ an $\mathcal{L}$-formula. Let $u_1, ..., u_k$ be variables which do not appear in $\varphi(t_1, ..., t_k, x_1, ..., x_n)$. Then the formula $u_1 \approx t_1, ..., u_k \approx t_k \rightarrow \varphi(u_1, ..., u_k, x_1, ..., x_n)$ is called a variable abstraction of $\varphi(t_1, ..., t_n)$.*

Lemma 2.3.2 (Abstraction) *Let $\mathcal{L}$ be a first-order language and $\varphi = \varphi(\bar{t}, \bar{x})$ an $\mathcal{L}$-formula. Let $\varphi_v(\bar{y}, \bar{x}) = y_1 \approx t_1, ..., y_k \approx t_k \rightarrow \varphi(y_1, ..., y_k, x_1, ..., x_n)$ be a variable abstraction of $\varphi(\bar{t}, \bar{x})$. Then it holds that φ and $\forall \bar{y}. \varphi_v(\bar{y}, \bar{x})$ are equivalent.*

Proof. Suppose that $\mathcal{A}, \bar{a} \models \varphi(\bar{t}, \bar{x})$. Fix some elements $\bar{b}$ of A as values of the variables $\bar{y}$. If there is an element b_i with $b_i \neq t_i^{\mathcal{A}}$ then $(\mathcal{A}, \bar{a}, \bar{b})$ trivially satisfies φ_v. Otherwise, it follows from the substitution lemma that $\mathcal{A}, \beta \models \varphi(\bar{t}, \bar{x})$ if and only if $\mathcal{A}, \beta \models \varphi(\bar{y}, \bar{x})$. For the other direction, let $\mathcal{A}, \bar{a} \models \forall \bar{y}. \varphi_v(\bar{y}, \bar{x})$. Let $b_i \in A$ be the element with $t_i^{\mathcal{A}}$. Then $\mathcal{A}, \bar{a}, \bar{b} \models \varphi$ and the claim follows from the substitution lemma again. □

The proof of the lemma depended strongly on the substitution lemma. The corresponding version for partial semantics does depend just as crucially on the substitution lemma for partial algebras.

Corollary 2.3.3 *Let $\mathcal{L}$ be a first-order language and $\varphi = \varphi(\bar{t}, \bar{x})$ an $\mathcal{L}$-formula. Let $\varphi_v(\bar{y}, \bar{x})$ be a variable term abstraction of $\varphi(\bar{t}, \bar{x})$. Then it holds that*

(1) $\varphi(\bar{t}, \bar{x}) \models_w \forall \bar{y}. \varphi_v(\bar{y}, \bar{x})$.

(2) If $\varphi(\bar{t})$ is a universal clause, then $\forall \bar{y}. \varphi_v(\bar{y}) \models_w \varphi(\bar{t})$.

(3) $\varphi(\bar{t}, \bar{x}) \models_s \forall \bar{y}. \varphi_v(\bar{y}, \bar{x})$ but not vice versa.

(4) Let $\bar{t}$ be ground terms and $\bar{c}$ new constants not appearing in $\varphi(\bar{t}, \bar{x})$. $\varphi(\bar{t}, \bar{x})$ has a weak (strong) partial model in which all terms $\bar{t}$ are defined if and only if $\bigwedge_i (c_i = t_i) \wedge \varphi(\bar{c}, \bar{x})$ has a weak (strong) partial model in which all terms $\bar{t}$ are defined.

(5) Suppose $\varphi(\bar{x})$ is a clause containing the negative literal $x_i \not\approx t(\bar{y})$, where $t(\bar{y})$ is a term in which the variable x_i does not occur. Let c be a constant not appearing in $\varphi(\bar{x})$ and $\varphi_c(\bar{x})$ be the clause that results from $\varphi(\bar{x})$ by replacing $x_i \not\approx t(\bar{y})$ with the two literals $x_i \not\approx c$ and $c \not\approx t(\bar{y})$. Then the universal clause $\forall \bar{x}. \varphi(\bar{x})$ has a weak partial model if and only if $\forall \bar{x}. \varphi_c(\bar{x})$ does.

Proof. 1) Let $(\mathcal{A}, \bar{a})$ be a weak partial model of $\varphi(\bar{t}, \bar{x})$. We want to show that $(\mathcal{A}, \bar{a}) \models_w \forall \bar{y}. \bigvee_i y_i \not\approx t_i \vee \varphi(\bar{y}, \bar{x})$. To that effect, fix some elements $\bar{b}$ of A. If there is some i with $(\mathcal{A}, \bar{a}, \bar{b}) \models_w y_i \not\approx t_i$ the claim follows immediately. Otherwise, by Observation 2.2.6.(2), all the terms t_i are defined and equal to b_i in $(\mathcal{A}, \bar{a})$. The claim follows now from the substitution lemma.
2) Let $\mathcal{A}$ be a weak partial model of $\forall \bar{y}. \varphi_v(\bar{y}, \bar{x})$ and $\beta : X \to A$ a valuation. If there is an abstraction term which is undefined in $(\mathcal{A}, \beta)$ the claim follows from Observation 2.2.6.(8). Otherwise we use the substitution lemma again.
3) This is similar to 1). Let $(\mathcal{A}, \bar{a})$ be a strong partial model of $\varphi(\bar{t}, \bar{x})$. We want to show that $(\mathcal{A}, \bar{a}) \models_s \forall \bar{y}. \bigvee_i y_i \not\approx t_i \vee \varphi(\bar{y}, \bar{x})$. To that effect, fix some elements $\bar{b}$ of A. If there is some i with $(\mathcal{A}, \bar{a}, \bar{b}) \models_s y_i \not\approx t_i$ the claim follows immediately. Otherwise, by Observation 2.2.6.(6), all the terms t_i are defined and equal to b_i in $(\mathcal{A}, \bar{a})$. The claim follows now from the substitution lemma.

As an example that strong partial models are not preserved under variable abstraction take $\varphi = f(t) \approx d$ where t is a term and d is a constant. Let $\mathcal{A}$ be a partial algebras with one element and $\mathcal{A}(f(t)) = \bot_u$. Trivially, $\mathcal{A} \models_s \forall y. y \approx d$ and, hence, $\forall y. y \approx d \to y \approx d$ but $\mathcal{A} \not\models_s d \not\approx f(t)$.
4) If $(\mathcal{A}, \beta)$ is a partial model of $\bigwedge_i (c_i = t_i) \wedge \varphi(\bar{c}, \bar{x})$ where all terms $\bar{t}$ are defined it follows from the substitution lemma that $(\mathcal{A}, \beta)$ is a partial model of $\varphi(\bar{t}, \bar{x})$. For the other direction, let $(\mathcal{A}, \beta)$ be a partial model of $\varphi(\bar{t}, \bar{x})$ where all terms $\bar{t}$ are defined. Expand $\mathcal{A}$ to $\mathcal{A}^+$ by defining $c_i^{\mathcal{A}^+} = (\mathcal{A}, \beta)(t_i)$. By the substitution lemma we have $(\mathcal{A}^+, \beta) \models_p \varphi(\bar{c}, \bar{x}) \Leftrightarrow (\mathcal{A}^+, \beta) \models_p \varphi(\bar{t}, \bar{x})$ and since the $\bar{c}$'s were fresh the right-hand side is equivalent to $\mathcal{A}, \beta \models_p \varphi(\bar{t}, \bar{x})$.
5) This is similar to 4). Suppose that $\mathcal{A}$ is a weak partial model of $\forall \bar{x}. \varphi_c(\bar{x})$ and let $\mathcal{A}^-$ be its reduct to the language without the constant c. Let β be any valuation for $\mathcal{A}^-$. We want to show that $\mathcal{A}^-, \beta \models_w \varphi(\bar{x})$. If $\beta(t(\bar{y}))$ is undefined we are done by Observation 2.2.6.(8). Otherwise the claim follows from $\mathcal{A}, \beta[x_i \mapsto c^{\mathcal{A}}] \models_w \varphi_c(\bar{x})$. For the other direction, let $\mathcal{A} \models_w \forall \bar{x}. \varphi(\bar{x})$ and β be any valuation for $\mathcal{A}$. Let $\mathcal{A}^+$ be the expansion of $\mathcal{A}$ with $c^{\mathcal{A}^+} := \beta(x_i)$. It follows that $\mathcal{A}^+, \beta \models_w \varphi_c(\bar{x})$, where β is considered as valuation for the expanded structure. □

2.4 Extensions of Theories

In what follows we will consider extensions of signatures by new *function symbols* and *extensions of theories by clauses* in the expanded language. We will always consider the new functions to be partial and the original ones to be total.

Let T_0 be an arbitrary theory in the signature $\Pi_0 = (\Sigma_0, \mathsf{Pred})$, where the set of function symbols is Σ_0 and the set of predicate symbols is Pred. We consider extensions T_1 of T_0 with signature $\Pi_1 = (\Sigma_0 \cup \Sigma_1, \mathsf{Pred})$, where the set of function symbols is $\Sigma_0 \cup \Sigma_1$. We call Σ_0 the base functions and Σ_1 the extension functions. Σ_1 is not supposed to contain any constants or to overlap with Σ_0. We assume that T_1 is obtained from T_0 by adding a set $\mathcal{K}$ of universally closed clauses.

Definition 2.4.1 (Weak partial model of a theory) *Let $\Pi_0 = (\Sigma_0, \mathsf{Pred})$ be a signature, Σ_1 a set of new function symbols of arity greater than 0, T_0 a Π_0-theory, $\mathcal{K}$ a set of universally closed clauses in the extended signature $\Pi_1 := (\Sigma_0 \cup \Sigma_1, \mathsf{Pred})$ and $T_1 := T_0 \cup \mathcal{K}$. A partial Π_1-algebra $\mathcal{A}$ is a* weak partial model *of T_1 with totally defined Σ_0-functions if*

(i) $\mathcal{A}\restriction_{\Pi_0}$ is a total model of T_0 and

(ii) $\mathcal{A}$ weakly satisfies all clauses in $\mathcal{K}$.

A partial Π_1-algebra $\mathcal{A}$ is a strong partial model of T_1 with totally defined Σ_0-functions if

(i) $\mathcal{A}\restriction_{\Pi_0}$ is a total model of T_0 and

(ii) $\mathcal{A}$ strongly satisfies all clauses in $\mathcal{K}$.

We denote the class of all weak partial models of T_1 with totally defined Σ_0-functions by $\mathsf{PMod}_w(\Sigma_1, T_1)$ and the class of strong partial models of T_1 with totally defined Σ_0-functions by $\mathsf{PMod}_s(\Sigma_1, T_1)$.

Embeddability. For theory extensions $T_0 \subseteq T_1 = T_0 \cup \mathcal{K}$, where $\mathcal{K}$ is a set of universally closed clauses and for the classes of partial algebras mentioned above we consider the following conditions.

(Emb_w)   Every $\mathcal{A} \in \mathsf{PMod}_w(\Sigma_1, T_1)$ weakly embeds into a total model of T_1.

(Emb_s)   Every $\mathcal{A} \in \mathsf{PMod}_s(\Sigma_1, T_1)$ weakly embeds into a total model of T_1.

We also define a stronger notion of embeddability, which we call *completability*:

(Comp_w)   Every $\mathcal{A} \in \mathsf{PMod}_w(\Sigma_1, T_1)$ weakly embeds into a total model $\mathcal{B}$ of T_1 such that $\mathcal{A}\restriction_{\Pi_0}$ and $\mathcal{B}\restriction_{\Pi_0}$ are isomorphic.

(Comp_s)   Every $\mathcal{A} \in \mathsf{PMod}_s(\Sigma_1, T_1)$ weakly embeds into a total model $\mathcal{B}$ of T_1 such that $\mathcal{A}\restriction_{\Pi_0}$ and $\mathcal{B}\restriction_{\Pi_0}$ are isomorphic.

Corresponding weaker conditions, which only refer to embeddability or completability of *finite* partial models, will be denoted by (Emb_w^f), (Emb_s^f), respectively (Comp_w^f), (Comp_s^f). We will also consider the embeddability of models with finite extension domains.

(Emb_w^{fd})   Every $\mathcal{A} \in \mathsf{PMod}_w(\Sigma_1, T_1)$ where all domains of extension functions are finite, weakly embeds into a total model of T_1.

As with total models, there is a syntactic characterization of embeddability which will prove useful. Recall that, given a partial algebra $\mathcal{A}$, we denote by $(\mathcal{A}, A)$ the expanded algebra which contains a name $\underline{a}$ for each element $a \in A$.

Definition 2.4.2 (Partial diagram) *Let $\mathcal{A}$ be a $\Pi = (\Sigma, \mathsf{Pred})$ partial algebra. Then the* partial diagram $\Delta_{\mathcal{A}}^P$ *of $\mathcal{A}$ is the following set of Σ_A-formulas.*

$$\Delta_{\mathcal{A}}^P := \{f(a_1, \ldots, a_n) \approx a \mid f \in \Sigma, f^{\mathcal{A}}(a_1, \ldots, a_n) \text{ is defined and its value is } a\}$$
$$\cup \{P(a_1, \ldots, a_n) \mid P \in \Pi, (a_1, \ldots, a_n) \in P^{\mathcal{A}}\}$$
$$\cup \{\neg P(a_1, \ldots, a_n) \mid P \in \Pi, (a_1, \ldots, a_n) \notin P^{\mathcal{A}}\}$$
$$\cup \{a \not\approx b \mid a \neq b\}$$

Lemma 2.4.3 (Partial diagram lemma) *Let Π be a signature, $\mathcal{A}$ a partial Π-algebra and $\mathcal{B}$ a total one. Then it is the case that $\mathcal{A}$ is weakly embedded in $\mathcal{B}$ if and only if there is an $\mathcal{L}_A$ expansion $\mathcal{B}'$ of $\mathcal{B}$ such that $\mathcal{B}' \models \Delta_{\mathcal{A}}^P$.*

Proof. Suppose first that there is a weak embedding $\varphi : \mathcal{A} \hookrightarrow \mathcal{B}$. We set $a^{\mathcal{B}'} := \varphi(a)$ for the additional constants. It follows directly from the definition of weak embeddings that $\mathcal{B}' \models \Delta_{\mathcal{A}}^P$. For the other direction, let $\mathcal{B}' \models \Delta_{\mathcal{A}}^P$. We construct a (weak) embedding $\varphi : \mathcal{A} \hookrightarrow \mathcal{B}$ by setting $\varphi(a) := a^{\mathcal{B}'}$. The last class of formulas in $\Delta_{\mathcal{A}}^P$ ensures that φ is one-one. We next check the homomorphism condition: let $f^{\mathcal{A}}(a_1, \ldots, a_n)$ be defined with value b. This means $\mathcal{B}' \models f(a_1, \ldots, a_n) \approx b$. It follows that

$$\varphi(f^{\mathcal{A}}(a_1, \ldots, a_n)) = \varphi(b) = b^{\mathcal{B}'} = f^{\mathcal{B}'}(a_1^{\mathcal{B}'}, \ldots, a_n^{\mathcal{B}'}) = f^{\mathcal{B}'}(\varphi a_1, \ldots, \varphi a_n).$$

Finally, from $(a_1, \ldots, a_n) \in P^{\mathcal{A}}$ it follows that $P(a_1, \ldots, a_n) \in \Delta_{\mathcal{A}}^P$. Hence, $(a_1^{\mathcal{B}'}, \ldots, a_n^{\mathcal{B}'}) = (\varphi a_1, \ldots, \varphi a_n) \in P^{\mathcal{B}'}$. Similarly, if $(a_1, \ldots, a_n) \notin P^{\mathcal{A}}$ then $\neg P(a_1, \ldots, a_n) \in \Delta_{\mathcal{A}}^P$. Thus, $(a_1^{\mathcal{B}'}, \ldots, a_n^{\mathcal{B}'}) = (\varphi a_1, \ldots, \varphi a_n) \notin P^{\mathcal{B}'}$. □

Sometimes we want to consider extensions of a theory T_0 by some extension formulas which are slightly more general than clauses (this was considered first in [SS05]).

Definition 2.4.4 (Augmented clause) *Let $\Pi_0 = (\Sigma_0, \mathsf{Pred})$ be a signature, Σ_1 a set of new function symbols of arity greater than 0, T_0 a Π_0-theory and $\Pi_1 := (\Sigma_0 \cup \Sigma_1, \mathsf{Pred})$. A Π_1-formula is called an* augmented clause *if it is of the form $\forall \bar{x}. (\Phi(\bar{x}) \vee C(\bar{x}))$ where $\Phi(\bar{x})$ is an arbitrary Π_0-formula and $C(\bar{x})$ is a Π_1-clause, which does contain a Σ_1-function symbol; if $\Phi(\bar{x})$ is universal for every $\varphi \in \mathcal{K}$, we speak of an* extension with universal augmented clauses.

In particular every extension clause is also an augmented clause.

2.5 Purification, Reduction and Flattening

Locality is a property of theory extensions. That is, it is a *syntactic* property. The particular axiomatization of a theory is crucial. We might have to transform the theory in order to show locality or we might have to transform the proof task in order to carry out a full reduction to the base theory. Henceforth, let Σ_C be an infinite set of fresh constants.

Purification. With the above notations, let Γ be a set of augmented Π_1-clauses. Let Γ^* be a set of instances of Γ with the property that variables do not occur below extension functions. *Purifying* Γ^* to a set $\Gamma_0 \cup D$ means separating all Σ_1-terms into the set D by using constant term abstraction. We introduce fresh constants $d_{f(c_1, \ldots, c_n)}$ for $f(c_1, \ldots, c_n)$ in a bottom-up manner and using these new names in Γ to get Γ_0. D only contains their definitions of the form $d_{f(c_1, \ldots, c_n)} \approx f(c_1, \ldots, c_n)$. Purifying increases the size of Γ only by a linear factor.

We may purify a set of clauses while maintaining satisfiability ([SS05]).

Lemma 2.5.1 (Reduction) *Let $\Pi_0 = (\Sigma_0, \mathsf{Pred})$ be a signature, Σ_1 a set of new function symbols of arity greater than 0, T_0 a Π_0-theory and $\Pi_1 := (\Sigma_0 \cup \Sigma_1, \mathsf{Pred})$. Let Γ be a set of augmented clauses and let G be a set of extension ground clauses, which may contain additional constants. Let Γ^* be a set of instances of Γ with the property that variables do not occur below extension functions. Let $\Gamma_0 \cup G_0 \cup D$ be the purified form of $\Gamma^* \cup G$, i.e., Σ_1-functions occur only in D in the form of ground unit clauses. Then the following are equivalent.*

(1) $T_0 \cup \Gamma^* \cup G$ has a weak (strong) partial model with totally defined Σ_0-functions in which all extension ground terms occurring in $\Gamma^* \cup G$ are defined.

(2) $T_0 \cup \Gamma_0 \cup G_0 \cup D$ has a weak (strong) partial model with totally defined Σ_0-functions in which all extension ground terms occurring in D are defined.

(3) $T_0 \cup \Gamma_0 \cup G_0 \cup N_0$ has a total model, where
$N_0 := \{ (\bigwedge_{i=1}^n c_i \approx d_i) \to c \approx d \mid f(c_1, ..., c_n) \approx c, f(d_1, ..., d_n) \approx d \in D \}$.

Remark 2.5.2 *The size increase of N_0 compared to D in the above lemma is at most quadratic. This is because an upper bound on the number of pairings of functions in D is $\frac{1}{2}n^2$ where n is the size of D.*

Flatness. With the above notations, we call a non-ground clause Σ_1-*flat* when it contains no nested functions with a Σ_1-symbol at root, i.e., all symbols occurring below a function symbol from Σ_1 are variables. A non-ground clause is Σ_1-*quasiflat* when all symbols below a function symbol of Σ_1 are variables or ground terms of the base signature Π_0.[3]

Similarly for ground clauses, except that here constants will have the role of variables. Thus, we call a ground clause Σ_1-*flat* if all symbols below a Σ_1-function are constants and we call a ground clause Σ_1-*quasiflat* if all symbols below a Σ_1-function are ground terms of the extended base language $\Pi_0 \cup \Sigma_C$.

Linearity. We call a non-ground clause Σ_1-*linear* if it is Σ_1-flat or Σ_1-quasiflat and whenever a variable occurs in two terms of the clause which start with the same Σ_1-function, the terms are identical, and none of these Σ_1-terms contains two occurrences of a variable. In other words, *a flat clause is linear if each variable which occurs in a Σ_1-term does so uniquely in the sense that it does not occur in any other Σ_1-term (that term, however, may appear multiple times)*.

We call a Σ_1-flat or quasiflat ground clause Σ_1-*linear* if whenever a constant occurs in two terms in the clause whose root symbol is in Σ_1, the two terms are identical, and if no term which starts with a Σ_1-function contains two occurrences of the same constant.

If Σ_1 is clear from the context, we will sometimes simply talk of flat or linear clauses instead of Σ_1-flat or Σ_1-linear clauses.

Example 2.5.3 *In the following examples, let f and g be the extension functions.*

(1) *$f(x,y) \approx f(y,x)$ is flat but not linear. We can transform it into an equi-satisfiable linear one by using variable abstraction: $\forall z_1, z_2.\, z_1 \approx y, z_2 \approx x \to f(x,y) \approx f(z_1, z_2)$.*

(2) *$f(x, g(c)) \approx g(x)$ is neither flat nor linear. We can transform it into an equi-satisfiable quasi-flat one: $\forall z_1.\, z_1 \approx g(c) \to f(x, z_1) \approx g(x)$. This clause is still not linear. Use abstraction again to get a linear one*
$\forall z_1, z_2.\, z_1 \approx g(c), z_2 \approx x \to f(x, z_1) \approx g(z_2)$.

(3) *The ground clause $g(f(c,c)) \approx g(c)$ can be transformed into the equi-satisfiable set of linear ground clauses $\{d_1 \approx c, d_2 \approx f(c, d_1), g(d_2) \approx g(c)\}$.*

---

[3]In the case of a set of quasiflat clauses it could happen that one of its clauses is ground. We still mean the same notion of (non-ground) flatness.

According to Corollary 2.3.3 we can always flatten and linearize a set of clauses without affecting satisfiability with regard to weak partial models and we can always flatten and linearize ground clauses without affecting the existence of a partial model, be it weak or strong, in which the abstracted terms are defined.

Chapter 3

Local Theory Extensions

The notion of *locality* was introduced by Givan and McAllester ([GM92, McA93]). They considered so-called *local inference systems* which have the property that the validity of ground Horn clauses can be checked in polynomial time. This is because for local inference systems only certain instances need to be considered in discharging a given proof task, viz. those instances which only contain ground terms already appearing in the inference system or the given proof task. Later, a more general notion of order locality was introduced by Basin and Ganzinger ([BG01]).

The notion of *locality* was generalized to equational theories and related to a semantical approach towards the uniform word problem by Harald Ganzinger in [Gan01]. A *local theory* is a set of Horn clauses $\mathcal{K}$ such that, for any ground Horn clause C, $\mathcal{K} \models C$ only if already $\mathcal{K}[C] \models C$ (where $\mathcal{K}[C]$ is the set of instances of $\mathcal{K}$ in which all terms are subterms of ground terms in either $\mathcal{K}$ or C). In [SS05] the notion of locality was lifted to *theory extensions*. Here one considers a base theory as fixed and extends it by a set of (universally closed) clauses $\mathcal{K}$, which do not need to be Horn, that specify the properties of new functions. With the notation of Section 2.4, let T_0 be a theory in the signature $\Pi_0 = (\Sigma_0, \mathsf{Pred})$, $\mathcal{K}$ a set of universally closed clauses in the signature $\Pi_1 = (\Sigma_0 \cup \Sigma_1, \mathsf{Pred})$. We want to answer the *clausal word problem* for this extension. That is, given some clause $\forall \bar{x}. C(\bar{x})$ we want to know if $T_0 \cup \mathcal{K} \models \forall \bar{x}. C(\bar{x})$. As often in model theory, it is more convenient to introduce new constants than to handle quantifiers. For this purpose, we introduce a fixed, countably infinite set Σ_C of new constants. No element of Σ_C may already occur in the signature Π_1. Given this new signature $\Pi_1^C = (\Sigma_0 \cup \Sigma_1 \cup \Sigma_C, \mathsf{Pred})$ the above problem is equivalent to $T_0 \cup \mathcal{K} \cup \neg C(\bar{c}) \models \bot$, where the constants $\bar{c}$ are taken from Σ_C. The negation $\neg C(\bar{c})$ of $C(\bar{c})$ is a set of ground literals. We will relax this a bit by considering sets of *ground clauses* in the extended signature with constants. This gives us the following setup.

Definition 3.0.4 (Local instances) *Let T_0 be a theory in the signature $\Pi_0 = (\Sigma_0, \mathsf{Pred})$, Σ_1 a set of new function symbols, $\mathcal{K}$ a set of clauses or augmented clauses in the extended signature $\Pi_1 = (\Sigma_0 \cup \Sigma_1, \mathsf{Pred})$ that are universally closed. Let G be a set of ground clauses in the signature $\Pi_1^C = (\Sigma_0 \cup \Sigma_1 \cup \Sigma_C, \mathsf{Pred})$ where Σ_C is a set of fresh constants. Let $\mathrm{st}(\mathcal{K}, G)$ be the set of ground terms which appear in $\mathcal{K}$ or in G.*

We denote by $\mathcal{K}[G]$ the set of all instances of $\mathcal{K}$ in which all terms starting with a Σ_1-function symbol are ground terms in the set $\mathrm{st}(\mathcal{K}, G)$. For technical reasons, we must first drop the universal quantifiers from a clause $C \in \mathcal{K}$ before employing a substitution σ. Then we universally close $C\sigma$

again. Formally,

$$\mathcal{K}[G] := \{C\sigma \mid C\sigma \text{ is universally closed and the universal closure}$$
$$\forall C \text{ of } C \text{ is in } \mathcal{K}, \text{for all terms } t \leq \cdot C\sigma \text{ with } \text{root}(t) \in \Sigma_1$$
$$\text{it holds that } t \in \text{st}(\mathcal{K}, G),$$
$$\text{and for each variable } x \text{ which does not occur}$$
$$\text{below a function symbol in } \Sigma_1 : \sigma(x) = x\}.$$

We call $\mathcal{K}[G]$ the set of local instances of $\mathcal{K}$ (w.r.t. G).

The following definition of locality is that introduced in [SS05].

Definition 3.0.5 (Local extension) *Let T_0 be a theory in the signature $\Pi_0 = (\Sigma_0, \mathsf{Pred})$, Σ_1 a set of new function symbols, $\mathcal{K}$ a set of universally closed clauses in the extended signature $\Pi_1 = (\Sigma_0 \cup \Sigma_1, \mathsf{Pred})$ and let $\Pi_1^C = (\Sigma_0 \cup \Sigma_1 \cup \Sigma_C, \mathsf{Pred})$ where Σ_C is a set of fresh constants. We call the extension $T_0 \cup \mathcal{K}$ of T_0 local if it holds for every set G of ground Π_1^C clauses that $T_0 \cup \mathcal{K} \cup G \models \perp$ if and only if $T_0 \cup \mathcal{K}[G] \cup G$ has no weak partial model (with total Σ_0-functions) in which all terms in $\mathsf{st}(\mathcal{K}, G)$ are defined. We call the extension $T_0 \cup \mathcal{K} \supseteq T_0$ finitely local if the above property holds for all finite sets of ground clauses G. We will abbreviate the property of locality and that of finite locality by* (Loc), (Loc^f) *respectively.*

Note that one direction in the definition of locality always holds: If there is no weak partial model for G and some instances $\mathcal{K}[G]$ of $\mathcal{K}$ there certainly is none for $\mathcal{K} \cup G$ because total models are also partial ones.

In the next sections we will prove the equivalence of locality and weak embeddability. We need to impose the syntactic restriction that the extension clauses be linear in order for this equivalence to hold. The equivalence of locality and embeddability was first established by Harald Ganzinger ([Gan01]) for the case of Horn clauses and later lifted to theory extensions by Viorica Sofronie-Stokkermans ([SS05]). We here present the proof in [SS05] because it will be the model for the proof in later chapters establishing links between generalized locality and embeddability.

3.1 Locality Implies Embeddability

Finite locality is enough to ensure embeddability as can be shown with the help of the diagram Lemma 2.4.3.

Theorem 3.1.1 (Sofronie-Stokkermans, [SS10]) *Let T_0 be a theory in the signature $\Pi_0 = (\Sigma_0, \mathsf{Pred})$, Σ_1 a set of new function symbols and $\mathcal{K}$ a set of universally closed clauses in the extended signature $\Pi_1 = (\Sigma_0 \cup \Sigma_1, \mathsf{Pred})$. Suppose that all the clauses in $\mathcal{K}$ are Σ_1-flat or that $\mathcal{K}$ does not contain any extension ground terms. If the extension $T_0 \subseteq T_0 \cup \mathcal{K}$ satisfies* (Loc^f) *then it satisfies* (Emb$_w$).

3.2 Embeddability Implies Locality

For the other direction it is necessary that the extension clauses are not only flat but also linear. The following theorem was proved by Viorica Sofronie-Stokkermans in [SS05] for the case of flat and linear extension clauses. The same proof works also for quasiflat and linear extension clauses and will serve as a model for similar results below.

Theorem 3.2.1 (cf. [SS05]) *Let T_0 be a theory in the signature $\Pi_0 = (\Sigma_0, \text{Pred})$, Σ_1 a set of new function symbols and $\mathcal{K}$ a set of universally closed clauses in the extended signature $\Pi_1 = (\Sigma_0 \cup \Sigma_1, \text{Pred})$. Suppose that all clauses in $\mathcal{K}$ are Σ_1-quasiflat and Σ_1-linear. Then if the extension $T_0 \subseteq T_0 \cup \mathcal{K}$ satisfies* (Emb$_w$) *then it satisfies* (Loc).

Proof. Let $T_1 := T_0 \cup \mathcal{K}$. Assume towards a contradiction that the extension were not local. That means that there would be a set of ground clauses G (with additional constants) such that $T_0 \cup \mathcal{K} \cup G \models \bot$ but there is a weak partial model $\mathcal{A}$ of $T_0 \cup \mathcal{K}[G] \cup G$ with total Σ_0-functions such that all terms in $\text{st}(\mathcal{K}, G)$ are defined.

From $\mathcal{A}$ we construct a weak partial model $\mathcal{B}$ of $T_0 \cup \mathcal{K} \cup G$. By the hypothesis $\mathcal{B}$ embeds into a total model $T_0 \cup \mathcal{K}$ which leads to a contradiction. The crucial step is to obtain a model of $\mathcal{K}$ from our model of $\mathcal{K}[G]$. We construct $\mathcal{B}$ from $\mathcal{A}$ by keeping the domain, i.e., $B := A$, and the base functions while restricting Σ_1-functions. For $f \in \Sigma_1$ we set

$$f^\mathcal{B}(a_1, ..., a_n) := \begin{cases} f^\mathcal{A}(t_1^\mathcal{A}, ..., t_n^\mathcal{A}) & \text{if there is a term } f(t_1, ..., t_n) \in \text{st}(\mathcal{K}, G) \\ & \text{such that } a_i = t_i^\mathcal{A}, \text{ for } i = 1, \ldots, n; \\ \text{undefined} & \text{otherwise.} \end{cases}$$

$\mathcal{B}$ and $\mathcal{A}$ do not differ on $\Sigma_0 \cup \Sigma_C$ and so $\mathcal{B}$ is also a model of T_0. Further, $\mathcal{A}$ and $\mathcal{B}$ agree on all terms in $\text{st}(\mathcal{K}, G)$. In particular, all terms of $\text{st}(\mathcal{K}, G)$ are defined in $\mathcal{B}$ too. Since $\mathcal{B}$ is a weak submodel of $\mathcal{A}$ it follows from Lemma 2.2.15 that $\mathcal{B} \models_w G$.

It remains to show that $\mathcal{B} \models_w \mathcal{K}$. Let D be a clause in $\mathcal{K}$. Consider first the case when D is ground. In that case we know that all terms in D are defined. Trivially, D is a member of $\mathcal{K}[G]$. Hence, $\mathcal{A} \models_w D$ and because all terms in D were defined in $\mathcal{A}$ it follows that $\mathcal{B} \models_w D$ and we are done. Now consider the case where D is not ground. Let $\beta : X \to B$ be an arbitrary valuation. Again, if there is a term t in D such that $t^\mathcal{B}[\beta]$ is undefined, we immediately have $\mathcal{B}, \beta \models_w D$ by Observation 2.2.6.(7). So let us suppose that all terms in D are defined. $\mathcal{K}$ is Σ_1-linear. This implies that a variable x either does not occur below a Σ_1-function at all or does so in a unique term (which may occur more than once). Concerning the latter case, if we have a Σ_1-term $t = f(...x...y...)$ of D we know from the fact that $\beta(t)$ is defined that there are ground terms which we will denote by t_x, t_y such that $\beta(x) = t_x$, $\beta(y) = t_y$, $\beta(t) = f^\mathcal{B}(...t_x^\mathcal{B}...t_y^\mathcal{B}...)$ and $f(...t_x...t_y...) \in \text{st}(\mathcal{K}, G)$. Using this notation we may define a substitution σ in the following manner.

$$\sigma(x) = \begin{cases} t_x & \text{if } x \text{ does occur below a } \Sigma_1\text{-function in } D \text{ and } \beta(x) = t_x^\mathcal{A}, \\ x & \text{if } x \text{ does not occur below a } \Sigma_1\text{-function in } D. \end{cases}$$

The above consideration shows that σ is well-defined and that $D\sigma \in \mathcal{K}[G]$. In particular, we have that $\mathcal{A}, \beta \models_w D\sigma$. By the substitution lemma, this is equivalent to $\mathcal{A}, (\beta \circ \sigma) \models_w D$. By construction we have that $(\beta \circ \sigma) = \beta$ and, hence, $\mathcal{A}, \beta \models_w D$. Remember that we are considering the case where all terms in D are defined in $(\mathcal{B}, \beta)$. We may therefore use Lemma 2.2.15 once again to conclude that $\mathcal{B}, \beta \models_w D$.

Finally, we use the assumption to obtain a total model $\mathcal{C}$ of T_1 into which $\mathcal{B}$ is embedded. By Lemma 2.2.14 we can expand $\mathcal{C}$ to a model of G and we have arrived at our contradiction. □

This proof technique also works for finite locality. The following generalizations were shown in [SSI07a] and [SS05] respectively.

Theorem 3.2.2 (Sofronie-Stokkermans) *Let T_0 be a theory in the signature $\Pi_0 = (\Sigma_0, \mathsf{Pred})$, Σ_1 a set of new function symbols and $\mathcal{K}$ a set of universally closed clauses in the extended signature $\Pi_1 = (\Sigma_0 \cup \Sigma_1, \mathsf{Pred})$. Suppose that all clauses in $\mathcal{K}$ are Σ_1-quasiflat and Σ_1-linear. Then*

(1) If $\mathcal{K}$ is additionally Σ_1-flat and the extension $T_0 \subseteq T_0 \cup \mathcal{K}$ satisfies ($\mathsf{Emb}_w^{\mathsf{fd}}$) then it satisfies ($\mathsf{Loc}^\mathsf{f}$).

(2) If $\mathcal{K}$ contains only finitely many extension ground terms, T_0 is universal and locally finite (i.e., each finitely generated model of T_0 is finite) and the extension $T_0 \subseteq T_0 \cup \mathcal{K}$ satisfies ($\mathsf{Emb}_w^\mathsf{f}$) then it satisfies ($\mathsf{Loc}^\mathsf{f}$).

Proof. (1) the proof is similar to the proof of the above theorem. We assume that there is a finite G such that $T_0 \cup \mathcal{K} \cup G \models \bot$ but there is a weak partial model $\mathcal{A} \in \mathsf{PMod}_w(\Sigma_1, T_1)$ of $T_0 \cup \mathcal{K}[G] \cup G$ such that all terms in $\mathrm{st}(\mathcal{K}, G)$ are defined. From this we construct $\mathcal{B}$ as before. Note that for an extension function f, the domain of $f^\mathcal{B}$ must be finite even when $\mathcal{K}$ is infinite because $\mathcal{K}$ is flat and not just quasiflat. It follows that $f(t) \in \mathrm{st}(\mathcal{K}, G)$ is the same as $f(t) \in \mathrm{st}(G)$. The rest of the proof is as before.

(2) is similar except that we use the set $\{t^\mathcal{A} \mid t \in \mathrm{Term}_{\Sigma_0}(\mathrm{st}(\mathcal{K}, G))\}$ as support for $\mathcal{B}$. The base functions are inherited from $\mathcal{A}$, the Σ_1-functions are defined as before. Because T_0 is universal, we have $\mathcal{B}\!\restriction_{\Pi_0} \models T_0$. It follows from the assumptions that $\mathcal{B}$ is finite. And as before we obtain $\mathcal{B} \models_w T_0 \cup \mathcal{K} \cup G$. By assumption, we obtain from this a total model of $T_0 \cup \mathcal{K} \cup G$. □

Remark 3.2.3 *The condition that $\mathcal{K}$ is in universal clause form is essential for the above theorem. Even weakening this constraint on $\mathcal{K}$ to negation normal form invalidates the implication from embeddability to locality.*

To show the above claim we proceeded by restricting a given partial model to the extension ground terms already appearing. Then we argue that a clause either contains an undefined term or it does not.

In the former case the clause is trivially satisfied due to weak semantics. In the latter case, we use the construction to show that the clause under the appropriate substitution must be in $\mathcal{K}[G]$ and therefore satisfied in both models. But the first prong does not work for negative normal form. For instance, if we have a conjunction, one term in some conjunct might be undefined but that does not mean the whole conjunction has the value $\frac{1}{2}$. As a counterexample, take the theory of a partial ordered set as our base theory T_0 and let N be the single formula

$$\forall x, y, z.\ h(z) = e \wedge (x \not\leq y \vee f(x) \leq f(y)),$$

where h, f are extension functions. We can embed any weak partial model $\mathcal{A}$ of $T_0 \cup N$ into a total model $\mathcal{B}$ of $T_0 \cup N$ in the following manner.

As carrier and order for $\mathcal{B}$ we take the Dedekind-MacNeille completion[1] $(\mathrm{DM}(A), \subseteq)$ of $(A, \leq)$ and set

$$h'(U) := \{e\}^l \text{ and } \bar{f}(U) := f(U)^{ul}$$

where $A^l := \{\, x \mid x \leq a, \text{ for all } a \in A\,\}$ and $A^u := \{\, x \mid x \geq a, \text{ for all } a \in A\,\}$.

Then $\mathcal{B} := (\mathrm{DM}(A), \subseteq, \{e\}^l, h', \bar{f})$ is a (total) model of $T_0 \cup N$ and the map $\varphi : a \mapsto \{b \mid b \leq a\}$ is a weak embedding from $\mathcal{A}$ into $\mathcal{B}$ (cf. Corollary 3.6.13). So we have embeddability of partial models of $T_0 \subseteq T_0 \cup N$ into total ones but the extension $T_0 \subseteq T_0 \cup N$ is not local. Take $G = \{c < c', f(c) > f(c')\}$. Then $T_0 \cup N \cup G$ is certainly unsatisfiable. Note that $N[G]$ is empty since h does not appear in any ground term. Trivially, $T_0 \cup G$ is weakly satisfiable. Hence, the extension is not local.

3.3 Stable Locality

Instead of considering those instances of an extension clause where every variable below an extension function must be instantiated in such a way that the *entire* resulting term already appears in the problem, we can consider those instances where those variables are instantiated by extension terms.

This will result in more instances. It turns out that the semantical counterpart for this notion of locality will be strong partial semantics. Another difference to weak locality is that we do not have to flatten or linearize the extension clauses in order to show locality (cf. [GSSW04, GSSW06, SS05]).

Definition 3.3.1 (Stably local instances) *Let T_0 be a theory in the signature $\Pi_0 = (\Sigma_0, \mathsf{Pred})$, Σ_1 a set of new function symbols, $\mathcal{K}$ a set of universally closed clauses in the extended signature $\Pi_1 = (\Sigma_0 \cup \Sigma_1, \mathsf{Pred})$ and G a set of ground clauses in the signature $\Pi_1^C = (\Sigma_0 \cup \Sigma_1 \cup \Sigma_C, \mathsf{Pred})$, where Σ_C is a set of fresh constants. Let $\mathrm{st}(\mathcal{K}, G)$ be the set of ground terms which appear in $\mathcal{K}$ or in G. We define the following set $\mathcal{K}^{[G]}$ of instances of $\mathcal{K}$*

$$\mathcal{K}^{[G]} := \{C\sigma \mid C\sigma \text{ is universally closed, the universal closure}$$
$$(\forall C) \text{ of } C \text{ is in } \mathcal{K}, \text{ for all variables } x: \text{ if } x \text{ appears below}$$
$$\text{an extension function in } C \text{ it holds that}$$
$$\sigma(x) \in \mathrm{Term}_{\Sigma_0}(\mathrm{st}(\mathcal{K}, G)) \text{ and otherwise } \sigma(x) = x\}.$$

We call $\mathcal{K}^{[G]}$ the set of stably local instances *of $\mathcal{K}$ (w.r.t. G).*

Definition 3.3.2 (Stably local extension) *Let T_0 be a theory in the signature $\Pi_0 = (\Sigma_0, \mathsf{Pred})$, Σ_1 a set of new function symbols, $\mathcal{K}$ a set of universally closed clauses in the extended signature*

---
[1]cf. Section 3.6.

$\Pi_1 = (\Sigma_0 \cup \Sigma_1, \mathsf{Pred})$ and let $\Pi_1^C = (\Sigma_0 \cup \Sigma_1 \cup \Sigma_C, \mathsf{Pred})$ where Σ_C is a set of fresh constants. We call the extension $T_0 \cup \mathcal{K} \supseteq T_0$ stably local if it holds for every set G of ground Π_1^C clauses that $T_0 \cup \mathcal{K} \cup G \models \bot$ if and only if $T_0 \cup \mathcal{K}^{[G]} \cup G$ has no strong partial model (with total Σ_0-functions) in which all terms in $\mathsf{st}(\mathcal{K}, G)$ are defined. We call the extension $T_0 \cup \mathcal{K} \supseteq T_0$ finitely stably local if the above property holds for all finite sets of ground clauses G. We will abbreviate the property of stable locality and that of finite stable locality by (SLoc), (SLoc^f) respectively.

Every local extension is stably local because $\mathcal{K}[G] \subseteq \mathcal{K}^{[G]}$ and every strong model of a set of clauses is also a weak one (Lemma 2.2.8).

3.4 Embeddability and Stable Locality

That embeddability of finite strong partial models is sufficient for stable locality for the case of Horn clauses was established by Harald Ganzinger ([Gan01]) and later generalized to theory extensions by Viorica Sofronie-Stokkermans ([SS05]). We present the proof here because a similar technique will be used later for Ψ-stable locality. Note that with Evans semantics no flattening is necessary.

Theorem 3.4.1 Let T_0 be a universal theory in the signature $\Pi_0 = (\Sigma_0, \mathsf{Pred})$, Σ_1 a set of new function symbols and $\mathcal{K}$ a set of universally closed clauses in the extended signature $\Pi_1 = (\Sigma_0 \cup \Sigma_1, \mathsf{Pred})$. If the extension $T_0 \subseteq T_0 \cup \mathcal{K}$ satisfies (Emb$_s$) then it satisfies (SLoc).

Proof. The proof is similar to the proof of Theorem 3.2.1. Assume towards a contradiction that the extension were not stably local. That means that there exists a set of ground clauses G (with additional constants) such that $T_0 \cup \mathcal{K} \cup G \models \bot$ but there is a strong partial model (with total Σ_0-functions and constants) $\mathcal{A}$ of $T_0 \cup \mathcal{K}^{[G]} \cup G$ such that all terms in $\mathsf{st}(\mathcal{K}, G)$ are defined. We construct a partial model $\mathcal{B}$ of $T_0 \cup \mathcal{K} \cup G$ from $\mathcal{A}$. Embedding this $\mathcal{B}$ into a total model $\mathcal{C}$ of $T_0 \cup \mathcal{K}$ will yield a contradiction.

As carrier of $\mathcal{B}$ we take $B := \{t^{\mathcal{A}} \mid t \in \mathrm{Term}_{\Sigma_0}(\mathsf{st}(\mathcal{K}, G))\}$ and keep all Σ_0-functions defined as in $\mathcal{A}$. We again want $f^{\mathcal{B}}$ to be a restriction of $f^{\mathcal{A}}$ for Σ_1-functions f, i.e., if $f^{\mathcal{B}}(\bar{a})$ is defined at all it is equal to $f^{\mathcal{A}}(\bar{a})$, in order to have $\mathcal{B}$ as a weak submodel of $\mathcal{A}$. For Σ_1-functions f we set

$$f^{\mathcal{B}}(t_1^{\mathcal{A}}, ..., t_n^{\mathcal{A}}) \text{ is defined} :\Leftrightarrow \exists t \in \mathrm{Term}_{\Sigma_0}(\mathsf{st}(\mathcal{K}, G)).\ f^{\mathcal{A}}(t_1^{\mathcal{A}}, ..., t_n^{\mathcal{A}}) = t^{\mathcal{A}}.$$

Because T_0 is universal and $\mathcal{B}\!\restriction_{\Pi_0}$ is a substructure of $\mathcal{A}\!\restriction_{\Pi_0}$, we have $\mathcal{B} \models T_0$ and we have $\mathcal{B} \models G$ because all terms are defined in $\mathcal{A}$. The crucial step, again, is to show that $\mathcal{B}$ is a model of $T_0 \cup \mathcal{K}$. In order to show that $\mathcal{B} \models_s \mathcal{K}$, let D be a clause in $\mathcal{K}$ and let $\beta : X \to A$ be a valuation. We know that $\beta(x) = t_x^{\mathcal{A}}$ for some $t_x \in \mathrm{Term}_{\Sigma_0}(\mathsf{st}(\mathcal{K}, G))$. We therefore can define a substitution σ by setting

$$\sigma(x) = \begin{cases} t_x & \text{if } x \text{ does occur below a } \Sigma_1\text{-function in } D, \\ x & \text{if } x \text{ does not occur below a } \Sigma_1\text{-function in } D. \end{cases}$$

with the property that $D\sigma \in \mathcal{K}^{[G]}$ and $\beta = \beta \circ \sigma$. By the substitution lemma, it follows that $\mathcal{A}, \beta \models_s D$. This means that there is a literal L in D with $\mathcal{A}, \beta \models_s L$. We will show that $\mathcal{B}, \beta \models_s L$.

If L is a negative equation or a predicate literal then $(\mathcal{B}, \beta)$ can only fail to strongly satisfy L if all the occurring terms are defined in $(\mathcal{B}, \beta)$ but do not stand in the relation expressed by L, according to Observation 2.2.6.(3) and 2.2.6.(5). But if all terms of L are defined in $(\mathcal{B}, \beta)$ they are defined in $(\mathcal{A}, \beta)$ a fortiori. Hence, it would follow that $\mathcal{A}, \beta \not\models_s L$ contrary to our assumption.

Thus, the only case left to consider is when L is a positive equation, say $L = s \approx t$. There are four cases to deal with. First, if both terms are undefined in $(\mathcal{B}, \beta)$ but all proper subterms are defined, we immediately get $\mathcal{B} \models_s s \approx t$. The same holds if there is a proper subterm of s or t which is undefined under $(\mathcal{B}, \beta)$. The third case is when both terms are defined in $(\mathcal{B}, \beta)$. This implies that both terms are also defined in $(\mathcal{A}, \beta)$. Thus, $s^{\mathcal{B}}[\beta] = s^{\mathcal{A}}[\beta] = t^{\mathcal{A}}[\beta] = t^{\mathcal{B}}[\beta]$.

Lastly, suppose that one term is defined in $\mathcal{B}$ while the other one is not although its proper subterms are. Let us agree that $t^{\mathcal{B}}[\beta]$ is defined. Then t is also defined in $(\mathcal{A}, \beta)$. Let $s = f(\bar{u})$. We know that $(\mathcal{B}, \beta)(\bar{u})$ is defined. By definition of $f^{\mathcal{B}}$, this would imply that s was defined in $(\mathcal{B}, \beta)$, too. Hence, this case cannot obtain and we may conclude that $(\mathcal{B}, \beta) \models_s L$.

Now we can use the assumption to obtain a total model $\mathcal{C}$ of $T_0 \cup \mathcal{K}$ into which $\mathcal{B}$ is embedded. We may use Lemma 2.2.15 to conclude that $\mathcal{C} \models G$. Contradiction.
$\square$

If the extension clauses are flat, this gives us the implications

$$(\mathsf{Loc}) \Rightarrow (\mathsf{Emb}_w) \Rightarrow (\mathsf{Emb}_s) \Rightarrow (\mathsf{SLoc}).$$

The first implication is an equivalence for linear extension clauses and the second holds because a strong model of $\mathcal{K}$ is also a weak model of $\mathcal{K}$ (cf. Lemma 2.2.8). The inclusion of locality into stable locality is proper. To see this consider the following example which is taken from [Gan01] with a different argument to show stable locality.

Example 3.4.2 (cf. [Gan01]) *We consider the following extension clauses over the empty theory.*

(Int) $p(x) \approx y \to s(y) \approx x$
$s(x) \approx y \to p(y) \approx x$

(Int) **is stably local but not local.** *Consider* $G = \{s(a) \approx s(b), a \not\approx b\}$. *Then we have* (Int), $G \models \bot$ *but* (Int)$[G]$ *is empty.* (Int) *is stably local because every strong partial model embeds into a total one. This is because if we have a partial model* $\mathcal{A} \models_s$ (Int) *we have that if* $p^{\mathcal{A}}(a)$ *is defined and equal to* b, *then* $s^{\mathcal{A}}(b)$ *is also defined and equal to* a. *The same holds dually. This allows us to complete these functions which are each other's inverse.*

3.5 Decidability and Complexity

In order to address the decidability of a theory extension in terms of the base theory we need the following definition.

Definition 3.5.1 (Fragments of a theory) *Let* Π *be a signature and* T *be a* Π-*theory. The* universal fragment of T (denoted by $T^\forall$) is the set of universal sentences implied by T. The $\forall\exists$-fragment of T is the set of $\forall\exists$-sentences implied by T.

Given a theory extension $T_0 \subseteq T_0 \cup \mathcal{K}$ we will call a variable x occurring in a clause D of $\mathcal{K}$ *shielded* if x occurs below an extension function in D (it need not appear exclusively so).

Corollary 3.5.2 ([SS05]) *Let T_0 be a theory in the signature $\Pi_0 = (\Sigma_0, \mathsf{Pred})$, Σ_1 a set of new function symbols and $\mathcal{K}$ a set of universally closed clauses in the extended signature $\Pi_1 = (\Sigma_0 \cup \Sigma_1, \mathsf{Pred})$. Assume that the theory extension $T_1 := T_0 \cup \mathcal{K} \supseteq T_0$ with finite $\mathcal{K}$ either has ($\mathsf{Loc_f}$) or it has both ($\mathsf{SLoc_f}$) and T_0 is locally finite. Then*

(1) If all variables in $\mathcal{K}$ are shielded by Σ_1-functions and $T_0^\forall$ is decidable then $T_1^\forall$ is decidable as well.

(2) If $T_0^{\forall\exists}$ is decidable then $T_1^\forall$ is decidable, too.

Corollary 3.5.3 ([SS06b]) *Let T_0 be a theory for which the satisfiability of a set of ground clauses of size n can be checked in time $g(n)$ and let $T_0 \subseteq T_0 \cup \mathcal{K}$ ($\mathcal{K}$ finite) be a local extension where all variables in $\mathcal{K}$ are shielded by Σ_1-functions. Then the validity of a set of clauses in T_1 can be checked in time $g(c \cdot n^k)$ where c is a constant and k is the maximum number of extension terms in a clause in $\mathcal{K}$ (but no smaller than 2).*

3.6 Applications

In this section we consider some concrete examples of local extensions. Theorem 3.2.1 is used to establish locality: any partial model of some theory extension (whose reduct is a total model of the underlying theory) embeds into a total model of said theory. Analogously, Theorem 3.2.2 is used to show finite locality: any partial model of some theory extension, such that all partial functions are defined on finitely many points only and whose reduct is a total model of the underlying theory, embeds into a total model of the theory.

The results in this section were published in [SSI07a, SSI07b, IJSS08].

3.6.1 Definitional Extensions

Definitional extensions are extensions where a new function is given by case distinctions such that in each case the definition is given without citing the new function. Definitional extensions have many real-life applications in verification, e.g., function updates used in loop invariants or modeling the insertion of new elements in a data structure. As we will see, it also has applications in multiple-valued logic.[2]

Example 3.6.1 ([IJSS08]) *Consider a parametric number m of processes. The priorities associated with the processes (non-negative real numbers) are stored in an array p. The states of the processes – enabled (1) or disabled (0) are stored in an array a. At each step only the process with maximal priority is enabled, its priority is set to x and the priorities of the waiting processes*

---
[2]This application is due to Viorica Sofronie-Stokkermans.

are increased by y. This can be expressed with the following set of axioms which we denote by Update(a, p, a', p')

$\forall i (1 \leq i \leq m \land \ (\forall j (1 \leq j \leq m \land j \neq i \rightarrow p(i) > p(j))) \longrightarrow a'(i) = 1)$
$\forall i (1 \leq i \leq m \land \ (\forall j (1 \leq j \leq m \land j \neq i \rightarrow p(i) > p(j))) \longrightarrow p'(i) = x)$
$\forall i (1 \leq i \leq m \land \neg (\forall j (1 \leq j \leq m \land j \neq i \rightarrow p(i) > p(j))) \longrightarrow a'(i) = 0)$
$\forall i (1 \leq i \leq m \land \neg (\forall j (1 \leq j \leq m \land j \neq i \rightarrow p(i) > p(j))) \longrightarrow p'(i) = p(i){+}y)$

where x and y are considered to be parameters. We may need to check whether if at the beginning the priority list is injective, i.e. formula (Inj)(p) holds:

Inj$(p) \quad \forall i, j (1 \leq i \leq m \land 1 \leq j \leq m \land i \neq j \rightarrow p(i) \neq p(j))$

then it remains injective after the update, i.e. check the satisfiability of:

$(\mathbb{Z} \cup \mathbb{R} \cup \{0, 1\}) \land$ Inj$(p) \land$ Update$(a, p, a', p') \land\ 1{\leq}c{\leq}m \land 1{\leq}d{\leq}m \land c{\neq}d \land p'(c){=}p'(d)$.

We may need to check satisfiability of the formula under certain assumptions on the values of x and y (for instance if $x = 0$ and $y = 1$), or to determine constraints on x and y for which the formula is (un)satisfiable.

We will pick up the above examples again in Section 6.9.

Theorem 3.6.2 (Sofronie-Stokkermans) *Let T_0 be a theory in the signature $\Pi_0 = (\Sigma_0, \text{Pred})$, Σ_1 a set of new function symbols and $\mathcal{K}$ a set of universally closed clauses in the extended signature $\Pi_1 = (\Sigma_0 \cup \Sigma_1, \text{Pred})$. Suppose $\mathcal{K} = \{\text{Def}_f \mid f \in \Sigma_1\}$ where Def_f is a conjunction of formulas*

$$\bigwedge_{i=1}^{k} \forall \overline{x}(\phi_i(x_1, \ldots, x_n) \rightarrow f(x_1, \ldots, x_n) = t_i(x_1, \ldots, t_n))$$

where t_i are Σ_0-terms and ϕ_i are Π_0-clauses such that for $i \neq j$, $\phi_i \land \phi_j$ is unsatisfiable w.r.t. T_0. Then the extension $T_0 \subseteq T_0 \cup \mathcal{K}$ is local.

We show below the usefulness of definitional extensions on the example of many-valued logics. Applications to array updates are presented later in Section 6.4. Definitional extensions provide an easy way to show the decidability of the universal theory of infinitely valued logics such as multiple-valued logics, Łukasiewicz logics, Gödel logics and product logics (cf. [SSI07a]).

Methods for automatically testing the validity of formulas in (in)finite-valued propositional Łukasiewicz and Gödel logics, and in propositional product logic are known (cf., e.g., [Häh03]). Definitional extensions yield a simple and easy-to-implement alternative decision procedure for the *universal theory* of the class $\mathcal{MV}$ of MV-algebras.

We use the fact that the class $\mathcal{MV}$, as a quasi-variety, is closed under products. Therefore, it is sufficient to give a decision procedure for the universal Horn theory of $\mathcal{MV}$ in order to obtain a decision procedure for the universal fragment. This is because we may assume that the universal formula to be decided is in clause normal form and since an atom is valid in a product if and only if it is valid in every factor[3], deciding the Horn fragment is tantamount to deciding the clause fragment (cf. [McK43]).

---
[3] In fact, this does not only hold for atoms but for Horn formulas in general, cf. [Hod93], Theorem 9.1.5.

The class $\mathcal{MV}$ is the quasi-variety[4] generated by the real unit interval $[0, 1]$ with the Łukasiewicz connectives $\{\vee, \wedge, \circ, \Rightarrow\}$, i.e., the algebra $[0, 1]_{\text{Ł}} = ([0, 1], \vee, \wedge, \circ, \Rightarrow)$ (cf. [GM05], Corollary 7.2), where the Łukasiewicz connectives are defined by the following formulas $\text{Def}_{\text{Ł}}$

($\text{Def}_\vee$)	$x \leq y \to x \vee y = y$	$x > y \to x \vee y = x$
($\text{Def}_\wedge$)	$x \leq y \to x \wedge y = x$	$x > y \to x \wedge y = y$
($\text{Def}_{\circ_{\text{Ł}}}$)	$x + y < 1 \to x \circ y = 0$	$x + y \geq 1 \to x \circ y = \min(1, x + y - 1)$
($\text{Def}_{\Rightarrow_{\text{Ł}}}$)	$x \leq y \to x \Rightarrow y = 1$	$x > y \to x \Rightarrow y = \min(1, 1 - x + y)$

Hence, the Łukasiewicz connectives $\{\vee, \wedge, \circ, \Rightarrow\}$ can be regarded as a definitional extension over the base signature $\{+, -, \leq\}$. Therefore, the following are equivalent:

(1) $\mathcal{MV} \models \forall \overline{x} \bigwedge_{i=1}^n s_i(\overline{x}) = t_i(\overline{x}) \to s(\overline{x}) = t(\overline{x})$

(2) $[0, 1]_{\text{Ł}} \models \forall \overline{x} \bigwedge_{i=1}^n s_i(\overline{x}) = t_i(\overline{x}) \to s(\overline{x}) = t(\overline{x})$

(3) $T_0 \cup \text{Def}_{\text{Ł}} \models \forall \overline{x} \bigwedge_{i=1}^n s_i(\overline{x}) = t_i(\overline{x}) \to s(\overline{x}) = t(\overline{x})$

(4) $T_0 \cup \text{Def}_{\text{Ł}} \wedge \bigwedge_{i=1}^n s_i(\overline{c}) = t_i(\overline{c}) \wedge s(\overline{c}) \neq t(\overline{c}) \models \bot$,

where T_0 is the theory of real numbers together with the constraint $\forall x. 0 \leq x \leq 1$.

Due to this reduction, we can use a solver for linear real arithmetic to decide the universal fragment of $\mathcal{MV}$. The program H-PILoT (cf. Chapter 6), which implements reductions in local theory extensions, has the above reduction as a special feature (cf. 6.6) (and will call a solver for the reals afterwards) thereby providing the user with an efficient method to handle multiple-valued logics.

Reasoning in the Gödel logic $[0, 1]_G = ([0, 1], \wedge, \vee, \circ_G, \Rightarrow_G)$ where $\circ_G, \Rightarrow_G$ are the Gödel connectives is similar. In this case, the signature of T_0 only needs to contain $\leq$; we obtain a reduction to testing the satisfiability of a set of ground Horn clauses in a restricted fragment of linear arithmetic over $[0, 1]$, where the atoms have the form $c \leq d$ or $c = d$.

For $[0, 1]_\Pi = ([0, 1], \wedge, \vee, \circ_\Pi, \Rightarrow_\Pi)$, where $\circ_\Pi, \Rightarrow_\Pi$ are the product logic operations one can proceed similarly. In this case, the signature of T_0 needs to contain $\{\leq, *, /\}$. Similar methods can be used for extensions with projection operators Δ, ∇, defined by $(\Delta(1) = 1) \wedge \forall x(x < 1 \to \Delta(x) = 0)$; respectively. $(\nabla(0) = 0) \wedge \forall x(x > 0 \to \nabla(x) = 1)$ (cf. [SSI07a]).

3.6.2 Monotone Functions

In this section we consider theory extensions with monotone functions. The corresponding base theory is – most generally – a poset, it could also be a linear order or a lattice.

A *partial order* or *poset* $P = (X, \leq)$ is a set together with a binary relation which is reflexive, transitive and anti-symmetric, i.e., it holds for all $x, y, z \in X$ that

---

[4]Quasi-varieties are modeled after varieties; the difference being that the former are defined by quasi-equations (Horn formulas with a positive atom) in lieu of equations. As a consequence, quasi-varieties are closed under isomorphisms, subalgebras and (reduced) products (and contain the trivial algebra), whereas varieties are closed under homomorphic images, subalgebras and products (cf. [Hod93], 9.2; [BS81], III.5 §2).

(1) $x \leq x$

(2) $x \leq y$ and $y \leq z$ implies $x \leq z$.

(3) $x \leq y$ and $y \leq x$ implies $x = y$.

If it additionally holds that $x \leq y \vee y \leq x$, for all $x, y \in X$, we call P (and the corresponding relation $\leq$) *linear* or *total*. A prominent partial order is a family of subsets of some set together with the subset relation, in general it is not total. Given a poset $P = (X, \leq)$, we will say $x \in P$ for an element $x \in X$ if this causes no confusion.

We also allow a many-sorted framework for monotone functions. By a monotone functions we mean the following.

Definition 3.6.3 (Monotone function) *Let $P = (X, \leq, f)$ be a poset with a partially defined n-ary function f on X and let $I \subseteq \{1, ..., n\}$ be a set of indices. We say that f is I-monotone if $(X, \leq, f)$ weakly satisfies the monotonicity axiom*

$$(\mathrm{Mon}^I_f) \qquad \bigwedge_{i \in I} x_i \leq y_i \wedge \bigwedge_{i \notin I} x_i = y_i \rightarrow f(x_1, ..., x_n) \leq f(y_1, ..., y_n).$$

Similarly, in a many-sorted framework we call an n-ary function from posets $P_1, ..., P_n$ with respective partial orders $\leq_j$ into a poset P_0 I-monotone, if it follows from $x_i \leq_i y_i$, for all $i \in I$, and $x_i = y_i$, for all $i \notin I$, that $f(x_1, ..., x_n) \leq_0 f(y_1, ..., y_n)$, if both $f(x_1, ..., x_n)$ and $f(y_1, ..., y_n)$ are defined. For ease of notation, we will also write $\prod_{i \in I} P_i \times \prod_{i \notin I} P_i$ for the domain of an I-monotone function even when I is not an initial sequence of $\{1, ..., n\}$.

We will need some basic notions from order theory. We will give a brief recap of the facts we will be needing. Most crucial is the notion of a *completion* of a poset. We will suitably adopt a given function on a poset to a corresponding function over its completion and thereby establish locality. For reference we cite [DP90] whose outline we follow.

Recall that the dual R^∂ of a relation R is the set $\{(y, x) \,|\, (x, y) \in R\}$. In the case of a poset $P = (X, \leq)$, its dual $P^\partial = (X, \leq^\partial) = (X, \geq)$ is best remembered as turning the Hasse diagram of P upside down. We want to use this result to expand the notion of a monotone function to the dual of a poset. This enables us to capture functions that are monotone in some components and antitone in others. In order to do this let us introduce the *sign* of a poset. For an element $x \in P$, define $x^\downarrow := \{y \in P \,|\, y \leq x\}$ and $x^\uparrow := \{y \in P \,|\, y \geq x\}$.

Definition 3.6.4 (Duality in a poset) *Let $P = (X, \leq)$ be a poset. We write P^+ ($\leq^+$) for P ($\leq$) and let P^- ($\leq^-$) denote the dual P^∂ ($\geq$). Similarly, for an element $x \in P$ define x^+ to be the set $x^\uparrow$ and x^- as the set $x^\downarrow$. If $\sigma \in \{+, -\}$ we will write $-\sigma$ for the opposite sign.*

Monotonicity in some arguments and antitonicity in other arguments is modeled by considering functions $f : P^{\sigma_1} \times ... \times P^{\sigma_n} \longrightarrow P$ with $\sigma_1, ..., \sigma_n \in \{+, -\}$. The corresponding monotonicity axiom is denoted by $(\mathrm{Mon}^{I,\sigma}_f)$ with $\sigma = (\sigma_1, ..., \sigma_n)$.

We call an element x of a poset $P = (X, \leq)$ *maximal* (*minimal*), if $x \leq y$ ($y \leq x$) implies $x = y$. Given a poset P and a subset A of P, let us write $x \leq A$ if it holds that $x \leq a$, for every $a \in A$. An element x of a poset $P = (X, \leq)$ is called the *greatest* element, if it holds that $x \geq X$. If a poset has a greatest element we denote it by 1. We define the *smallest element* of a poset dually and denote it by 0. Note that the greatest element is always maximal in a poset but not vice versa.

For two elements x, y of a poset P, if the supremum of $\{x, y\}$ exists, we will denote it by $x \vee y$ and call it the *join* of x and y. If the join of two elements always exists in a poset we will call the poset a *join-semilattice*. Dually, the infimum of $\{x, y\}$, if it exists, is denoted by $x \wedge y$ and is called the *meet* of x and y. If the meet of two elements always exists in a poset we will call the poset a *meet-semilattice*; a poset where each join and meet exists is called a *lattice*. Similarly, for a subset A of P, we will write $\bigvee A$ for the supremum of A, if it exists, and if the infimum of A exists, we will denote it by $\bigwedge A$.

Given a poset P and a subset A of P, we call A *join-dense* in P, if for every $x \in P$ there is a subset B of A such that $x = \bigvee_P B$. The dual of join-dense is *meet-dense*. We call a subset of a poset *dense* if it is both join-dense and meet-dense.

We denote the set of upper bounds of A by A^u, i.e., $A^u = \{x \mid x \geq A\}$. Similarly, the set of lower bounds of A is $A^l = \{x \mid x \leq A\}$. A *complete lattice* L is a lattice such that for any subset $A \subseteq L$ the infimum $\bigwedge A$ and the supremum $\bigvee A$ exist (that implies that the lattice has 0 and 1 because $\bigwedge \emptyset = 1$ and $\bigvee \emptyset = 0$). Trivially, every finite lattice is complete.

Lemma 3.6.5 (cf. [DP90], Lemma 2.32) *Let $P = (X, \leq)$ be a poset.*

(1) For all $x \in P$, we have $(x^\downarrow)^{ul} = x^\downarrow$.

(2) If the supremum $\bigvee A$ exists for an $A \subseteq P$, then $A^{ul} = (\bigvee A)^\downarrow$.

In order to establish finite locality, it is sufficient according to Theorem 3.2.2.(1) to show the embeddability of models in which the extension functions are defined on finitely many points only. Suppose we have a partial monotone function f into a join-semilattice P that has a finite definition domain, then we can transform f into a total function $\bar{f}$ by setting $\bar{f}(x) := \bigvee f(x^\downarrow)$. The only complication is that f might not be defined on any points smaller or equal to x. We therefore consider join-semilattices with 0 to cover that eventuality. As always with posets, the same argument works for the dual, too. This gives us the following lemma (which is joint work with Viorica Sofronie-Stokkermans).

Lemma 3.6.6 *Let $P_1, P_2, \ldots, P_n$ be posets, P a total structure endowed with a partial order $\leq$, such that $(P_1, P_2, \ldots, P_n, P, f)$ is a weak partial model of Mon_f^σ, i.e., such that $f : \prod_{i \in I} P_i^{\sigma_i} \times \prod_{j \notin I} P_i \to P$ is a partial function weakly satisfying Mon_f^σ. Suppose that the reduct $(P, \leq)$ of P is a join-semilattice with 0 or, alternately, a meet-semilattice with 1 and that the definition domain of f is finite, then f has a total extension, $\bar{f} : \prod_{i \in I} P_i^{\sigma_i} \times \prod_{j \notin I} P_i \to P$ satisfying Mon_f^σ.*

In particular, if SLat is the theory of join-semilattices with 0 or, dually, the theory of meet-semilattice with 1, and T_0 is any theory such that $T_0 \supseteq \mathsf{SLat}$, then the extension $T_0 \subseteq T_0 \cup \mathsf{Mon}_f^\sigma$ is finitely local.

As was pointed out to us by Viorica Sofronie-Stokkermans, the same argument works for full-fledged lattices without 0 or 1. For example, let f be a function which is monotone in its first components, antitone in its third components and fixed in its second. If the domain of f is empty, choose some arbitrary element x_{in} and set $\bar{f}(x, y, z) := x_{in}$. If the domain of f is not empty, set $\bar{f}(x,y,z) := \bigvee f(x^\downarrow, y, z^\uparrow)$, if the set $f(x^\downarrow, y, z^\uparrow)$ is not empty and $\bar{f}(x,y,z) := \bigwedge f(x^\uparrow, y, z^\downarrow)$, otherwise.

Example 3.6.7 *In [SS02], Viorica Sofronie-Stokkermans considers numerical information associated with concepts in the context of description logics, so-called* bridging functions. *For example, given a bounded lattice of sets* $(S, \cup, \cap, \emptyset, X)$, *with* $S \subseteq \wp(X)$, *consider a* maxcost *function associating each set* $A \in S$ *with a real value in* $[0,1]$. *If the* maxcost-*function is monotone, then the extension of the theory of (bounded) lattices with maxcost is finitely local.*

In order to be able to handle locality for monotone functions in general, we need to consider completions of posets. By the *completion of a poset* P we mean an embedding $\varphi : P \to L$ of P into a complete lattice L. The canonical completion of a poset P is the *Dedekind-MacNeille* completion DM(P), consisting of the subsets of P which are closed under the closure operator ^{ul}, i.e., $A^{ul} = A$, ordered by inclusion. The map $x \mapsto x^\downarrow$ embeds P into DM(P); it also preserves infima and suprema if they exist.

Given a dense subset P of a complete lattice L, it holds that $L \cong DM(P)$. It follows that if the lattice L is already complete, its Dedekind-MacNeille completion is isomorphic to L. In particular, this means that each finite lattice is isomorphic to its Dedekind-MacNeille completion.

Lemma 3.6.8 (cf. [DP90], Theorem 2.33 & 2.36) *Let* $P = (X, \leq)$ *be a poset and let* $\varphi : P \to DM(P)$ *be defined by* $\varphi(x) := x^\downarrow$, *for all* $x \in X$.

(1) DM(P) is a completion of P via the map φ.

(2) φ preserves all infima and suprema that exists in P.

(3) $\varphi(P)$ is dense in DM(P).

(4) Let L be a complete lattice and let P be a dense subset of L. Then $L \cong DM(P)$ via an order isomorphism which agrees with φ on P.

For later use, we want to establish that the Dedekind-MacNeille completion of a linear poset is linear again.

Lemma 3.6.9 *Let* $P = (X, \leq)$ *be a linear order and let* $(DM(P), \subseteq)$ *be its Dedekind-MacNeille completion. Then* $(DM(P), \subseteq)$ *is a linear order.*

Proof. In this proof all infima, suprema and upper bounds are taken in DM(P). Assume towards a contradiction, that there were two elements $\tilde{a}, \tilde{b}$ of DM(P) that are incomparable, i.e., neither $\tilde{a} \subseteq \tilde{b}$ nor $\tilde{b} \subseteq \tilde{a}$. From Lemma 3.6.8.(3), we know that the set $\{x^\downarrow \mid x \in P\}$ is dense in DM(P). In particular, there are set $Q_{\tilde{a}}, Q_{\tilde{b}} \subseteq P$ such that $\tilde{a} = \bigvee\{x^\downarrow \mid x \in Q_{\tilde{a}}\}$ and $\tilde{b} = \bigvee\{x^\downarrow \mid x \in Q_{\tilde{b}}\}$. Set $A := \{x^\downarrow \mid x \in Q_{\tilde{a}}\}$ and $B := \{x^\downarrow \mid x \in Q_{\tilde{b}}\}$.

Note first, that there cannot be a $b_m \in B$ that is strictly bigger (w.r.t. to the order $\subseteq$) than every element in A, i.e., $b_m \supset a$, for all $a \in A$. For if there were, it would follow that $\bigvee B \supseteq b_m \supset A$ which implies $\tilde{b} = \bigvee B \supseteq \bigvee A = \tilde{a}$, contradicting our assumption. We therefore know that for each $b \in B$, there is some $a_b \in A$ such that $b \subseteq a_b$ or b and a_b are incomparable. The latter cannot occur, however, because $b = r^\downarrow$, for some $r \in Q_{\tilde{b}}$, and $a_b = q^\downarrow$, for some $q \in Q_{\tilde{a}}$, and since the underlying order was linear, r and q must have been comparable: it holds that $r \leq q$ if and only if $r^\downarrow \subseteq q^\downarrow$. Hence, for every $b \in B$ there is some $a_b \in A$ such that $b \subseteq a_b$.

Our next claim is that $A^u \subseteq B^u$. Let $a \supseteq A$. Suppose there were a $b \in B$ such that $a \not\supseteq b$. From the above considerations, we know that there is an $a_b \in A$ such that $b \subseteq a_b$. It follows that $b \subseteq a_b \subseteq a$. This contradiction establishes our claim. From $A^u \subseteq B^u$ it follows at once that $\tilde{a} = \bigvee A \supseteq \bigvee B = \tilde{b}$. Contradiction. □

Regarding monotone functions, we note first that duality and Dedekind-MacNeille completions work smoothly together and that monotonicity is preserved under completions.

Lemma 3.6.10 *The Dedekind-MacNeille completion of the dual P^∂ of a poset P consists of the subsets of P which are closed w.r.t. to the hull operator ^{lu} (ordered by inclusion). Furthermore, it is isomorphic to the dual of the Dedekind-MacNeille completion of P. The map $^l : \mathrm{DM}(P^\partial) \longrightarrow \mathrm{DM}(P)^\partial$, sending a set to the set of its lower bounds, is an isomorphism (its inverse is the map ^{u}).*

Lemma 3.6.11 *Let $P_1, ..., P_n, P$ be posets, $I \subseteq \{1, ..., n\}$ and $f : P_1 \times ... \times P_n \longrightarrow P$ be a (partial) I-monotone function. Then the map $\hat{f} : \prod_{i \in I} \mathrm{DM}(P_i) \times \prod_{i \notin I} P_i \longrightarrow \mathrm{DM}(P)$ defined by*

$$\hat{f}(C_1, ..., C_n) := \{f(x_1, ..., x_n) \mid x_1 \in C_1, ..., x_n \in C_n, f(x_1, ..., x_n) \text{ defined}\}^{ul}$$
$$= f(C_1, ..., C_n)^{ul}$$

is also I-monotone. Further, if $f(...x_i...x_j...x_k...)$ is defined ($i, k \in I$) it holds that $\hat{f}(...x_i^\downarrow...x_j...x_k^\downarrow...) = f(...x_i...x_j...x_k...)^\downarrow$.

Proof. Let $C_i \subseteq D_i, ..., C_k \subseteq D_k$, $i, k \in I$. Then we trivially have $f(...C_i...\{x\}...C_k...) \subseteq f(...D_i...\{x\}...D_k...)$ and since ^{ul} is a hull operator it follows that

$$f(...C_i...\{x\}...C_k...)^{ul} \subseteq f(...D_i...\{x\}...D_k...)^{ul}.$$

For the additional claim note that it follows from monotonicity that the supremum of the set $f(...x_i^\downarrow...\{x_j\}...x_k^\downarrow...)$ is $f(...x_i...x_j...x_k...)$ because the latter was supposed to be defined.

By definition we have $\hat{f}(...x_i^\downarrow...x_j...x_k^\downarrow...) = f(...x_i^\downarrow...\{x_j\}...x_k^\downarrow...)^{ul}$. It follows from Lemma 3.6.5.(2) that

$$\hat{f}(...x_i^\downarrow...x_j...x_k^\downarrow...) = f(...x_i...x_j...x_k...)^\downarrow.$$

□

Lemma 3.6.12 *Let $P, P_1, ..., P_n$ be posets, $f : P_1^{\sigma_1} \times ... \times P_n^{\sigma_n} \longrightarrow P$, with $\sigma_1, ..., \sigma_n \in \{+, -\}$, be a partial (I, σ)-monotone function. Let $max : \wp(P) \to P$ be a function which returns a maximal element of a subset of a partial order P if it has one and a fixed element $a_{in} \in P$ otherwise. Let $\hat{f}$ be as in Lemma 3.6.11. Let $\overline{f} : \mathrm{DM}(P_1)^{\sigma_1} \times ... \times \mathrm{DM}(P_n)^{\sigma_n} \longrightarrow \mathrm{DM}(P)$ be defined by*

$$\overline{f}(C_1, ..., C_n) := \hat{f}(u_1(C_1), ..., u_n(C_n))$$

with $u_i = \begin{cases} u & \text{if } i \in I \text{ and } \sigma_i \text{ is negative,} \\ \text{id} & \text{if } i \in I \text{ and } \sigma_i \text{ is positive,} \\ \max & \text{if } i \notin I. \end{cases}$

Then $\overline{f}$ is (I, σ)-monotone. This gives us the following diagram.

$$\begin{array}{ccc} \prod_{i \in I} \text{DM}(P_i^{\sigma_i}) \times \prod_{i \notin I} P_i & \xrightarrow{\hat{f}} & \text{DM}(P) \\ {\scriptstyle (u_1, ..., u_n)} \uparrow & & \downarrow {\scriptstyle \text{id}} \\ \prod_{i \in I} \text{DM}(P_i)^{\sigma_i} \times \prod_{i \notin I} \text{DM}(P_i) & \xrightarrow{\overline{f}} & \text{DM}(P) \end{array}$$

Proof. Consider sets $A_i \subseteq^{\sigma_i} A'_i$ for $i \in I$ and $A_i = A'_i$ for $i \notin I$. Note again that ^{u} is antitone, i.e., $A^u \supseteq B^u$ if $A \subseteq B$. Hence, we always have $f \circ (u_1, ..., u_n) \, (A_1, ..., A_n) \subseteq f \circ (u_1, ..., u_n)(A'_1, ..., A'_n)$. It holds that

$$\begin{aligned} \overline{f}(A_1, ..., A_n) &:= \quad (\hat{f} \circ (u_1, ..., u_n)) \, (A_1, ..., A_n) \\ &= \quad [(f \circ (u_1, ..., u_n)) \, (A_1, ..., A_n)]^{ul} \\ &\subseteq \quad [(f \circ (u_1, ..., u_n)) \, (A'_1, ..., A'_n)]^{ul} \quad (^{ul} \text{ is monotone}) \\ &= \quad (\hat{f} \circ (u_1, ..., u_n)) \, (A'_1, ..., A'_n) \\ &= \quad \overline{f}(A'_1, ..., A'_n). \end{aligned}$$

$\square$

Corollary 3.6.13 *Let* $P_1, P_2, \ldots, P_n, P$ *be posets*, I *a subset of* $\{1, \ldots, n\}$. *Let* $(P_1, P_2, \ldots, P_n, P, f)$ *be a weak partial model of an* (I, σ)*-monotone partial function* $f : P_1^{\sigma_1} \times \ldots \times P_n^{\sigma_n} \longrightarrow P$. *Let* $\overline{f}$ *be defined as in Lemma 3.6.12. Then the map* $(x_1, \ldots, x_n) \mapsto (x_1^{\downarrow}, \ldots, x^{\downarrow})$ *induces a many-sorted weak embedding*

$$\iota : (P_1, P_2, \ldots, P_n, P, f) \longrightarrow (\text{DM}(P_1), \text{DM}(P_2), \ldots, \text{DM}(P_n), \text{DM}(P), \overline{f}).$$

Proof. Suppose that $f(x_1, ..., x_n)$ is defined. We have to show that $f(x_1, ..., x_n)^{\downarrow} = \overline{f}(x_1^{\downarrow}, ..., x_n^{\downarrow})$. Observe that $u_i(x_i^{\downarrow}) = x_i^{-\sigma_1}$ if $i \in I$ and $u_i(x_i^{\downarrow}) = x_i$ if $i \notin I$, by definition of u_i.

By definition we have $\overline{f}(x_1^{\downarrow}, ..., x_n^{\downarrow}) = [(f \circ (u_1, ..., u_n)) \, (x_1^{\downarrow}, ..., x_n^{\downarrow})]^{ul}$. We use Lemma 3.6.5.(2) again which says that $(\bigvee A)^{\downarrow} = A^{ul}$ if the supremum exists. By construction, the supremum of the set $(f \circ (u_1, ..., u_n)) \, (x_1^{\downarrow}, ..., x_n^{\downarrow})$ is simply $f(x_1, ..., x_n)$ because of f's I-monotonicity. Therefore, $[(f \circ (u_1, ..., u_n)) \, (x_1^{\downarrow}, ..., x_n^{\downarrow})]^{ul} = [f(x_1, ..., x_n)]^{\downarrow}$.

$\square$

The following result generalizes [SS05] to the case of general monotone functions and appears also in [SSI07a, SSI07b].

Corollary 3.6.14 *Let T_0 be one of the following theories:*

(1) $\mathcal{P}$, the theory of posets,

(2) $\mathcal{T}$, the theory of totally-ordered sets,

(3) $\mathcal{DO}$, the theory of dense totally-ordered sets,

(4) $\mathcal{S}$, the theory of semi-lattices,

(5) Lat, the theory of lattices,

and let Mon_f be a monotonicity axiom for an n-ary function f:

$$\bigwedge_{i=1}^n x_i \leq^{\sigma_i} y_i \to f(x_1,...,x_n) \leq f(y_1,...,y_n) \quad \text{with } \sigma_i \in \{+,-\}.$$

Then any partial model of $T_1 = T_0 \cup \mathsf{Mon}_f \supseteq T_0$ weakly embeds into a total model of T_1. In particular, $T_0 \cup \mathsf{Mon}_f \supseteq T_0$ is a local extension.

Proof. (1) is just Corollary 3.6.13, (2) follows from (1) and Lemma 3.6.9. For (3) we need to show that the Dedekind-MacNeille completion of a linear, dense ordering is linear and dense again. The former was settled by Lemma 3.6.9. So suppose we have two ^{ul}-closed sets A and B with $A \subset B$. We need to find a third (closed) set C such that $A \subset C \subset B$. To do this, we offer the observation that A and B cannot differ by just one element, i.e., there are two elements $x, y \in B \setminus A$, say $x < y$. Note further that any ^{ul}-closed set is downward closed in particular. This means $z > A$ for all $z \in B \setminus A$. From this the claim follows since we have $A = A^{ul} \subset x^{\downarrow} \subset B^{ul} = B$. To establish the observation, assume the contrary, say $B = A \cup \{b\}$ with $b \notin A$.

It follows from the density of the order that $(b^{\downarrow} \setminus \{b\})^u = b^{\uparrow}$. For the non-trivial direction, suppose $a \geq b^{\downarrow} \setminus \{b\}$. If it held that $a < b$, it followed from density that there were some c such that $a < c < b$. In particular, $c \in b^{\downarrow} \setminus \{b\}$ and, hence, $a \geq c$. By linearity we conclude that $a \geq b$.

Thus, $B = B^{ul} = (A \cup \{b\})^{ul} = b^{\uparrow l} = b^{\downarrow}$ (the third equation holds because of $b > A$). It follows that $A = A^{ul} = (b^{\downarrow} \setminus \{b\})^{ul} = b^{\uparrow l} = b^{\downarrow} = B$. Contradiction.

(4) and (5) follow from the fact that a Dedekind-MacNeille completion is a complete lattice and the embedding preserves all existing infima and suprema.

□

3.6.3 Bounded Functions

We now consider extensions with functions satisfying boundedness conditions and possibly also monotonicity.

Theorem 3.6.15 (Sofronie-Stokkermans, [SSI07a]) *Let T_0 be a theory in the signature $\Pi_0 = (\Sigma_0, \mathsf{Pred})$, Σ_1 a set of new function symbols and $\mathcal{K}$ a set of universally closed clauses in the extended signature $\Pi_1 = (\Sigma_0 \cup \Sigma_1, \mathsf{Pred})$. Let Pred contain a reflexive binary predicate symbol $\leq$. Then the extension $T_0 \subseteq T_0 \cup \{\mathsf{GBound}(f) \mid f \in \Sigma_1\}$ is local, where $(\mathsf{GBound}(f))$ specifies piecewise boundedness of f:*

$$(\text{GBound}(f)) \quad \bigwedge_{i=1}^{k} \forall \bar{x}(\phi_i(\bar{x}) \to t_i(\bar{x}) \leq f(\bar{x}) \leq t'_i(\bar{x})),$$

where t_i, t'_i are Π_0-terms and ϕ_i are Π_0-clauses such that for every i, if $i \neq j$ then $\phi_i \wedge \phi_j$ is unsatisfiable w.r.t. T_0 and $T_0 \models \forall x.(\phi_i(\bar{x}) \to s_i(\bar{x}) \leq t_i(\bar{x}))$.

Theorem 3.6.16 (Sofronie-Stokkermans, [SSI07a]) *Let T_0 be a Σ_0-theory consisting of a class of $\vee$-semilattice-ordered (possibly many-sorted) structures, and let Σ_1 be a set of new function symbols. Then the extension $T_0 \subseteq T_0 \cup \text{Mon}_f^\sigma \cup \text{Bound}_f^\sigma$ is finitely local.*

$$(\text{Bound}_f^t) \quad \forall x_1, \ldots, x_n(f(x_1, \ldots, x_n) \leq t(x_1, \ldots, x_n)),$$

where $t(x_1, \ldots, x_n)$ is a term in the base signature Π_0 with the same monotonicity as f, i.e. satisfying

$$\forall \bar{x}.(\bigwedge_{i=1}^{n} x_i \leq^{\sigma_i} y_i \to t(x_1, \ldots, x_n) \leq t(y_1, \ldots, y_n)).$$

Example 3.6.17 ([SSI07a]) *Let $T_1 = \mathcal{MV}$ be the theory of MV-algebras, and T_2 be the extension of T_1 with a binary function f, decreasing in the first and increasing in the second argument, and bounded by $\Rightarrow$, i.e., satisfying*

$$(\text{Mon}_f^{-+}) \quad x_1 \geq x_2 \wedge y_1 \leq y_2 \to f(x_1, y_1) \leq f(x_2, y_2)$$
$$(\text{Bound}_f^\Rightarrow) \quad f(x, y) \leq (x \Rightarrow y).$$

We want to prove that

$$T_2 \models \forall x, x', y, y', z. (z \leq f(x, y) \wedge x' \leq x \wedge y \leq y' \to x' \circ z \leq y'),$$

or equivalently, that the (skolemized, i.e. ground) negation of the formula above is unsatisfiable w.r.t. T_2:

$$G: \quad c \leq f(a, b) \quad \wedge \quad a' \leq a \quad \wedge \quad b \leq b' \quad \wedge \quad a' \circ c \not\leq b'.$$

As f and $\Rightarrow$ satisfy the same type of monotonicity, the extension $T_1 = \mathcal{MV} \subseteq \mathcal{MV} \cup (\text{Mon}_f^{-+}) \cup (\text{Bound}_f^\Rightarrow) = T_2$ is local. Therefore we only need to consider those instances of $(\text{Mon}_f^{-+}) \cup (\text{Bound}_f^\Rightarrow)$ which only contain the ground terms occurring in G. These are trivial instances of monotonicity of f and the following instance of $(\text{Bound}_f^\Rightarrow)$:

$$(\text{Bound}_f^\Rightarrow)[G] \quad f(a, b) \leq a \Rightarrow b.$$

It is sufficient to check the satisfiability of $T_1 \wedge G \wedge (\text{Bound}_f^\Rightarrow)[G]$. We flatten $G \wedge (\text{Bound}_f^\Rightarrow)[G]$ by introducing a new constant e for the extension term $f(a, b)$, together with its definition $e = f(a, b)$. We thus obtain a conjunction of a formula in the base theory $G_0 \wedge (\text{Bound}_f^\Rightarrow)[G]_0$ and a formula D, containing the definitions of extension terms

D	$G_0 \wedge (\mathsf{Bound}_f^{\Rightarrow})[G]_0$
$e = f(a,b)$	$c \leq e \wedge a' \leq a \wedge b \leq b' \wedge a' \circ c \not\leq b'$
	$e \leq (a \Rightarrow b)$

D is now replaced by the set $\mathsf{Con}[D]$ of functionality axioms corresponding to the instances $f(c_1, \ldots, c_n$ c in D. As only one extension term occurs in D, $\mathsf{Con}[D]$ contains only redundant clauses. It is sufficient to check that $G_0 \wedge (\mathsf{Bound}_f^{\Rightarrow})[G]_0$ is satisfiable in the theory of MV-algebras.

Note that checking the satisfiability of $G_0 \wedge (\mathsf{Bound}_f^{\Rightarrow})[G]_0$ w.r.t. the theory of MV-algebras is equivalent to checking whether

$$\mathcal{MV} \models z \leq u \ \wedge \ x' \leq x \ \wedge \ y \leq y' \ \wedge \ u \leq (x \Rightarrow y) \rightarrow x' \circ z \leq y'.$$

We can check this by checking whether

$$T_0 \cup \mathsf{Def}_{\text{Ł}} \wedge G_0 \wedge (\mathsf{Bound}_f^{\Rightarrow})[G]_0 \models \bot,$$

where T_0 is the theory of the unit interval $[0,1]$ with the operation $+$ and the predicate $\leq$ inherited from the real numbers, and $\mathsf{Def}_{\text{Ł}}$ is the set of definitions for the Łukasiewicz connectives. We introduce new constants denoting the terms starting with the Łukasiewicz connectives, and add the appropriate (flattened and purified) instances $\mathsf{Def}_{\text{Ł}0}$ of $\mathsf{Def}_{\text{Ł}}$ and functionality axioms:

$D_{\text{Ł}}$	$(G_0 \wedge (\mathsf{Bound}_f^{\Rightarrow})[G]_0)_0 \wedge \mathsf{Def}_{\text{Ł}0}$
$p = a' \circ c$	$e \leq q \ \wedge \ c \leq e \ \wedge \ a' \leq a \ \wedge \ b \leq b' \ \wedge \ p \not\leq b'$
$q = (a \Rightarrow b)$	$(a' + c < 1 \rightarrow p = 0)$
	$(a' + c \geq 1 \rightarrow p = a' + c - 1)$
	$(a \leq b \rightarrow q = 1)$
	$(a > b \rightarrow q = 1 - a + b)$

The satisfiability of $(G_0 \wedge (\mathsf{Bound}_f^{\Rightarrow})[G]_0)_0 \wedge \mathsf{Def}_{\text{Ł}0}$ w.r.t. T_0 can be checked, e.g., with a $DPLL(T)$ method for SAT-solving modulo the theory of reals.

Chapter 4

Generalized Locality

In a local extension we may replace the universally quantified extension clauses by a set of their instances without losing completeness: An extension clause is instantiated using all the ground terms appearing in the extension clauses or in the given proof task. This set of instances then replaces the original clause. If the theory extension is local, we may prove or disprove the given task using these instances alone (modulo the background theory).

For some applications more instances of the extension clauses are needed in order to discharge arbitrary proof tasks. This chapter considers such cases. A pertinent example, where more ground terms are needed as instances of universal clauses, is that of *arrays*. For the theory of arrays the notion of *minimal locality* is introduced. With minimal locality the idea is to consider those instances $C\sigma$ of an extension clause C where each extension term $f(x)$ appearing in C is instantiated to $f(t)$ where t is a ground term appearing below an extension function g in this or another extension clause.

This important example of verification by using the ground terms occurring in the problem as a basis for, instead of the whole set of, the instances required inspired the notion of Ψ-*locality*, which will be developed in Section 4.6 and which generalizes minimal locality. The approach taken is to employ a closure operator Ψ on ground terms for generating all the instances needed.

In the case of stable locality the approach of using a closure operator on ground terms is inherently more complicated. This is due to the required closure properties of such an operator. However, it can still guide the way of how practical verification tasks can be solved that require stable locality. An example of this will be given in Section 4.8: the theory of *pointers*.

4.1 Minimal Locality

Careful inspection of the proof of Theorem 3.2.1 – that embeddability implies locality – reveals that the embeddability of all partial models is more than was needed. What was actually needed was the embeddability of the restricted "term model", where an extension function f is defined on a point a if and only if a is named by some constant c, such that $f(c)$ is a ground term of the extension clauses or a ground term occurring in the proof task under consideration. We capture this "forgetting of values" in the following notion.

Definition 4.1.1 (Minimal model) Let T_0 be a theory in the signature $\Pi_0 = (\Sigma_0, \mathsf{Pred})$, Σ_1 a set of new function symbols, $\mathcal{K}$ a set of universally closed clauses in the extended signature $\Pi_1 = (\Sigma_0 \cup \Sigma_1, \mathsf{Pred})$ and G a set of ground clauses in the signature $\Pi_1^C = (\Sigma_0 \cup \Sigma_1 \cup \Sigma_C, \mathsf{Pred})$, where Σ_C is a set of fresh constants. Let $T_1 := T_0 \cup \mathcal{K}$ and let Θ be a set of ground terms in the signature $\Sigma_0 \cup \Sigma_C$ such that Θ contains all the base ground terms, i.e., ground terms in the signature Π_0, of $\mathcal{K}$. A partial model $\mathcal{A} \in \mathsf{PMod}_w(\Sigma_1, T_1)$ is called Θ-**minimal** if we have, for all extension functions $f \in \Sigma_1$, that

$$f^{\mathcal{A}}(a_1, ..., a_n) \text{ is defined } \Leftrightarrow \exists t_1, ..., t_n. \forall i.\ t_i \in \Theta \wedge t_i^{\mathcal{A}} = a_i.$$

We will adapt our chief properties accordingly. The terminology borrows from [BMS06].

Definition 4.1.2 (Minimal instances) Let T_0 be a theory in the signature $\Pi_0 = (\Sigma_0, \mathsf{Pred})$, Σ_1 a set of new function symbols, $\mathcal{K}$ a set of universally closed clauses in the extended signature $\Pi_1 = (\Sigma_0 \cup \Sigma_1, \mathsf{Pred})$ and G a set of ground clauses in the signature $\Pi_1^C = (\Sigma_0 \cup \Sigma_1 \cup \Sigma_C, \mathsf{Pred})$, where Σ_C is a set of fresh constants. The read set $\mathcal{R}(G)$ of G is the set of ground terms appearing below some Σ_1-function in G. Let $\mathsf{st}(\mathcal{K}, \mathcal{R}(G))$ be the set of ground $(\Sigma_0 \cup \Sigma_C)$-terms in $\mathcal{K}$ or $\mathcal{R}(G)$. Also, for any set Θ of $(\Sigma_0 \cup \Sigma_C)$-ground terms we will write $\Theta^{(1)}$ for the set $\{f(t_1, ..., t_n) \mid t_i \in \Theta, f \in \Sigma_1\}$ (the "one-step closure" under Σ_1). In general for a set of ground terms Θ let

$\mathcal{K}{<}\Theta{>} := \{\varphi\sigma \mid \varphi\sigma \text{ is universally closed, the universal closure}$
$(\forall \varphi) \text{ of } \varphi \text{ is in } \mathcal{K}, \text{ for all terms } t \leq \cdot \varphi\sigma:$
$\text{if } t \text{ has a } \Sigma_1\text{-function as root then } t \in \Theta^{(1)},$
$\text{and for each variable } x \text{ which does not occur}$
$\text{below a function symbol in } \Sigma_1 : \sigma(x) = x\}.$

We will write $\mathcal{K}_{[G]}$ for $\mathcal{K}{<}\mathsf{st}(\mathcal{K}, \mathcal{R}(G)){>}$.

We now introduce the corresponding notions of *minimal* locality and embeddability (with the same notation as in the definitions above).

(MEmb) For every non-empty set Θ of ground $(\Sigma_0 \cup \Sigma_C)$-terms containing the ground Σ_0-terms of $\mathcal{K}$ it holds that every Θ-minimal $\mathcal{A} \in \mathsf{PMod}_w(\Sigma_1, T_1)$ weakly embeds into a total model of T_1.

(MLoc) For every set G of ground clauses in $\Sigma_1 \cup \Sigma_C$ containing at least one Σ_1-term, it holds that $T_1 \cup G \models \bot$ if and only if $T_0 \cup \mathcal{K}_{[G]} \cup G$ has no weak partial model in which all terms in $\mathsf{st}(\mathcal{K}, \mathcal{R}(G))^{(1)}$ are defined.

Theorem 4.1.3 Let T_0 be a theory in the signature $\Pi_0 = (\Sigma_0, \mathsf{Pred})$, Σ_1 a set of new function symbols and $\mathcal{K}$ a set of universally closed clauses in the extended signature $\Pi_1 = (\Sigma_0 \cup \Sigma_1, \mathsf{Pred})$. Suppose that $\mathcal{K}$ is Σ_1-quasiflat and Σ_1-linear. Then (MEmb) implies (MLoc).

Proof. The proof is similar to the proof of Theorem 3.2.1. Assume towards a contradiction that there were a set G of ground $(\Sigma_1 \cup \Sigma_C)$-clauses (with $\mathcal{R}(G) \neq \emptyset$) such that $T_1 \cup G$ was inconsistent but such that there was a partial model $\mathcal{A}$ of $T_0 \cup \mathcal{K}_{[G]} \cup G$ with defined $\mathsf{st}(\mathcal{K}, \mathcal{R}(G))^{(1)}$ terms and whose Σ_0-functions are total. For brevity, let us write Θ for the set $\mathsf{st}(\mathcal{K}, \mathcal{R}(G))$ in the following. Let $\mathcal{B}$ be a Θ-minimal submodel of $\mathcal{A}$ which inherits the carrier and the interpretation of base functions from $\mathcal{A}$. Because $\Theta^{(1)}$ is defined in $\mathcal{A}$ there is such a submodel.

By construction we have $\mathcal{B} \models T_0$. Because the extension ground terms of G are contained in $\Theta^{(1)}$ we also obtain $\mathcal{B} \models G$. We want to show that $\mathcal{B}$ is also a partial model of $\mathcal{K}$. Let D be a clause in $\mathcal{K}$. In case D is ground, we trivially have $D \in \mathcal{K}{<}\Theta{>} = \mathcal{K}_{[G]}$ and therefore $\mathcal{B} \models_w D$. If D is not ground, let β be a valuation for $\mathcal{B}$. If there is a term t in D such that $\beta(t)$ is undefined then $(\mathcal{B}, \beta)$ trivially satisfies D. Otherwise, because $\mathcal{K}$ is linear, we know that every variable x which appears under a Σ_1-function does so in a unique term $u_x = f(...x...)$ (which may occur repeatedly). Since $\beta(u_x)$ was defined, there must be a ground term t_x in Θ with $\beta(x) = t_x^{\mathcal{A}}$. This allows us to define a substitution

$$\sigma(x) = \begin{cases} x & \text{if } x \text{ does not occur below a } \Sigma_1\text{-function in D,} \\ t_x & \text{if } x \text{ does occur below a } \Sigma_1\text{-function.} \end{cases}$$

It is easy to check that $D\sigma \in \mathcal{K}_{[G]}$. Hence, we have $\mathcal{A}, \beta \models_w D\sigma$. This is equivalent to $\mathcal{A}, (\beta \circ \sigma) \models_w D$. By construction we have that $(\beta \circ \sigma) = \beta$. Thus, by Lemma 2.2.9, $\mathcal{A}, \beta \models_w D$ and, because all terms in D are defined in $(\mathcal{B}, \beta)$, we may conclude that $\mathcal{B}, \beta \models_w D$. Now that we have shown that $\mathcal{B}$ is a partial model of $T_0 \cup \mathcal{K}$, we may use the assumption to obtain a total model $\mathcal{C}$ of $T_0 \cup \mathcal{K}$ into which $\mathcal{B}$ embeds. Since all terms in G are defined in $\mathcal{B}$ by construction (and G is quantifier-free) it follows from Lemma 2.2.15 that $\mathcal{C} \models G$. Contradiction. □

4.2 The Array Property Fragment

The *array property fragment* (APF) was introduced as a decidable fragment of the theory of arrays by Bradley, Manna and Sipma ([BMS06]). In this section we will present their result in a locality setting. This allows us to integrate the array property fragment into a unifying framework, enabling us, among other things, to use arrays as a link in a chain of theory extensions.

The theory of arrays is considered in a many-sorted setting. There are three sorts: elements, arrays and indices (integers). We have two functions 'read' and 'write' of sort Array × Index → Element and Array × Index × Element → Array, respectively. The theory T_A has two axioms ('read-over-write'): the universal closure of

$$\text{read}(\text{write}(a, i, e), i) = e,$$
$$j \neq i \rightarrow \text{read}(\text{write}(a, i, e), j) = \text{read}(a, j).$$

The index theory will always be fixed to be linear integer arithmetic, known as *Presburger arithmetic* (cf. [BMS06]), i.e., the theory of integers $\mathbb{Z}$ in the signature $\Pi_{Ar} := \{+, -, 0, 1, \leq\}$. The reason for this is that Presburger arithmetic is known to be complete and decidable (cf. [Pre29] and [End02], §3.2, for a modern account). In contrast, the type Element will not be fixed but will be regarded as a parameter. In this section, our base theory T_0 will be fixed as the combination of Presburger arithmetic, the parametric element theory and the read-over-write axioms. Accordingly, our base signature will be the combination of the signatures of said theories. A set of fresh constants will again be denoted by Σ_C. We consider arrays as extension functions Σ_1 from the integers into the element theory. Array reads like $read(a, j)$ become simply $a(j)$.

As in [BMS06], array writes are eliminated from a given proof task by introducing new array names before the decision procedure is employed. That is, we replace a term $write(a, i, e)$ by a fresh array symbol a' everywhere it occurs and add the new formulas $a'(i) = e$ and $\forall j.j \leq i-1 \vee i+1 \leq j \to b(j) = a(j)$. (In this way the second formula will conform to the syntactic restrictions given below.) This transformation clearly preserves satisfiability.

The array property fragment is defined as follows.

Definition 4.2.1 (Array property, [BMS06]) *With the notations just introduced, consider the following.*

(1) An index guard *is a positive Boolean combination (only '$\wedge$' and '$\vee$' are used) of atoms of the form $t \leq u$ or $t = u$ where t and u are either a variable or a ground term of $\Pi_{Ar} \cup \Sigma_C$.*

(2) A universal formula *of the form $(\forall \bar{x})(\varphi_I(\bar{x}) \to \varphi_V(\bar{x}))$ is an* array property *if it is Σ_1-quasiflat, i.e., there are no nestings of array reads such as $a(b(x))$, if φ_I is an index guard, $\varphi_V(\bar{x})$ is quantifier-free and if variables x only occur as direct array reads $a(x)$ in φ_V.*

The array property fragment *consists of all existentially-closed Boolean combinations of array property formulas and quantifier-free formulas.*

Because we are concerned with satisfiability problems, we could equivalently treat the free variables as constants in the definition of the array property fragment, instead of employing the existential closure.

Remark 4.2.2 *Our definition of the array property fragment is slightly more restrictive than the one given in [BMS06]. There, the array property fragment is defined as (the existential closure) of Boolean combinations of array properties and quantifier free array formulas. In a locality setting, however, it is more natural to consider the array property formulas separately from the quantifier-free formulas in a problem from the array property fragment. The former will be considered as extension clauses and the latter as the proof task.*

Note that to a large extent we can rewrite formulas φ of the more general definition of the array property fragment to fit our format. We may assume that φ is in negation normal form. The negation of an array property can be skolemized, while a disjunction can be resolved by fusing the disjuncts. We can always fuse two array properties into one. Say we have $(\forall \bar{x})(\varphi_I^1(\bar{x}) \to \varphi_V^1(\bar{x})) \vee (\forall \bar{x})(\varphi_I^2(\bar{x}) \to \varphi_V^2(\bar{x}))$. We may change the bound variables so that they do not overlap: $(\forall \bar{x})(\varphi_I^1(\bar{x}) \to \varphi_V^1(\bar{x})) \vee (\forall \bar{y})(\varphi_I^2(\bar{y}) \to \varphi_V^2(\bar{y}))$. Now this is equivalent to $(\forall \bar{x})(\forall \bar{y})(\neg \varphi_I^1(\bar{x}) \vee \varphi_V^1(\bar{x}) \vee \neg \varphi_I^2(\bar{y}) \vee \varphi_V^2(\bar{y}))$. This we may rewrite as $(\forall \bar{x})(\forall \bar{y})(\varphi_I^1(\bar{x}) \wedge \varphi_I^2(\bar{y}) \to \varphi_V^1(\bar{x}) \vee \varphi_V^2(\bar{y}))$. This is again an array property because index guard are closed under conjunctions.

We can also fuse the disjunction of an array property with a ground formula provided the ground formula is flat, which can always be achieved without affecting satisfiability.

All the actual examples of a problem in the array property fragment given in [BMS06, BM07] fit our format.

Recall that we called a partial model $\mathcal{A}$ Θ-minimal, if we have for all extension functions f, that $f^\mathcal{A}(a_1, ..., a_n)$ is defined if and only if there are terms $t_i \in \Theta$, such that $t_i^\mathcal{A} = a_i$. We can use minimal locality to handle the array property fragment (and therefore subsume it).

Definition 4.2.3 (Projection) *With the above notations, let Θ be a non-empty set of ground integer terms and let $\mathcal{A}$ be a (total) model of Presburger arithmetic. A map $\pi : \mathbb{Z} \to \Theta^\mathcal{A}$ is called a $(\Theta, \mathcal{A})$-projection if it has the properties*

(1) $\pi(t^\mathcal{A}) = t^\mathcal{A}$, for all $t \in \Theta$, and

(2) $i \leq j \to \pi(i) \leq \pi(j)$, for all $i, j \in \mathbb{Z}$.

We will usually drop the qualification for $(\Theta, \mathcal{A})$-projections if that is unambiguous. As an example of a projection, we could always choose the nearest neighbor in $\Theta^\mathcal{A}$ with a preference for smaller. That is set

$$\pi(i) := \begin{cases} \max(\{\, t^\mathcal{A} \mid t \in \Theta, t^\mathcal{A} \leq i \,\}) & \text{if the set is non-empty,} \\ \min(\{\, t^\mathcal{A} \mid t \in \Theta, t^\mathcal{A} > i \,\}) & \text{otherwise.} \end{cases}$$

In general, suppose $\Theta^\mathcal{A}$ consists of the integers $x_1 < x_2 < \ldots < x_k$. Then it must hold, for any projection π, that $\pi(y) = x_1$, for all $y \leq x_1$; and $\pi(y) = x_k$, for all $y \geq x_k$. Projections may differ on the value they assign to an integer between x_i and x_{i+1} ($1 < i < k$), or rather, they may differ on whether and if so on what point in the interval (x_i, x_{i+1}) the value of π changes from x_i to x_{i+1}. The value might never change and be constantly x_i (as in the example above), it might be constantly x_{i+1} or it might change at a integer $j \in (x_i, x_{i+1})$. See Figure 4.1 for an illustration. (In case $\Theta^\mathcal{A}$ has no minimal element x_1, or no maximal element x_k, or both, we do not have to treat the case $y \leq x_1$ or $y \geq x_k$ differently.)

In this section we will commonly write $a, b, c, \ldots$ for extension functions because the extension functions are considered to be arrays.

Definition 4.2.4 $((\Theta, \pi)$-Completion) *With the above notations, let Θ be a non-empty set of ground integer terms. Let $T_0 \subseteq T_0 \cup \mathcal{K}$ be an extension by a set of array properties, let $\mathcal{A} \in \mathsf{PMod}_w(\Sigma_1, T_1)$ be Θ-minimal and let $\pi : \mathbb{Z} \to \Theta^\mathcal{A}$ be a $(\Theta, \mathcal{A})$-projection. We call an algebra $\hat{\mathcal{A}}$ the (Θ, π)-completion of $\mathcal{A}$ if it is exactly like $\mathcal{A}$ except that*

$$a^{\hat{\mathcal{A}}}(i_1, ..., i_n) := a^\mathcal{A}(\pi(i_1), ..., \pi(i_n)), \quad \text{for all } a \in \Sigma_1 \text{ and } i_1, \ldots, i_n \in \mathbb{Z}.$$

Remark 4.2.5 *In a similar fashion, Ge and de Moura ([GdM09]) extract a monotone projection function in order to decide the array property fragment. In an abstraction step, they then use a non-monotonic projection function for a fragment lacking index guards, the so-called essentially uninterpreted formulas. In essence, this is the fragment where variables only appear below extension functions.*

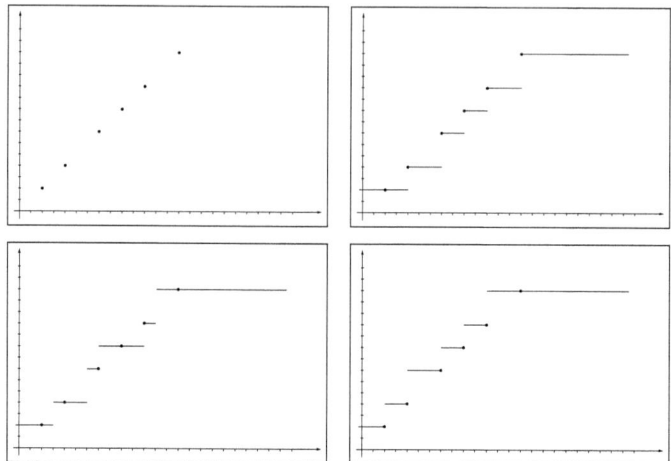

Figure 4.1: Projections. Clockwise from top left: $\Theta^{\mathcal{A}}$, a projection with preference for the right neighbor, a projection with preference for the left neighbor and an example of a projection function without a simple preference. The (discrete) projections are drawn continuously.

The aim of this section is to prove the following theorem.

Theorem 4.2.6 *With the above notations, let $T_0 \subseteq T_0 \cup \mathcal{K}$ be an extension by a set of array properties. Let Θ be a non-empty set of ground integer terms containing the ground Σ_0-terms of $\mathcal{K}$ and let $\mathcal{A} \in \mathsf{PMod}_w(\Sigma_1, T_1)$ be Θ-minimal. Let π be any projection. For the (Θ, π)-completion $\hat{\mathcal{A}}$ of $\mathcal{A}$ it holds that $\mathcal{A}$ is a weak submodel of $\hat{\mathcal{A}}$, i.e., the identity is a weak embedding, and $\hat{\mathcal{A}}$ is a total model of $T_0 \cup \mathcal{K}$.*

From this and Theorem 4.1.3 we immediately get:

Corollary 4.2.7 *Let $\mathcal{K}$ be a set of Σ_1-quasiflat and Σ_1-linear array properties. Then the extension $T_0 \subseteq T_0 \cup \mathcal{K}$ is minimally local.*

We will need the following lemma. Recall that by the notation $t^{\mathcal{A}}[\bar{a}]$ we mean the value of the term $t(\bar{x})$ in an algebra $\mathcal{A}$ under any valuation β with $\beta\bar{x} = \bar{a}$ (see page 11).

Lemma 4.2.8 *Let π, $\mathcal{A}$ be as above and let $\hat{\mathcal{A}}$ be the (Θ, π)-completion of $\mathcal{A}$. Let t be any Σ_1-quasiflat term whose $\Pi_{Ar} \cup \Sigma_C$-subterms are contained in Θ. It holds that*

(1) $\pi(\pi(i)) = \pi(i)$.

(2) $t^{\hat{\mathcal{A}}}[\pi(\bar{i})] = t^{\mathcal{A}}[\pi(\bar{i})]$.

(3) If additionally t has variables only below Σ_1-functions, we have $t^{\hat{\mathcal{A}}}[\bar{i}] = t^{\mathcal{A}}[\pi(\bar{i})]$.

Proof. (1) is a trivial consequence of 4.2.3.1.
We show the other two claims simultaneously. Note first, that if t contains no Σ_1-functions then (2) is trivial and for (3) we have that t is a ground term of $(\Sigma_0 \cup \Sigma_C)$ and therefore $t^{\hat{\mathcal{A}}}[\pi(\bar{i})] = t^{\hat{\mathcal{A}}} = t^{\mathcal{A}} = t^{\mathcal{A}}[\pi(\bar{i})]$. In general, if t is ground, (3) is trivial and (2) follows from 4.2.3.1 and the fact that

t is Σ_1-quasiflat. Let us therefore assume that t is not ground and contains a Σ_1-function. We may further assume that t has a Σ_1-function at root, say a. With the above observation we get

$$t^{\hat{\mathcal{A}}}[\pi(\bar{i})] = a^{\hat{\mathcal{A}}}(\pi(\bar{i})) := a^{\mathcal{A}}(\pi(\pi(\bar{i}))) = a^{\mathcal{A}}(\pi(\bar{i})) = t^{\mathcal{A}}[\pi(\bar{i})].$$

for (2) and

$$t^{\hat{\mathcal{A}}}[\bar{i}] = a^{\hat{\mathcal{A}}}(\bar{i}) := a^{\mathcal{A}}(\pi(\bar{i})) = a^{\mathcal{A}}(\pi(\pi(\bar{i}))) = a^{\hat{\mathcal{A}}}(\pi(\bar{i})) = t^{\hat{\mathcal{A}}}[\pi(\bar{i})].$$

for (3). □

We are now in a position to prove Theorem 4.2.6.

Proof of theorem. We first check that the identity is a weak embedding from $\mathcal{A}$ into $\hat{\mathcal{A}}$. Let $a^{\mathcal{A}}(a_1, ..., a_n)$ be defined. Since $\mathcal{A}$ was Θ-minimal it follows that there are terms $t_1, ..., t_n \in \Theta$ such that $a_i = t_i^{\mathcal{A}}$ and we have

$$a^{\hat{\mathcal{A}}}(t_1^{\hat{\mathcal{A}}}, ..., t_n^{\hat{\mathcal{A}}}) := a^{\mathcal{A}}(\pi(t_1^{\hat{\mathcal{A}}}), ..., \pi(t_n^{\hat{\mathcal{A}}})) = a^{\mathcal{A}}(t_1^{\mathcal{A}}, ..., t_n^{\mathcal{A}}) = a^{\mathcal{A}}(a_1, ..., a_n).$$

We trivially have $\hat{\mathcal{A}} \models T_0$. So what is left to check is that $\hat{\mathcal{A}} \models \mathcal{K}$. Let $(\forall \bar{x})(\varphi_I(\bar{x}) \to \varphi_V(\bar{x}))$ be an array property from $\mathcal{K}$. We fix some $\bar{i} \in \mathbb{Z}^*$. We assume that $\hat{\mathcal{A}} \models \varphi_I[\bar{i}]$ and need to show that $\hat{\mathcal{A}} \models \varphi_V[\bar{i}]$. It follows that $\hat{\mathcal{A}} \models \varphi_I[\pi(\bar{i})]$ by induction on the structure of φ. To see this, consider the base case. The atoms allowed in φ_I are either $t = u$ or $t \leq u$ where t, u are either ground terms of $\mathcal{L}_{Ar}$ or simple variables. If t, u are both variables the claim follows from the monotonicity of π. If they are both ground terms there is nothing to show. That leaves the remaining case. Say t is ground and u is the variable x. If we have that $t^{\mathcal{A}} = i$ we get $\pi(i) = \pi(t^{\mathcal{A}}) = t^{\hat{\mathcal{A}}}$ by definition; and, similarly, if we have that $t^{\mathcal{A}} \leq i$ it follows that $\pi(i) \geq \pi(t^{\mathcal{A}}) = t^{\hat{\mathcal{A}}}$. This covers the base case. Since φ_I is a positive combination of these atoms, the induction step is easy.

From $\hat{\mathcal{A}} \models \varphi_I[\pi(\bar{i})]$ we trivially get $\mathcal{A} \models \varphi_I[\pi(\bar{i})]$. It follows by assumption that $\mathcal{A} \models \varphi_V[\pi(\bar{i})]$. We now show by induction that the last fact is equivalent to $\hat{\mathcal{A}} \models \varphi_V[\pi(\bar{i})]$. The base case is immediate from Lemma 4.2.8.(2) and the induction step is straightforward because φ_V is quantifier-free. The last claim is that $\hat{\mathcal{A}} \models \varphi_V[\pi(\bar{i})]$ is equivalent to $\hat{\mathcal{A}} \models \varphi_V[\bar{i}]$ and the main claim then follows. We again proceed by induction on φ_V. The base case is covered by Lemma 4.2.8.(3) and the induction step is again clear. □

Theorem 4.2.6 establishes the array property fragment as an instance of (generalized) local reasoning. Aside from offering a unified framework, regarding the array property fragment as a local extension allows one to consider the array property fragment as a link in a chain of local extensions and thereby to extend it (cf. [IJSS08]).

4.3 Example

We demonstrate how to use locality for arrays on an example from Bradley, Manna and Sipma [BMS06]. We slightly modify the proof task for our purposes. As base theory T_0 we take Presburger arithmetic, in the same signature $\Pi_{Ar} = \{+, -, 0, 1, \leq\}$ as above.

We want to show the unsatisfiability of the following proof task w.r.t. our base theory T_0: An array a is sorted after being updated twice in two different ways.

$$w < x < y < z \land 0 < k < l < n \land 3 < l - k$$
$$\land \operatorname{sorted}(0, n - 1, \operatorname{write}(\operatorname{write}(a, k, w), l, x))$$
$$\land \operatorname{sorted}(0, n - 1, \operatorname{write}(\operatorname{write}(a, k, y), l, z))$$

where $\operatorname{sorted}(0, n - 1, a)$ is shorthand for $(\forall i, j)(0 \leq i \leq j \leq n - 1 \to a[i] \leq a[j])$, a is a constant of type array; and w, x, y, z, k, l and n are integer constants. Equivalently, since we are concerned with a satisfiability problem, we can regard a, w, x, y, z, k, l and n as existentially quantified.

A formula $x < y$ is seen as an abbreviation for the formula $x + 1 \leq y$ which is equivalent w.r.t. Presburger arithmetic. The extension of the base language consists of some functions $\Sigma_1 = \{a, b, c, d, e\}$ which will serve as arrays (and array updates). Our set $\mathcal{K}$ of extension clauses looks as follows.

$$\left. \begin{array}{l} (\forall i, j)(0 \leq i \leq j \leq n - 1 \to c[i] \leq c[j]), \quad (1) \\ (\forall i, j)(0 \leq i \leq j \leq n - 1 \to e[i] \leq e[j]), \quad (2) \\ (\forall i)(i \neq l \to b[i] = c[i]), \quad (3) \\ (\forall i)(i \neq k \to a[i] = b[i]), \quad (4) \\ (\forall i)(i \neq l \to d[i] = e[i]), \quad (5) \\ (\forall i)(i \neq k \to a[i] = d[i]). \quad (6) \end{array} \right\} \mathcal{K}$$

These clauses express that the arrays c and e are sorted where e is just like d, except maybe at position d, and d is just like a, but for position k, and similarly for c, b and a.

Our proof task (set of ground clauses) G looks like this.

$$\left. \begin{array}{l} w < x < y < z, \\ 0 < k < l < n, \\ k + 3 < l, \\ c[l] = x, \\ b[k] = w, \\ e[l] = z, \\ d[k] = y. \end{array} \right\} G$$

We have to rewrite the clauses a bit in order to fulfill the syntactic requirements laid out in the last section. First, index guards must be positive. We change an expression $i \neq l$ where i is the (universally quantified) variable to $i \leq l - 1 \lor l + 1 \leq i$. We have to rewrite it like this because the universally quantified variable i must not appear below a function in the index guard. This gives us the following set of clauses.

$$\left.\begin{aligned}&(\forall i,j)(0 \leq i \leq j \leq n-1 \rightarrow c[i] \leq c[j]), \quad (1)\\&(\forall i,j)(0 \leq i \leq j \leq n-1 \rightarrow e[i] \leq e[j]), \quad (2)\\&(\forall i)(i \leq l-1 \rightarrow b[i] = c[i]), \quad (3)\\&(\forall i)(l+1 \leq i \rightarrow b[i] = c[i]), \quad (4)\\&(\forall i)(i \leq k-1 \rightarrow a[i] = b[i]), \quad (5)\\&(\forall i)(k+1 \leq i \rightarrow a[i] = b[i]), \quad (6)\\&(\forall i)(i \leq l-1 \rightarrow d[i] = e[i]), \quad (7)\\&(\forall i)(l+1 \leq i \rightarrow d[i] = e[i]), \quad (8)\\&(\forall i)(i \leq k-1 \rightarrow a[i] = d[i]), \quad (9)\\&(\forall i)(k+1 \leq i \rightarrow a[i] = d[i]). \quad (10)\end{aligned}\right\} \mathcal{K}'$$

$\mathcal{K}'$ is flat but not Σ_1-linear. We therefore need to make it so.

$$\left.\begin{aligned}&(\forall i,j)(0 \leq i \leq j \leq n-1 \rightarrow c[i] \leq c[j]), \quad (1)\\&(\forall i,j)(0 \leq i \leq j \leq n-1 \rightarrow e[i] \leq e[j]), \quad (2)\\&(\forall i,j)(i = j \wedge i \leq l-1 \rightarrow b[i] = c[j]), \quad (3)\\&(\forall i,j)(i = j \wedge l+1 \leq i \rightarrow b[i] = c[j]), \quad (4)\\&(\forall i,j)(i = j \wedge i \leq k-1 \rightarrow a[i] = b[j]), \quad (5)\\&(\forall i,j)(i = j \wedge k+1 \leq i \rightarrow a[i] = b[j]), \quad (6)\\&(\forall i,j)(i = j \wedge i \leq l-1 \rightarrow d[i] = e[j]), \quad (7)\\&(\forall i,j)(i = j \wedge l+1 \leq i \rightarrow d[i] = e[j]), \quad (8)\\&(\forall i,j)(i = j \wedge i \leq k-1 \rightarrow a[i] = d[j]), \quad (9)\\&(\forall i,j)(i = j \wedge k+1 \leq i \rightarrow a[i] = d[j]). \quad (10)\end{aligned}\right\} \mathcal{K}''$$

Here we finally can express that b resulted from a after w was written at position k and c is the update of b where x was written at position l and analogously for a, d and e.

$\mathcal{K}''$ contains the Σ_{Ar}-ground terms $\{0, n-1, k-1, k+1, l-1, l+1\}$ and the read set of G is $\{k, l\}$. Let us abbreviate the set $\text{st}(\mathcal{K}, \mathcal{R}(G))$ as Θ, then we get

$$\begin{aligned}\Theta^{(1)} = \{&a[0], a[n-1], a[k-1], a[k+1], a[l-1], a[l+1], a[k], a[l],\\&b[0], b[n-1], b[k-1], b[k+1], b[l-1], b[l+1], b[k], b[l],\\&c[0], c[n-1], c[k-1], c[k+1], c[l-1], c[l+1], c[k], c[l],\\&d[0], d[n-1], d[k-1], d[k+1], d[l-1], d[l+1], d[k], d[l],\\&e[0], e[n-1], e[k-1], e[k+1], e[l-1], e[l+1], e[k], e[l]\}.\end{aligned}$$

By Corollary 4.2.7, we know that the extension $T_0 \subseteq T_0 \cup \mathcal{K}''$ is minimally Θ-local. This means for the above G that $T_1 \cup G \models \bot$ if and only if $T_0 \cup \mathcal{K}''_{[G]} \cup G$ has no weak partial model in which all terms in $\Theta^{(1)}$ are defined.

The program *H-PILoT* presented in Section 6 will perform the necessary transformations of the clauses shown here automatically, calculate the required instances of said clauses and delegate the arithmetic part to a dedicated prover. For the array property fragment we thus have a full decision procedures implemented in a general purpose local reasoning tool.

For now, let us check manually that the instances of $\mathcal{K}''_{[G]}$ do indeed suffice to prove inconsistency of $T_0 \cup \mathcal{K}'' \cup G$. Consider

$$0 \leq k \leq k+1 \leq n-1 \rightarrow c[k] \leq c[k+1], \qquad (1)$$
$$k \leq l-1 \rightarrow b[k] = c[k], \qquad (2)$$
$$0 \leq k+1 \leq l \leq n-1 \rightarrow c[k+1] \leq c[l], \qquad (3)$$
$$0 \leq k+1 \leq l \leq n-1 \rightarrow e[k] \leq e[k+1], \qquad (4)$$
$$k \leq l-1 \rightarrow e[k] = d[k], \qquad (5)$$
$$0 \leq k+1 \leq l \leq n-1 \rightarrow e[k+1] \leq e[l], \qquad (6)$$
$$k+1 \leq l-1 \rightarrow b[k+1] = c[k+1], \qquad (7)$$
$$k+1 \leq l-1 \rightarrow b[k+1] = a[k+1], \qquad (8)$$
$$k+1 \leq l-1 \rightarrow e[k+1] = d[k+1], \qquad (9)$$
$$k+1 \leq l-1 \rightarrow d[k+1] = a[k+1], \qquad (10)$$

By arithmetic we get $G \models_{T_0} k+1 \leq l \leq n-1$ and $G \models_{T_0} k+3 \leq l-1 \models_{T_0} k \leq k+1 \leq l-1$.

Putting thing together we get:

$$w =_G b[k] =_{(2)} c[k] \leq_{(1)} c[k+1] \leq_{(3)} c[l] =_G x < y =_G d[k] =_{(5)} e[k]$$
$$\leq_{(4)} e[k+1] =_{(9)} d[k+1] =_{(10)} a[k+1] =_{(8)} b[k+1] =_{(7)} c[k+1].$$

Therefore, $c[k+1] < c[k+1]$. Contradiction. This shows the classical inconsistency of $T_0 \cup \mathcal{K}'' \cup G$.

4.4 The Λ-Array Property Fragment

Looking at the array property fragment, the most severe restriction is certainly that no arithmetic whatsoever is allowed on variables. Even expressions like $i + 1$ are not allowed - neither in the guard nor in the value. In fact, Bradley, Manna and Sipma have shown that this would result in an undecidable fragment of the theory of arrays (cf. [BMS06]). In this section we will loosen this restraint, if in a somewhat piecemeal fashion.

Definition 4.4.1 (Λ-array property fragment) *Let Σ_C be a set of constant symbols, $\mathcal{L}_{Ar+C}$ the language of arithmetic with signature $\{+, -, 0, 1, \leq\} \cup \Sigma_C$. Let Λ be a set of non-empty ground terms of $\mathcal{L}_{Ar+C}$ and let Σ_1 be a set of fresh function symbols.*

(1) An Λ-index guard is a positive Boolean combination of atoms of the form $t \leq u$ or $t = u$

where t and u are either a variable or a ground term of $\mathcal{L}_{Ar+C}$, or one of them is a ground term and the other is in the form $x + \lambda$, for a variable x and a $\lambda \in \Lambda$.

(2) A universal formula of the form $(\forall \bar{x})(\varphi_I(\bar{x}) \to \varphi_V(\bar{x}))$ *is a* Λ*-array property if it is* Σ_1*-quasiflat,* φ_I *is a* Λ*-index guard,* φ_V *is quantifier-free and if all variables* x *only occur as direct array reads* $a(x)$ *in* φ_V, $a \in \Sigma_1$.

The Λ-array property fragment *consists of all existentially-closed (equivalently, ground) Boolean combinations of Λ-array property formulas and quantifier-free formulas.*

We use our recently gained insights into projection functions to modify our Definition 4.2.3 in order to cope with this new fragment. For this new fragment we have to consider projections whose range is infinite.

Definition 4.4.2 (($\Theta, \Lambda, \mathcal{A}$)-projection) *With the above notations, let Θ be a non-empty set of ground integer terms that is closed under subtractions of terms in Λ, i.e., if $t \in \Theta$, $\lambda \in \Lambda$ then $t - \lambda \in \Theta$, and let $\mathcal{A}$ be a structure with total Σ_{Ar}-functions. A map $\pi : \mathbb{Z} \to \Theta^{\mathcal{A}}$ is called a $(\Theta, \Lambda, \mathcal{A})$-projection if it has the properties*

(1) $\pi(t^{\mathcal{A}}) = t^{\mathcal{A}}$, *for all* $t \in \Theta$;

(2) $i \leq j \Rightarrow \pi(i) \leq \pi(j)$, *for all* $i, j \in \mathbb{Z}$;

(3) $i + \lambda^{\mathcal{A}} \leq t^{\mathcal{A}} \Rightarrow \pi(i) + \lambda^{\mathcal{A}} \leq t^{\mathcal{A}}$, *for all* $i \in \mathbb{Z}$, $\lambda \in \Lambda$, $t \in \Theta$;

(4) $t^{\mathcal{A}} \leq i + \lambda^{\mathcal{A}} \Rightarrow t^{\mathcal{A}} \leq \pi(i) + \lambda^{\mathcal{A}}$, *for all* $i \in \mathbb{Z}$, $\lambda \in \Lambda$, $t \in \Theta$.

It is perhaps not as obvious as in Section 4.2 that there exists a projection function with the above properties. We inquire.

Lemma 4.4.3 *With the above notations, let Θ be a non-empty set of ground integer terms that is closed under subtractions of terms in Λ and let $\mathcal{A}$ be a structure with total Σ_{Ar}-functions where all terms of Θ are defined. Then there exists a $(\Theta, \Lambda, \mathcal{A})$-projection $\pi : \mathbb{Z} \to \Theta^{\mathcal{A}}$.*

Proof. If Λ is empty or $\Lambda = \{\lambda\}$ and $\lambda^{\mathcal{A}} = 0$ the claim reduces to the existence of a $(\Theta, \mathcal{A})$-projection as defined in Section 4.2.

Consider next the case where there is a $\lambda \in \Lambda$ such that $\lambda^{\mathcal{A}} > 0$. Then we set $\pi(i) := \max(\{\, t^{\mathcal{A}} \mid t \in \Theta, t^{\mathcal{A}} \leq i\,\})$, that is, we always choose the left neighbor. This is well-defined because Θ is not empty and contains for each term u also the term $u - \lambda$. Because $\mathbb{Z}$ is Archimedean, for every $i \in \mathbb{Z}$, we can find an element $u \in \Theta$ such that $u^{\mathcal{A}} < i$.

In particular, we have $\pi(i) \leq i$ for all $i \in \mathbb{Z}$. This implies $\pi(i) + \lambda^{\mathcal{A}} \leq i + \lambda^{\mathcal{A}}$. This settles 3). It is easy to see that π satisfies 1) and 2). Concerning 4), observe that $t^{\mathcal{A}} \leq i + \lambda^{\mathcal{A}}$ implies $\pi(t^{\mathcal{A}} - \lambda^{\mathcal{A}}) \leq \pi(i)$ by 2). Since both t and $t - \lambda$ are in Θ we further have $\pi(t^{\mathcal{A}} - \lambda^{\mathcal{A}}) = t^{\mathcal{A}} - \lambda^{\mathcal{A}}$, establishing 4).

The reasoning for the remaining case where $\lambda^{\mathcal{A}} < 0$, for all $\lambda \in \Lambda$, is similar but take $\pi(i) := \min(\{\, t^{\mathcal{A}} \mid t \in \Theta, t^{\mathcal{A}} \geq i\,\})$ instead. □

We now define the completion $\hat{\mathcal{A}}$ of a partial algebra $\mathcal{A}$ just as in Definition 4.2.4 by setting $a^{\hat{\mathcal{A}}}(i_1, ..., i_n) := a^{\mathcal{A}}(\pi(i_1), ..., \pi(i_n))$, for arrays a. Note also that a $(\Theta, \Lambda, \mathcal{A})$-projection function is also a projection function in the sense of Section 4.2. This means in particular that we can reuse Lemma 4.2.8.

Theorem 4.4.4 *Let $T_0 \subseteq T_0 \cup \mathcal{K}$ be an extension by a set of Λ-array properties, Θ a non-empty set of ground integer terms containing the base ground terms of $\mathcal{K}$, with the property that if $t \in \Theta$ then $t - \lambda \in \Theta$, for all $\lambda \in \Lambda$, and let $\mathcal{A} \in \mathsf{PMod}_w(\Sigma_1, T_1)$ be Θ-minimal. Let π be any $(\Theta, \Lambda, \mathcal{A})$-projection. For the (Θ, π)-completion $\hat{\mathcal{A}}$ of $\mathcal{A}$ it holds that $\mathcal{A}$ is a weak submodel of $\hat{\mathcal{A}}$, i.e., the identity is a weak embedding, and $\hat{\mathcal{A}}$ is a total model of $T_0 \cup \mathcal{K}$.*

Proof. The proof is similar to the proof of Theorem 4.2.6. The projection function once again ensures that $\mathcal{A}$ is a weak submodel of $\hat{\mathcal{A}}$ and $\hat{\mathcal{A}} \models T_0$ is clear. What we need to show is $\hat{\mathcal{A}} \models (\forall \bar{x})(\varphi_I(\bar{x}) \to \varphi_V(\bar{x}))$, for a Λ-array property from $\mathcal{K}$. To this end, let us fix some $\bar{i} \in \mathbb{Z}^*$. We assume that $\hat{\mathcal{A}} \models \varphi_I[\bar{i}]$ and need to show that $\hat{\mathcal{A}} \models \varphi_V[\bar{i}]$.

It follows again by induction that $\hat{\mathcal{A}} \models \varphi_I[\pi(\bar{i})]$. We have two additional cases to cover: atoms of the form $x + \lambda \leq t$ or $t \leq x + \lambda$ (the case $x + \lambda = t$ is reducible to these two). However, this is immediate from the definition of $(\Theta, \Lambda, \mathcal{A})$-projections.

From $\hat{\mathcal{A}} \models \varphi_I[\pi(\bar{i})]$ we trivially get $\mathcal{A} \models \varphi_I[\pi(\bar{i})]$. It follows by assumption that $\mathcal{A} \models \varphi_V[\pi(\bar{i})]$. With the help of Lemma 4.2.8.(2) we see that this is equivalent to $\hat{\mathcal{A}} \models \varphi_V[\pi(\bar{i})]$, which in turn, according to Lemma 4.2.8.(3) and a trivial induction, is equivalent to $\hat{\mathcal{A}} \models \varphi_V[\bar{i}]$. This is what we wanted. □

Although we can embed partial models of the Λ-array property fragment into total ones, Theorem 4.1.3 is not sufficient to establish minimal locality. That is because we imposed restrictions on our set Θ: the closure under subtraction of terms in Λ. We therefore need a yet more general notion of locality. This led to the development of the notion of Ψ-locality which will employ a full-fledged *closure operator* on ground terms instead of a fixed set thereof. This notion will be flexible enough to accommodate the Λ-array fragment of this section. We postpone the proof of the locality of the Λ-array property fragment until then and give an example of the usage of this fragment first.

4.5 Example

In this section we give an example when and how to use the Λ-array property fragment. We present a simple case where $\Lambda = \{1\}$ but which does already lie outside the standard array property fragment and which might occur in a real-life verification task.

Consider inserting a new element x into a sorted array a. We naturally want to do so in such a fashion that resulting array a' will still be sorted. This time we will take a more algorithmical viewpoint: We scan the sorted array until we encounter the appropriate position p for inserting the new element x. We then insert $\dot{x}$ at position p of a and shift the elements at position bigger than p to the right. A case like this may come up when we want to prove an insertion algorithm correct.

We define a predicate 'insert' expressing that the array a' resulted from array a by inserting an element x at position p and shifting the elements right of p one position to the right.

$$\text{insert}(a, l, u, x, p, a') \leftrightarrow l \leq p \leq u+1 \wedge a'[p] = x$$
$$\wedge \forall i.(l \leq i < p \rightarrow a'[i] = a[i]) \wedge \forall i.(u \geq i \geq p \rightarrow a'[i+1] = a[i])$$

If the array a is sorted, the insertion should take place in such a manner that the resulting array is sorted again. This is achieved if p is the first position such that $a[p] \geq x$. The verification condition now looks like this.

$$\text{sorted}(a, l, u) \wedge \text{insert}(a, l, u, x, p, a')$$
$$\wedge \forall i.(l \leq i < p \rightarrow a[i] < x) \wedge x \leq a[p] \rightarrow \text{sorted}(a', l, u+1).$$

Expressed as a satisfiability problem this gives us:

$$\text{sorted}(a, l, u) \wedge \text{insert}(a, l, u, x, p, a') \wedge \forall i.(l \leq i < p \rightarrow a[i] < x)$$
$$\wedge x \leq a[p] \wedge \exists m, n.(l \leq m \leq n \leq u+1 \wedge a'(m) \not\leq a'(n)) \models \bot.$$

Spelt out, this gives us the following clauses:

$$\left. \begin{array}{ll} (\forall i, j)(l \leq i \leq j \leq u \rightarrow a[i] \leq a[j]), & (1) \\ (\forall i)(l \leq i < p \rightarrow a'[i] = a[i]), & (2) \\ (\forall i)(p \leq i \leq u \rightarrow a'[i+1] = a[i]), & (3) \\ (\forall i)(l \leq i < p \rightarrow a[i] < x). & (4) \end{array} \right\} \mathcal{K}$$

And the following proof task.

$$\left. \begin{array}{l} l \leq p \leq u+1, \\ a'[p] = x, \\ x \leq a[p], \\ l \leq m \leq n \leq u+1, \\ a'[m] \not\leq a'[n]. \end{array} \right\} \mathcal{G}$$

In order to meet the syntactic requirements of the Λ-array property fragment, we replace $<$ with $\leq$ and flatten the third clause.

$$\left. \begin{array}{ll} (\forall i, j)(l \leq i \leq j \leq u \rightarrow a[i] \leq a[j]), & (1) \\ (\forall i)(l \leq i \leq p-1 \rightarrow a'[i] = a[i]), & (2) \\ (\forall i, j)(p \leq i \leq u, j = \lceil i+1 \rceil \rightarrow a'[j] = a[i]), & (3) \\ (\forall i)(l \leq i \leq p-1 \rightarrow a[i] \leq x-1), & (4) \end{array} \right\} \mathcal{K}'$$

Note that the antecedent of the third clause does not fulfill the requirements for an index guard

(Λ or otherwise), because $j = i+1$ is not permitted for variables i and j. We therefore rewrite it by introducing a fresh constant c. This we may do without affecting (weak) satisfiability by Corollary 2.3.3.(5). We also linearize the second clause.

$$\left.\begin{array}{lr}(\forall i, j)(l \leq i \leq j \leq u \to a[i] \leq a[j]), & (1) \\ (\forall i, j)(l \leq i \leq p-1, j = i \to a'[i] = a[j]), & (2) \\ (\forall i, j)(p \leq i \leq u, j = c, \boxed{c = i+1} \to a'[j] = a[i]), & (3) \\ (\forall i)(l \leq i \leq p-1 \to a[i] \leq x - 1), & (4)\end{array}\right\} \mathcal{K}''$$

Now the third clause (and therefore $\mathcal{K}''$) lies in the Λ-array property fragment for $\Lambda = \{1\}$. It does not lie, however, in the standard array property fragment since $c = i+1$ is only permissible for a Λ-index guard.

$\mathcal{K}''$ contains the (maximal) Σ_{Ar}-ground terms $\{p, p-1, c, l, u\}$ and the read set of G is $\{p, m, n\}$. So our set Θ is

$$\begin{aligned}\Theta = \{\ & p, p-1, c, l, u, m, n, \\ & p-2, c-1, l-1, u-1, m-1, n-1, \\ & p-3, c-2, l-2, u-2, m-2, n-2, \\ & p-4, c-3, l-3, u-3, m-3, n-3, \\ & \vdots \\ & \vdots \quad\}\end{aligned}$$

We quickly make sure that these instances do indeed suffice to derive a contradiction. First note, that it follows from G that $m < n$. There are three cases to consider: p is strictly bigger than both m and n, p is strictly smaller than both m and n or $m \leq p \leq n$. In the first case we get

$$m < n < p \models_{(2)} a'[m] = a[m] \wedge a'[n] = a[n] \models_{(1)} a'[m] = a[m] \leq a[n] = a'[n].$$

In the second case we get

$$\begin{aligned}p < m < n &\models_{(3)} a'[m] = a[m-1] \wedge a'[n] = a[n-1] \\ &\models_{(1)} a'[m] = a[m-1] \leq a[n-1] = a'[n].\end{aligned}$$

Notice that here we had to use additional ground terms of $\text{st}(\mathcal{K}, \mathcal{R}(G)) - 1$.

The third case subdivides into another three cases. First, suppose that $m = p$. It follows that

$$a'[m] = a'[p] = x \leq a[p] \leq_{(1)} a[n-1] =_{(3)} a'[n].$$

Next suppose that $n = p$. It follows that

$$a'[m] =_{(2)} a[m] <_{(4)} x = a'[p] = a'[n].$$

Finally, suppose that $m < p < n$. Then

$$a'[n] =_{(3)} a[n-1] \geq_{(1)} a[p] \geq x >_{(3)} a[m] =_{(2)} a'[m].$$

Thus, in all cases do we get $a'[m] \leq a'[n]$ which contradicts G.

4.6 Ψ-Locality

Regarding the above sections about arrays, we see that in some real-life examples it might be necessary to consider a bit more instances than in standard locality. We need a general framework for these eventualities.

We generalize locality by considering closure operator on ground terms. In this way we are more flexible in case more instances are needed for completeness than in locality simpliciter. Throughout this section, let T_0 be an arbitrary theory with signature $\Pi_0 = (\Sigma_0, \mathsf{Pred})$, where the set of function symbols is Σ_0. Let $\Pi_1 = (\Sigma_0 \cup \Sigma_1, \mathsf{Pred})$ be an extension by a nonempty set of function symbols and $\mathcal{K}$ be a set of universally closed clauses in the extended signature. Let Σ_C be a fixed nonempty set of fresh constants, $\Pi_0^C = (\Sigma_0 \cup \Sigma_C, \mathsf{Pred})$ and $\Pi_1^C = (\Sigma_0 \cup \Sigma_1 \cup \Sigma_C, \mathsf{Pred})$.

Recall from Definition 2.4.4 that if T_0 is extended by a set $\mathcal{K}$ of formulas of the form $\varphi := \forall \bar{x}.(\Phi(\bar{x}) \vee C(\bar{x}))$, where $\Phi(\bar{x})$ is an arbitrary formula of Π_0 and $C(\bar{x})$ is a Π_1-clause where a Σ_1-function symbol does occur, we speak of an extension with augmented clauses; if $\Phi(\bar{x})$ is universal for every $\varphi \in \mathcal{K}$, we speak of an extension with universal augmented clauses.

The material in this section is joint work with Viorica Sofronie-Stokkermans.

Definition 4.6.1 (Term closure operator) *With the above notations, let Ψ be a map associating a set of extension clauses or augmented clauses $\mathcal{K}$ and a set of Σ_1^C-ground terms Γ with a set $\Psi_\mathcal{K}(\Gamma)$ of Σ_1^C-ground terms. Let $\mathrm{est}(\mathcal{K}, \Gamma)$ be the set of extension ground terms in $\mathcal{K}$ or Γ in which a Σ_1-function symbol appears at root. We call $\Psi_\mathcal{K}$ a term closure operator if the following holds for all sets of ground terms Γ, Δ*

(1) $\mathrm{est}(\mathcal{K}, \Gamma) \subseteq \Psi_\mathcal{K}(\Gamma)$,

(2) $\Gamma \subseteq \Delta \Rightarrow \Psi_\mathcal{K}(\Gamma) \subseteq \Psi_\mathcal{K}(\Delta)$,

(3) $\Psi_\mathcal{K}(\Psi_\mathcal{K}(\Gamma)) \subseteq \Psi_\mathcal{K}(\Gamma)$.

(4) $\Psi_\mathcal{K}$ *is taut, i.e., if $\mathcal{K}$ is Σ_1-quasiflat and Γ is Σ_1-flat, then all terms in $\Psi_\mathcal{K}(\Gamma)$ are Σ_1-quasiflat and all terms in $\Psi_\mathcal{K}(\Gamma)$ have a Σ_1-function at root.*

(5) $\Psi_\mathcal{K}$ *is invariant under renaming of ground base terms, i.e., for any map $h : \mathrm{GTerm}_{\Pi_0^C} \to \mathrm{GTerm}_{\Pi_0^C}$, it holds that $\bar{h}(\Psi_\mathcal{K}(\Gamma)) = \Psi_{\bar{h}\mathcal{K}}(\bar{h}(\Gamma))$, where $\bar{h}$ is the canonical extension of h to extension ground terms and $\bar{h}\mathcal{K}$ is the result of applying the renaming of ground terms to $\mathcal{K}$.*

We will write $\Psi_\mathcal{K}(G)$ for $\Psi_\mathcal{K}(\mathrm{est}(G))$.

We generalize our definition of local instances (Definition 3.0.5) in the following way.

Definition 4.6.2 (Θ-instances) *Let $\Pi_0 = (\Sigma_0, \mathsf{Pred})$ be a signature, Σ_1 a set of new function symbols, $\mathcal{K}$ a set of universally closed clauses or augmented clauses in the extended signature*

$\Pi_1 = (\Sigma_0 \cup \Sigma_1, \mathsf{Pred})$, Σ_C a set of fresh constants and let Θ be an arbitrary set of ground terms in the extended signature $\Pi_1^C = (\Sigma_0 \cup \Sigma_1 \cup \Sigma_C, \mathsf{Pred})$. Define

$$\mathcal{K}[\Theta] := \{\varphi\sigma \mid \varphi\sigma \text{ is universally closed, the universal closure}$$
$$\forall \varphi \text{ of } \varphi \text{ is in } \mathcal{K}, \text{ for all terms } t \leq \cdot \varphi\sigma \text{ whose root is in } \Sigma_1,$$
$$\text{it holds that } t \in \Theta;$$
$$\text{and for all variables } x \text{ which do not appear below}$$
$$\text{some } \Sigma_1\text{-function in } \varphi, \text{ it holds that } \sigma(x) = x\}.$$

If $\mathcal{A}$ is a partial Σ_1-algebra with total Σ_0-functions in which all terms in Θ are defined, we define $\mathcal{A}_\Theta$ to be the partial algebra such that $\mathcal{A}_\Theta\!\restriction_{\Pi_0} = \mathcal{A}\!\restriction_{\Pi_0}$ and such that for functions $f \in \Sigma_1$ it holds that

$$f^{\mathcal{A}_\Theta}(a_1, ..., a_n) \text{ is defined} \iff \exists t_1, ..., t_n.\ a_i = t_i^{\mathcal{A}} \land f(t_1, ..., t_n) \in \Theta.$$

If $\Psi_\mathcal{K}$ is term closure operator we write $\mathcal{K}[\Psi]$ for $\mathcal{K}[\Psi_\mathcal{K}(G)]$.

As in the proof that embeddability implies locality (Theorem 3.2.1), the restricted model $\mathcal{A}_\Theta$ is a model of $T_0 \cup \mathcal{K}$ if $\mathcal{A}$ is a model of $T_0 \cup \mathcal{K}[\Theta]$.

Lemma 4.6.3 *Let T_0 be a theory in the signature $\Pi_0 = (\Sigma_0, \mathsf{Pred})$. Let $\Pi_1 = (\Sigma_1, \mathsf{Pred}) \supseteq \Pi_0$ be an extension by function symbols and let $\mathcal{K}$ be a set of Σ_1-quasiflat and Σ_1-linear clauses or augmented clauses in the signature Π_1 that are universally closed. Let G be a set of ground extension clauses (with additional constants), Θ a set of ground terms such that $\mathrm{est}(\mathcal{K}, G) \subseteq \Theta$ and $\mathcal{A}$ a weak partial model of $T_0, \mathcal{K}[\Theta], G$ with total Σ_0-functions in which all terms of Θ are defined. Then $\mathcal{A}_\Theta$ is a weak partial model of $T_0 \cup \mathcal{K} \cup G$ in which all Σ_0-functions are total and in which all terms of Θ are defined. In particular, all terms appearing in G are defined in $\mathcal{A}_\Theta$.*

Proof. By definition of $\mathcal{A}_\Theta$ we immediately get $\mathcal{A}_\Theta \models_w T_0$. Because of $\mathrm{est}(G) \subseteq \mathrm{est}(\mathcal{K}, G) \subseteq \Theta$, $\mathcal{A}$ and $\mathcal{A}_\Theta$ agree on all terms in G and this implies $\mathcal{A}_\Theta \models G$. So the part requiring work is to show that $\mathcal{A}_\Theta \models_w \mathcal{K}$. We show this for the case of an extension with augmented clauses to which the case of extension with clauses can be reduced. Take an augmented clause $\Phi \lor D \in \mathcal{K}$, where Φ is a formula of the base language, and let β be a valuation $\beta : X \to A$.

If there is a term u in D such that $u^{\mathcal{A}_\Theta}[\beta]$ is undefined, we trivially have $\mathcal{A}_\Theta, \beta \models_w \Phi \lor D$. So let us suppose that all terms in D are defined. $\mathcal{K}$ was Σ_1-linear. This implies that a variable x either does not occur in D below a Σ_1-function at all or it does so in a unique term (that may occur more than once). Concerning the latter case, if we have a Σ_1-term $u = f(s_1, ..., s_n)$ of D, where the terms s_i are either variables or ground terms of the base signature, we know from the fact that $\beta(t)$ is defined and by the definition of $\mathcal{A}_\Theta$ that there are ground terms t_i with $\beta(s_i) = t_i^{\mathcal{A}}$ such that $\beta(t) = f^{\mathcal{A}_\Theta}(t_1^{\mathcal{A}}, ..., t_n^{\mathcal{A}})$ and $f(t_1, ..., t_n) \in \Theta$. As before in the proof of Theorem 3.2.1, this allows us to define a substitution σ in the following manner.

$$\sigma(x) = \begin{cases} x & \text{if } x \text{ does not occur below a } \Sigma_1\text{-function in } D, \\ t & \text{if } x \text{ does occur below a } \Sigma_1\text{-function in } D \text{ and } \beta(x) = t^{\mathcal{A}}. \end{cases}$$

The above consideration shows that σ is well-defined. If a term u of D is ground, it follows that $u \in \text{est}(\mathcal{K})$ and $u\sigma = u$, otherwise, if u is not ground, it follows that $u\sigma \in \Theta$. In sum, we may conclude that $(\Phi \vee D)\sigma \in \mathcal{K}[\Theta]$.

In particular, we have that $\mathcal{A}, \beta \models_w (\Phi \vee D)\sigma$. By the substitution lemma, this is equivalent to $\mathcal{A}, (\beta \circ \sigma) \models_w \Phi \vee D$. By construction we also have that $(\beta \circ \sigma) = \beta$ and, hence, $\mathcal{A}, \beta \models_w \Phi \vee D$.

Remember that we are considering the case where all terms in D are defined in $(\mathcal{A}_\Theta, \beta)$. Hence, $\mathcal{A}$ and $\mathcal{A}_\Theta$ coincide on D (under β) as they do on Φ and we therefore have $\mathcal{A}_\Theta, \beta \models_w \Phi \vee D$. □

By the *table* of a partial algebra $\mathcal{A}$ we mean the set of all extension ground terms which are defined in $\mathcal{A}$. We assume w.l.o.g. that our fixed set of fresh variables Σ_C is chosen large enough to contain a constant a for each element a of a given algebra $\mathcal{A}$.

Definition 4.6.4 (Table of a partial algebra) *With the above notations, Let $\mathcal{A}$ be a partial Π_1^C-model with total Σ_0-functions. The table of $\mathcal{A}$ is the following set of ground $\mathcal{L}_\mathcal{A}$-terms*

$$\mathcal{D}(\mathcal{A}) := \{f(a_1, ..., a_n) \mid f \in \Sigma_1, a_i \in A, i = 1, \ldots, n, f^\mathcal{A}(a_1, ..., a_n) \text{ is defined }\}.$$

We are now able to state the definition of Ψ-locality formally. With the above notations, let $\Psi_\mathcal{K}$ be a term closure operator and $T_1 := T_0 \cup \mathcal{K}$.

PMod_w^Ψ $\mathsf{PMod}_w^\Psi(\Sigma_1, T_1)$ denotes the class of all weak partial models $\mathcal{A}$ of T_1 in which the Σ_1-functions are partial and all other functions are total and where all terms in $\Psi_\mathcal{K}(\mathcal{D}(\mathcal{A}))$ are defined.

(Emb_w^Ψ)   Every $\mathcal{A} \in \mathsf{PMod}_w^\Psi(\Sigma_1, T_1)$ weakly embeds into a total model of T_1.

(EEmb_w^Ψ)   For every $\mathcal{A} \in \mathsf{PMod}_w^\Psi(\Sigma_1, T_1)$ there is a total model $\mathcal{B}$ of T_1 and a weak embedding $\varphi: \mathcal{A} \to \mathcal{B}$
such that $(\mathcal{A}|_{\Pi_0}, \bar{a})_{\bar{a} \in A} \equiv (\mathcal{B}|_{\Pi_0}, \varphi\bar{a})_{\bar{a} \in A}$.
In other words, the embedding $\varphi: \mathcal{A}|_{\Pi_0} \to \mathcal{B}|_{\Pi_0}$ is elementary.

(Comp_w^Ψ)   Every $\mathcal{A} \in \mathsf{PMod}_w^\Psi(\Sigma_1, T_1)$ weakly embeds into a total model $\mathcal{B}$ of T_1 such that $\mathcal{A}|_{\Pi_0}$ and $\mathcal{B}|_{\Pi_0}$ are isomorphic.

The definitions for finite algebras: ($\mathsf{Emb}_w^{f,\Psi}$), ($\mathsf{EEmb}_w^{f,\Psi}$), ($\mathsf{Comp}_w^{f,\Psi}$) and for algebras where the domain of each extension function is finite: ($\mathsf{Emb}_w^{fd,\Psi}$), ($\mathsf{EEmb}_w^{fd,\Psi}$), ($\mathsf{Comp}_w^{fd,\Psi}$), are analogous.

Since every isomorphism is an elementary embedding we have the implications (Comp_w^Ψ) → (EEmb_w^Ψ) → (Emb_w^Ψ) and (Comp_w) → (EEmb_w) → (Emb_w) (and similar for finite algebras or algebras with finite extension domains).

Remark 4.6.5 (Flatness of goals) *When considering locality modulo a term closure operator $\Psi_\mathcal{K}$ we have to restrict ourselves to flat proof tasks G. This is no major restriction because we can always flatten a given proof task without affecting satisfiability (cf. 2.3.3.(5)).*

In standard locality we may assume w.l.o.g. that a given proof task G is flat or even flat and linear. This is because it suffices to show locality for flat proof tasks, then locality for all proof tasks follows, provided $\mathcal{K}$ is flat (cf. [Gan01, SS05]).

This is easy to see as follows. Let $\mathcal{K}$ be our extension clauses, T_0 our base theory, G our proof task and G' derived from G by a process of term abstraction, e.g., flattening or flattening and linearization. Suppose $T_0, \mathcal{K}, G \models \bot$. Then $T_0, \mathcal{K}, G' \models \bot$, because term abstraction does not affect satisfiability. It follows, by our assumption, that $T_0, \mathcal{K}[G'], G'$ has no weak partial models where all subterms of $\mathcal{K}$ and G' are defined. This implies in turn that $T_0, \mathcal{K}[G], G$ has no weak partial models where all subterms of $\mathcal{K}$ and G are defined, either, because we can roll back the abstraction operations and reinsert the original terms.

However, if we use Ψ-locality instead, we cannot argue in this fashion. Here is an example of a term closure operator where $T_0, \mathcal{K}[\Psi_\mathcal{K}(G')], G'$ does not imply $T_0, \mathcal{K}[\Psi_\mathcal{K}(G)], G$. Consider

$$\Psi_\mathcal{K}(\Gamma) := \text{est}(\mathcal{K}, \Gamma) \cup \{f(t) |\ f \in \Sigma_1, g(t) \in \Gamma$$

$$\text{for some } g \in \Sigma_1 \text{ and some base ground term } t\}$$

It is easy to check that this does indeed define a term closure operator.

As our (flat) extension clauses $\mathcal{K}$ take the universal closure of the following clauses (f, g are both extension functions).

(1) $y = f(x) \rightarrow g(y) = x$,

(2) $y = g(x), z = f(x) \rightarrow f(y) = g(z)$.

Our proof task G is the following set of ground clauses.

(1) $f(g(c)) = d$

(2) $f(f(c)) \neq c$

(3) $c \neq d$

We flatten G to the set G':

(1) $d_1 = g(c)$

(2) $d_2 = f(c)$

(3) $f(d_1) = d$

(4) $f(d_2) \neq c$

(5) $c \neq d$

We have

$$\Psi_\mathcal{K}(G') = \{g(c), f(c), f(d_1), f(d_2), g(d_1), g(d_2)\} \text{ and}$$
$$\Psi_\mathcal{K}(G) = \{f(g(c)), f(f(c)), g(c), f(c)\} = \text{est}(\mathcal{K}, G).$$

In particular, the following clauses are members of $\mathcal{K}[\Psi_\mathcal{K}(G')]$.

(1) $d_2 = f(c) \rightarrow g(d_2) = c$,

(2) $d_1 = g(c), d_2 = f(c) \rightarrow f(d_1) = g(d_2)$.

From this and G' it follows that
$$d = f(d_1) = g(d_2) = c,$$
showing the unsatisfiability of $\mathcal{K}[\Psi_\mathcal{K}(G')] \cup G'$.

On the other hand, $\mathcal{K}[\Psi_\mathcal{K}(G)]$ consists of the following clauses.

(1) $c = f(c) \rightarrow g(c) = c,$
(2) $c = f(g(c)) \rightarrow g(c) = g(c),$
(3) $c = f(f(c)) \rightarrow g(c) = f(c),$
(4) $c = g(c), c = f(c) \rightarrow f(c) = g(c).$
(5) $f(c) = g(c), c = f(c) \rightarrow f(f(c)) = g(c).$
(6) $g(c) = g(c), c = f(c) \rightarrow f(g(c)) = g(c).$

It follows that $\mathcal{K}[\Psi_\mathcal{K}(G)] \cup G$ is satisfiable.

We define Ψ-locality w.r.t. flat proof tasks.

(Loc$^\Psi$) Let $T_0 \cup \mathcal{K} \supseteq T_0$ be an extension by clauses.
For every set G of *flat* ground clauses in $\Pi_1 \cup \Sigma_C$ it holds that
$T_0 \cup \mathcal{K} \cup G \models \bot$ if and only if $T_0 \cup \mathcal{K}[\Psi] \cup G$ has no weak partial model in which all terms in $\Psi_\mathcal{K}(G)$ are defined.

(ELoc$^\Psi$) Let $T_0 \cup \mathcal{K} \supseteq T_0$ be an extension by augmented clauses.
For every set of formulas $\Gamma = \Gamma_0 \cup G$, where Γ_0 is a Π_0-sentence and G is a set of *flat* ground clauses in Π_1^C, it holds that
$T_0 \cup \mathcal{K} \cup \Gamma \models \bot$ if and only if $T_0 \cup \mathcal{K}[\Psi] \cup \Gamma$ has no weak partial model in which all terms in $\Psi_\mathcal{K}(G)$ are defined.

The notions (Loc$^{f,\Psi}$) and (ELoc$^{f,\Psi}$) for finite proof tasks G are defined similarly. We want to establish relationships between Ψ-locality and embeddability.

Corollary 4.6.6 *Let T_0 be a theory in the signature $\Pi_0 = (\Sigma_0, \text{Pred})$, Σ_1 a set of new function symbols and $\mathcal{K}$ a set of universally closed clauses or augmented clauses in the extended signature $\Pi_1 = (\Sigma_0 \cup \Sigma_1, \text{Pred})$ that are Σ_1-quasiflat. Let G be a set of Σ_1-flat ground extension clauses with additional constants, $\Psi_\mathcal{K}$ a term closure operator, $\Theta := \Psi_\mathcal{K}(G)$, $\mathcal{A}$ a weak partial model of $T_0 \cup \mathcal{K}[\Psi] \cup G$ with total Σ_0-functions in which all terms of $\Psi_\mathcal{K}(G)$ are defined and let $\mathcal{A}_\Theta$ be as in Definition 4.6.2. Then all the terms in $\Psi_\mathcal{K}(\mathcal{D}(\mathcal{A}_\Theta))$ are defined in $\mathcal{A}_\Theta$.*

Proof. We first claim that $\mathcal{D}(\mathcal{A}_\Theta) = \bar{h}(\Theta)$, where $h : \text{GTerm}_{\Pi_0^C} \rightarrow \text{GTerm}_{\Pi_0^C}$ is the map that sends a base ground term t to the constant a such that $t^{\mathcal{A}_\Theta} = a$ (recall that we chose our set of constants big enough to incorporate all constants a for elements $a \in A$). Now suppose $f(a_1, \ldots, a_n) \in \mathcal{D}(\mathcal{A}_\Theta)$. This means that there are some terms $t_1, \ldots, t_n$ (with $t_i^{\mathcal{A}_\Theta} = a_i$) such that $f(t_1, \ldots, t_n) \in \Theta = \Psi_\mathcal{K}(G)$. Because $\mathcal{K}$ is quasiflat, G is flat and $\Psi_\mathcal{K}$ is taut, it follows that the terms $\bar{t}$ must be base ground terms. It follows that $f(\bar{a}) = \bar{h}(f(\bar{t}))$.

For the other inclusion, let $f(\bar{t}) \in \Theta$. According to Lemma 4.6.3, all terms in Θ are defined in $\mathcal{A}_\Theta$. Let $a_i := t_i^{\mathcal{A}_\Theta}$. Then we have $f(\bar{a}) \in \mathcal{D}(\mathcal{A}_\Theta)$ and $f(\bar{a}) = \bar{h}(f(\bar{t}))$. This establishes the claim.

Note also that we have $\bar{h}\bar{h} = \bar{h}$ by definition of $\bar{h}$. Next, it follows from the definition of a term closure operator that

$$\begin{aligned}
\bar{h}(\Psi_\mathcal{K}(\mathcal{D}(\mathcal{A}_\Theta))) &= \bar{h}(\Psi_\mathcal{K}(\bar{h}\Theta)) & \text{(Claim)} \\
&= \Psi_{\bar{h}\mathcal{K}}(\bar{h}\bar{h}\Theta) & \text{(Definition 4.6.1.(5))} \\
&= \Psi_{\bar{h}\mathcal{K}}(\bar{h}\Theta) & \\
&= \bar{h}(\Psi_\mathcal{K}(\Theta)) & \text{(Definition 4.6.1.(5))} \\
&= \bar{h}(\Psi_\mathcal{K}(\Psi_\mathcal{K}(G))) & \text{(Definition of } \Theta) \\
&= \bar{h}(\Psi_\mathcal{K}(G)) & \text{(Definition 4.6.1.(3))} \\
&= \mathcal{D}(\mathcal{A}_\Theta). & \text{(Claim)}
\end{aligned}$$

Now, let $f(\bar{t}) \in \Psi_\mathcal{K}(\mathcal{D}(\mathcal{A}_\Theta))$. It follows that $f(\bar{h}\bar{t}) \in \mathcal{D}(\mathcal{A}_\Theta)$ which implies that $f(\bar{t})$ is defined in $\mathcal{A}_\Theta$. □

Theorem 4.6.7 *Let T_0 be a theory in the signature $\Pi_0 = (\Sigma_0, \mathsf{Pred})$. Let $\Pi_1 = (\Sigma_1, \mathsf{Pred}) \supseteq \Pi_0$ be an extension by function symbols and let $\mathcal{K}$ be a set of universally closed Σ_1-quasiflat and Σ_1-linear clauses in the signature Π_1 and let $\Psi_\mathcal{K}$ be a term closure operator. If the extension $T_0 \subseteq T_0 \cup \mathcal{K}$ satisfies (Emb_w^Ψ) then it satisfies (Loc^Ψ).*

Proof. We proceed again by contradiction. Suppose that the extension were not local, i.e., that there is a set of flat ground clauses G (with additional constants) such that $T_0 \cup \mathcal{K} \cup G$ is inconsistent although there is a weak partial model $\mathcal{A}$ of $T_0 \cup \mathcal{K}[\Psi_\mathcal{K}(G)] \cup G$ (with total Σ_0-functions) in which all terms in $\Psi_\mathcal{K}(G)$ are defined. Let $\Theta := \Psi_\mathcal{K}(G)$. We know from Corollary 4.6.6 that all terms in the set $\Psi_\mathcal{K}(\mathcal{D}(\mathcal{A}_\Theta))$ are defined in $\mathcal{A}_\Theta$. By Lemma 4.6.3, $\mathcal{A}_\Theta$ is a weak partial model of $T_0 \cup \mathcal{K}$. Thus, by (Emb_w^Ψ) we obtain a total model $\mathcal{B}$ of $T_0 \cup \mathcal{K}$ into which $\mathcal{A}_\Theta$ weakly embeds. Since $\mathcal{A}_\Theta$ is a model of G where all terms of G are defined and embeddings preserve literals, we conclude that $\mathcal{B}$ is also a model of G, which contradicts our assumption. □

Theorem 4.6.8 *Let T_0 be a theory in the signature $\Pi_0 = (\Sigma_0, \mathsf{Pred})$. Let $\Pi_1 = (\Sigma_1, \mathsf{Pred}) \supseteq \Pi_0$ be an extension by function symbols and let $\mathcal{K}$ be a set of universally closed Σ_1-quasiflat and Σ_1-linear augmented clauses in the signature Π_1 and let $\Psi_\mathcal{K}$ be a term closure operator. If the extension $T_0 \subseteq T_0 \cup \mathcal{K}$ satisfies (EEmb_w^Ψ) then it satisfies (ELoc^Ψ).*

Proof. The proof is similar to the one above. Assume again towards a contradiction that there were an extended proof task $\Gamma = \Gamma_0 \cup G$, where Γ_0 is a Π_0-sentence and G is a set of flat ground clauses in Π_1^C, such that $T_0, \mathcal{K}, \Gamma \models \bot$, but there is a partial algebra $\mathcal{A}$ with total Π_0-functions and $\mathcal{A} \models_w T_0, \mathcal{K}[\Psi], \Gamma$ in which all terms of $\Psi_\mathcal{K}(G)$ are defined. Set $\Theta := \Psi_\mathcal{K}(G)$. By Lemma 4.6.3, $\mathcal{A}_\Theta$ is a weak partial model of $T_0 \cup \mathcal{K} \cup G$.

This enables us to use elementary embeddability to arrive at a model $\mathcal{B}$ of $T_0 \cup \mathcal{K}$ such that $\mathcal{A}_\Theta$ weakly embeds into $\mathcal{B}$, and $\mathcal{A}_\Theta {\restriction}_{\Pi_0} \preceq \mathcal{B} {\restriction}_{\Pi_0}$. In particular, $\mathcal{A}_\Theta {\restriction}_{\Pi_0} \equiv \mathcal{B} {\restriction}_{\Pi_0}$. By the last item: $\mathcal{B} \models \Gamma_0$. Because all subterms of G were defined in $\mathcal{A}_\Theta$ we also have $\mathcal{B} \models G$. Contradiction. □

If we choose $\Psi_{\mathcal{K}}(G) := \text{est}(\mathcal{K}, G)$ we obtain the

Corollary 4.6.9 *Let T_0 be a theory in the signature $\Pi_0 = (\Sigma_0, \text{Pred})$. Let $\Pi_1 = (\Sigma_1, \text{Pred}) \supseteq \Pi_0$ be an extension by function symbols and let $\mathcal{K}$ be a set of universally closed Σ_1-quasiflat and Σ_1-linear augmented clauses in the signature Π_1. Then (EEmb_w) implies (ELoc).*

Similarly, we obtain the analogue for finite locality (cf. [SS10, ISS10a]).

Corollary 4.6.10 *Let T_0 be a theory in the signature $\Pi_0 = (\Sigma_0, \text{Pred})$, Σ_1 a set of new function symbols and $\mathcal{K}$ a set of universally closed clauses in the extended signature $\Pi_1 = (\Sigma_0 \cup \Sigma_1, \text{Pred})$. Suppose that all clauses in $\mathcal{K}$ are Σ_1-quasiflat and Σ_1-linear. Then*

(1) If $\mathcal{K}$ is additionally Σ_1-flat and the extension $T_0 \subseteq T_0 \cup \mathcal{K}$ satisfies $(\text{EEmb}_w^{\text{fd}})$ then it satisfies (ELoc^{f}).

(2) If $\mathcal{K}$ contains only finitely many extension ground terms, T_0 is universal and locally finite (i.e., each finitely generated model of T_0 is finite) and the extension $T_0 \subseteq T_0 \cup \mathcal{K}$ satisfies $(\text{EEmb}_w^{\text{f}})$ then it satisfies (ELoc^{f}).

It is also the case that Ψ-locality implies the embeddability of partial models into total ones.

Theorem 4.6.11 *Let T_0 be a theory in the signature $\Pi_0 = (\Sigma_0, \text{Pred})$, Σ_1 a set of new function symbols and $\mathcal{K}$ a set of universally closed clauses or augmented clauses in the extended signature $\Pi_1 = (\Sigma_0 \cup \Sigma_1, \text{Pred})$. Let $\Psi_{\mathcal{K}}$ be a term closure operator. Then*

(1) If $\mathcal{K}$ is a set of clauses and $T_0 \subseteq T_0 \cup \mathcal{K}$ satisfies (Loc^Ψ) then the extension satisfies (Emb_w^Ψ).

(2) If $T_0 \subseteq T_0 \cup \mathcal{K}$ satisfies (ELoc^Ψ) then it satisfies (EEmb_w^Ψ).

Proof. (1) Let $\mathcal{A} \in \text{PMod}_w^\Psi(\Sigma_1, T_1)$. We want to embed $\mathcal{A}$ into a total model of $T_0 \cup \mathcal{K}$. By the partial diagram lemma (Lemma 2.4.3), it suffices to show that the set of formulas $T_0 \cup \mathcal{K} \cup \Delta_{\mathcal{A}}^P$ is satisfiable. Assume it were not. It follows from compactness of first-order logic that there is a finite subset G of $\Delta_{\mathcal{A}}^P$ such that $T_0 \cup \mathcal{K} \cup G$ is unsatisfiable. $\Delta_{\mathcal{A}}^P$ consists of literals. Hence, G is a set of flat clauses. Therefore, by Ψ-locality, $T_0 \cup \mathcal{K}[\Psi_{\mathcal{K}}(G)] \cup G$ cannot have a weak partial model in which all terms in $\Psi_{\mathcal{K}}(G)$ are defined. But $(\mathcal{A}, A)$ is just such a model. We know from $\text{est}(G) \subseteq \mathcal{D}(\mathcal{A})$ and monotonicity of Ψ that $\Psi_{\mathcal{K}}(\text{est}(G)) \subseteq \Psi_{\mathcal{K}}(\mathcal{D}(\mathcal{A}))$ and all terms of $\Psi_{\mathcal{K}}(\mathcal{D}(\mathcal{A}))$ were defined in $\mathcal{A}$ by assumption. Since all terms of $\Psi_{\mathcal{K}}(G)$ are defined in $\mathcal{A}$ it also follows that $\mathcal{A} \models_w \mathcal{K}[\Psi_{\mathcal{K}}(G)]$ by $\forall$-elimination (Corollary 2.2.10). Thus we have arrived at a contradiction.

(2) is analogous to (1). The only difference is that we allow augmented clauses $\mathcal{K}$ now and that we consider the set $T_0 \cup \mathcal{K} \cup \Delta_{\mathcal{A}}^P \cup \Delta^{el}$ to be unsatisfiable, where Δ^{el} is the elementary diagram of $\mathcal{A}|_{\Pi_0}$. By compactness we obtain $T_0 \cup \mathcal{K} \cup G \cup \varphi_0 \models \bot$, with G as above and φ_0 a sentence in the signature $\Pi_0^{\mathcal{A}}$. It follows from extended Ψ-locality that $T_0 \cup \mathcal{K}[\Psi] \cup G \cup \varphi_0$ cannot have a weak partial model where all terms in $\Psi_{\mathcal{K}}(G)$ are defined. But, again, $(\mathcal{A}, A)$ is just such a model. Therefore, $T_0 \cup \mathcal{K} \cup \Delta_{\mathcal{A}}^P \cup \Delta^{el}$ has a model $\mathcal{B}$. The additional claim that $\mathcal{A}|_{\Pi_0} \preccurlyeq \mathcal{B}|_{\Pi_0}$ follows from Lemma 2.1.8. □

In sum, we have the relations among the properties studied as depicted in Figure 4.2, for quasiflat and linear extensions, where Ψ is an arbitrary but fixed term closure operator.

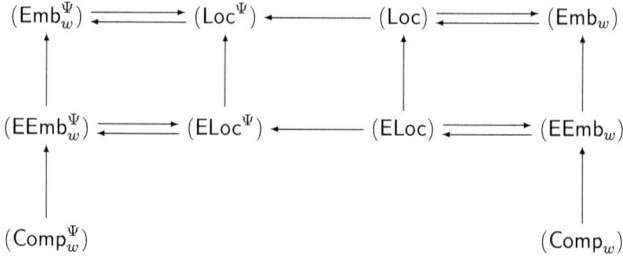

Figure 4.2: Relations between the properties.

4.7 Arrays Revisited

We have used the array property fragment and the Λ-array property fragment, together with the associated notion of minimal locality, as a motivation for arriving at a more general notion of locality, namely Ψ-locality. There is a difference, however, between the two notions. In minimal locality, we demand that the definition domain of all extension functions is equal to some set of ground terms, whereas in Ψ-locality, as in locality simpliciter, we only demand that the partial model be defined on the ground terms occurring in the extending clauses $\mathcal{K}$ or the proof task G - it may be defined elsewhere too. This difference turns out to be inessential due to the model $\mathcal{A}_\Theta$ developed in the last section.

For the array property fragment consider the following closure operator

$$\Psi_\mathcal{K}(G) := \{f(t) \mid f \in \Sigma_1, g(t) \leq \cdot\; G \text{ for some } g \in \Sigma_1 \text{ or } t \in \mathsf{st}(\mathcal{K})\}$$

or with the more succinct notation of Section 4.2

$$\Psi_\mathcal{K}(G) := \mathsf{st}(\mathcal{K}, \mathcal{R}(G))^{(1)}.$$

It is easy to check that this does indeed define a term closure operator.

Similarly for the Λ-array property fragment. For a set of ground terms Θ, let us write $\Lambda(\Theta)$ for the closure of Θ under subtraction of Λ, i.e., if $t \in \Lambda(\Theta)$ then $t - \lambda \in \Lambda(\Theta)$, for all $\lambda \in \Lambda$, as well. Then the term closure operator needed is

$$\Psi_\mathcal{K}(G) := [\Lambda(\mathsf{st}(\mathcal{K}, \mathcal{R}(G)))]^{(1)}.$$

Corollary 4.7.1 *Let $T_0 \subseteq T_0 \cup \mathcal{K}$ be an extension by a set of array properties or Λ-array properties as in Sections 4.2 and 4.4, respectively. Let $\Psi_\mathcal{K}(G)$ be the appropriate term closure operator as defined above. Then the extension $T_0 \subseteq T_0 \cup \mathcal{K}$ is Ψ-local.*

Proof. We show both claims simultaneously. Suppose the extension were not Ψ-local. This means that there were a set of ground clauses G such $T_0 \cup \mathcal{K} \cup G$ is unsatisfiable and a weak partial model $\mathcal{A}$ of $T_0 \cup \mathcal{K}[\Psi] \cup G$ in which all terms in $\Psi_\mathcal{K}(G)$ were defined. Let us write Θ for $\Psi_\mathcal{K}(G)$. Consider the model $\mathcal{A}_\Theta$ of Definition 4.6.2. It follows from Lemma 4.6.3 that $\mathcal{A}_\Theta$ is a weak partial model of $T_0 \cup \mathcal{K} \cup G$. Hence, by Theorems 4.2.6 and 4.4.4 respectively, we may conclude that the π-completion $\hat{\mathcal{A}}_\Theta$ of $\mathcal{A}_\Theta$ is a total model of $T_0 \cup \mathcal{K} \cup G$, for a projection π. Contradiction. □

4.8 Pointers Directly

In [MN05] McPeak and Necula investigate reasoning in pointer data structures. The language used has sorts p (pointer) and s (scalar). In contrast to their account, we will allow more than one pointer type and allow functions with domains of pointer sort to have arity bigger than one. We will also loosen their syntactic constraints (see below).[1]

We will denote the different (disjoint) pointer types by $\mathsf{P} = \{\mathsf{p}_1, \ldots, \mathsf{p}_n\}$, $n \geq 1$. Accordingly, we will have a constant null_i, for every pointer sort p_i, denoting the null pointer. Having different pointer types might make modeling of systems easier by allowing different unconnected lists to be specified with different types, see Section 6.8. For simplicity, we will consider only one scalar sort s.

We distinguish two types of extension functions both of which will only allow pointer types as input sorts. Functions Σ^p of arity $\mathsf{p}_{i_1}, \ldots, \mathsf{p}_{i_m} \to \mathsf{p}_k$ with $\mathsf{p}_k, \mathsf{p}_{i_j} \in \mathsf{P}$, for $1 \leq j \leq m$, which have a pointer type as output sort and functions Σ^s of arity $\mathsf{p}_{i_1}, \ldots, \mathsf{p}_{i_m} \to s$ with $\mathsf{p}_{i_j} \in \mathsf{P}$, for $1 \leq j \leq m$, which have the scalar type as output sort. The only predicate of sort p_i, $1 \leq i \leq n$, is equality. We write Π_1 for the signature $\Pi_\mathsf{s} \cup \Sigma^\mathsf{p} \cup \Sigma^\mathsf{s} \cup \{\mathsf{null}_i \mid \mathsf{p}_i \in \mathsf{P}\}$. Let Σ_C be a fixed set of (fresh) constants as before.

The axioms considered in [MN05] are of the form

$$(4.1) \qquad \forall \bar{p}. \; \mathcal{E} \vee \mathcal{C}$$

where $\bar{p}$ is a set of pointer variables containing all the pointer variables occurring in $\mathcal{E} \vee \mathcal{C}$, $\mathcal{E}$ contains disjunctions of pointer equalities and $\mathcal{C}$ is a disjunction of scalar constraints (i.e., literals of type s). $\mathcal{E} \vee \mathcal{C}$ may also contain free variables of scalar type or, equivalently, free scalar constants.

In order to rule out null pointer errors, Necula and McPeak demand that pointer terms appearing below a function should not be null. In our setting this means that for all terms $t = f(t_1, \ldots, t_n)$, $f \in \Sigma^p \cup \Sigma^s$, occurring in an axiom, the axiom also contains the disjunction $t' = \mathsf{null}_j$, for any proper subterm t' of t with type p_j. We will call pointer/scalar formulas complying with this restriction *nullable*.

As an examples of nullable axioms (for doubly linked data structures with priorities) considered by Necula and McPeak take

(4.2) $\quad \forall p \;\; p \neq \mathsf{null} \wedge \mathsf{next}(p) \neq \mathsf{null} \;\to\; \mathsf{prev}(\mathsf{next}(p)) = p$
(4.3) $\quad \forall p \;\; p \neq \mathsf{null} \wedge \mathsf{prev}(p) \neq \mathsf{null} \;\to\; \mathsf{next}(\mathsf{prev}(p)) = p$
(4.4) $\quad \forall p \;\; p \neq \mathsf{null} \wedge \mathsf{next}(p) \neq \mathsf{null} \;\to\; \mathsf{priority}(p) \geq \mathsf{priority}(\mathsf{next}(p))$

(the first two axioms state that **prev** is a left inverse for **next**, the third axiom is a monotonicity condition on the function **priority**).

---

[1] The material in this section consists of continuing joint work with Viorica Sofronie-Stokkermans.

We now give our less restrictive definition of a pointer fragment, where we allow not only more than one pointer type but also general formulas - instead of disjunctions - combined with pointer equalities.

Definition 4.8.1 (Pointer fragment) *With the above notations, given pointer types* $\mathsf{P} = \mathsf{p}_1, \ldots, \mathsf{p}_r$ $n \geq 1$ *and a scalar type* s, *we call formulas of the form*

$$\forall \bar{p}. \ (\mathcal{E} \vee \varphi)(\bar{p})$$

an extended pointer clause *if the following holds.*

(1) $\bar{p}$ *are variables of pointer type which contain all the free variables of both* $\mathcal{E}$ *and* φ,

(2) $\mathcal{E}$ *consists of disjunctions of pointer equalities,*

(3) $(\mathcal{E} \vee \varphi)$ *is nullable, i.e., for all terms* $t = f(t_1, \ldots, t_n)$, $f \in \Sigma^\mathsf{p} \cup \Sigma^\mathsf{s}$, *occurring in it,* $\mathcal{E}$ *contains the disjunction* $t' = \mathsf{null}_j$, *for any proper subterm* t' *(of type* p_j*) of* t,

(4) φ *is an* arbitrary *formula in the signature* Π_1, *such that functions of type* Σ^p *appear only below functions of type* Σ^s.

The presence of types helps to reduce the complexity of the pointer fragment. As a result, even though we can not use a general notion of Ψ-stable local extensions due to the inherent complexity of closure operators on ground term for strong partial semantics, we are able to give a direct proof of stable locality for extensions with extended pointer clauses.

In particular, the fact that we allow only universal variables of pointer sort in the fragment allows us to constrain the instances needed. Given a set Φ of extended pointer clauses and a set of ground clauses G in the signature $\Pi_1 \cup \Sigma_C$, let $\mathrm{st}[\Phi, G]_\mathsf{p}$ be the set of all pointer ground terms, i.e., ground terms whose type is among $\mathsf{p}_1, \ldots, \mathsf{p}_n$, appearing in Φ or G. Similarly, let $\mathrm{st}[\Phi, G]_{\mathsf{p}_i}$ be the set of all pointer ground terms of type p_i appearing in Φ or G. Due to nullability we may always assume that $\mathsf{null}_i \in \mathrm{st}[\Phi, G]_\mathsf{p}$, otherwise the extension would be trivial. We now consider a set of complete instances for a set of extended pointer clauses Φ w.r.t. a set G ground clauses in the signature $\Pi_1 \cup \Sigma_C$.

$$\Phi^{[\mathsf{P}]} := \{\varphi\sigma \mid \varphi\sigma \text{ is closed}, (\forall \bar{p}.\varphi) \in \Phi,$$
$$\text{for all variables } p \text{ of } \varphi \text{ it holds that } \sigma(p) \in \mathrm{st}[\Phi, G]_\mathsf{p}\}$$

Also, define

$$\Theta_\Phi(G) := \mathrm{st}[\Phi, G] \cup \{f_s(t_1, \ldots, t_n) \mid f_s \in \Sigma^\mathsf{s}, t_i \in \mathrm{st}[\Phi, G] \setminus \{\mathsf{null}_j\}, 1 \leq j \leq n\}.$$

A similar result to the one below was published in [IJSS08].

Theorem 4.8.2 *With the notations of this section, let* T_0 *be a theory in the signature* Π_s, Φ *a set of extended pointer clauses of the form* $\forall \bar{p}. \ (\mathcal{E} \vee \varphi)$ *and* G *a set of ground clauses in the signature* $\Pi_1 \cup \Sigma_C$. *Then it holds that* $T_0 \cup \Phi \cup G$ *is unsatisfiable if and only if* $T_0 \cup \Phi^{[\mathsf{P}]} \cup G$ *has no strong partial model with total* Σ_s-*functions in which all terms of* $\Theta_\Phi(G)$ *are defined.*

Proof. The direction from right to left is clear. For the other direction, assume towards a contradiction that there were a set of ground clauses G such that $T_0 \cup \Phi \cup G$ had no model, but there were a strong partial model $\mathcal{A}$ of $T_0 \cup \Phi^{[\text{P}]} \cup G$ with total Σ_s-functions in which all terms of $\Theta_\Phi(G)$ were defined. Our goal is to construct a total model $\mathcal{B}$ of $T_0 \cup \Phi \cup G$ from $\mathcal{A}$. Let A_s, $A_{\text{p}_1}, \ldots, A_{\text{p}_n}$ be the scalar and pointer sorts of $\mathcal{A}$ respectively. As carrier for $\mathcal{B}$ we keep A_s for the scalar elements and for the pointer elements we take $B_{\text{p}_i} := \{t^\mathcal{A} \mid t \in \text{st}[\Phi, G]_{\text{p}_i}\}$. We also keep the scalar functions and predicates from Π_s of $\mathcal{A}$. It follows that $\mathcal{B} \models T_0$. We define the functions of $\Sigma^\text{p} \cup \Sigma^\text{s}$ for $\mathcal{B}$ in the following manner.

For f_p of arity $\text{p}_{i_1}, \ldots, \text{p}_{i_m} \to \text{p}_j$ define

$$f_p^\mathcal{B}(t_1^\mathcal{A}, \ldots, t_m^\mathcal{A}) := \begin{cases} u^\mathcal{A} & \text{if there is a } u \in \text{st}[\Phi, G]_{\text{p}_j} \text{ such that} \\ & f_p^\mathcal{A}(t_1^\mathcal{A}, \ldots, t_m^\mathcal{A}) \text{ is defined and equal to } u^\mathcal{A}, \\ \text{null}_j^\mathcal{A} & \text{otherwise.} \end{cases}$$

and for f_s of type $\text{p}_{i_1}, \ldots, \text{p}_{i_m} \to \text{s}$ define

$$f_s^\mathcal{B}(t_1^\mathcal{A}, \ldots, t_m^\mathcal{A}) := f_s^\mathcal{A}(t_1^\mathcal{A}, \ldots, t_m^\mathcal{A}).$$

Note that functions of this type are total by definition of $\Theta_\Phi(G)$.

It is immediate from the construction that $t^\mathcal{A} = t^\mathcal{B}$ for any $t \in \text{st}[\Phi, G]$. Hence, $\mathcal{B} \models G$. It remains to be shown that $\mathcal{B} \models \Phi$. For that purpose, fix a valuation β and let $D \in \Phi$. D is of the form $\forall \bar{x}.\, \mathcal{E} \vee \varphi$, where all variables $\bar{x}$ are of pointer type. We know that $\beta(x) = t_x^\mathcal{A}$ for some $t_x \in \text{st}[\Phi, G]_{\text{p}_i}$ and some pointer type p_i. We therefore can define a substitution $\sigma : x \mapsto t_x$ such that $(\mathcal{E} \vee \varphi)\sigma \in \Phi^{[\text{P}]}$ and $\beta = \beta \circ \sigma$. By the substitution lemma it follows that $\mathcal{A}, \beta \models_s \mathcal{E} \vee \varphi$.

We therefore know that $(\mathcal{A}, \beta)$ either (strongly) satisfies one of the literals in $\mathcal{E}$ or it satisfies φ. Suppose $(\mathcal{A}, \beta)$ satisfies a pointer equality in $\mathcal{E}$, say $t \approx u$. We have to consider the three cases of how an equality comes out true in strong partial semantics. First, if both sides are defined in $(\mathcal{A}, \beta)$ they must be equal. If both $(\mathcal{B}, \beta)(u)$ and $(\mathcal{B}, \beta)(t)$ are equal to $\text{null}_i^\mathcal{A}$ we are done. Suppose now that $(\mathcal{B}, \beta)(t)$ is equal to some $\tilde{t}^\mathcal{A}$, $\tilde{t} \in \Theta_\Phi(G)$ with $\tilde{t}^\mathcal{A} = t^\mathcal{A}$. By assumption we have $t^\mathcal{A} = u^\mathcal{A}$ and therefore $u^\mathcal{A} = \tilde{t}^\mathcal{A}$. Hence, $u^\mathcal{B} = \tilde{t}^\mathcal{A} = t^\mathcal{B}$.

Second, the equation could be satisfied because a proper subterm on either side is undefined under $(\mathcal{A}, \beta)$, say $t = f(t'_1, \ldots, t'_m)$ and $(\mathcal{A}, \beta)(t'_j)$ is undefined. By nullability, $\mathcal{E}$ then contains the equation $t'_j = \text{null}_i$ (note that t' must be of some pointer type p_i). By construction it then follows that $\mathcal{B}, \beta \models t'_j \approx \text{null}_i$. The remaining case is when all proper subterms are defined in $(\mathcal{A}, \beta)$ but both t and u are not. In that case we obtain $(\mathcal{B}, \beta)(t) = \text{null}_i^\mathcal{A} = (\mathcal{B}, \beta)(u)$.

Now suppose that $(\mathcal{A}, \beta)$ strongly satisfies φ. We distinguish two cases. First, if there is a term $t = f(t'_1, \ldots, t'_m)$ in φ which is undefined in $(\mathcal{A}, \beta)$, then the t'_j must be of some pointer type p_i. By nullability, $\mathcal{E}$ contains the equations $t'_j \approx \text{null}_i$. In particular, if t'_j is undefined in $(\mathcal{A}, \beta)$ it follows that $(\mathcal{B}, \beta) \models t'_j \approx \text{null}_i$. On the other hand, if all terms t'_j were defined but $f(t'_1, \ldots, t'_m)$ was not, then not all t'_j could be equal in $(\mathcal{A}, \beta)$ to a term in $\text{st}[\Phi, G]$ other than null_i. For if it were it would follow from the definition of $\Theta_\Phi(G)$ that $f(t'_1, \ldots, t'_m)$ would be defined too. Thus, there must be a term t'_j that is equal to null_i w.r.t. $(\mathcal{A}, \beta)$. It follows that $\mathcal{B}, \beta \models t'_j \approx \text{null}_i$ and, hence, $\mathcal{B}, \beta \models (\mathcal{E} \vee \varphi)$.

The second case is that all the terms appearing in φ are defined. But since $\mathcal{B}$ and $\mathcal{A}$ agree on scalar terms we immediately obtain $\mathcal{B}, \beta \models \varphi$. In conclusion, we have shown that $\mathcal{B}, \beta \models (\mathcal{E} \vee \varphi)$ and this establishes $\mathcal{B} \models T_0 \cup \Phi \cup G$. Contradiction! □

Chapter 5

Combinations of Theories

Up to this point we have addressed the question of how to handle the complexity of proof tasks by using hierarchical reasoning. Local extensions, in one flavor or another, allow the replacement of universally quantified (extension) clauses by a set of their instances which, then, leads to the reduction to an underlying theory. In case that tools, preferably decision procedures, for that underlying theory are available, local/hierarchical reasoning thus allows the extension of said tools to new verification tasks. In this chapter we will consider the related question of when and how different theories can be combined.

Obviously such a modular approach, if it can be made to work, is of great practical value. Real-life verification tasks often mix several theories or types each of which might well be tractable individually and there might be off-the-shelf solvers for each of them. Nevertheless, obtaining a decision procedures for their combination is a non-trivial task even in quite simple cases.

Pioneering work in this area was done by Nelson and Oppen ([NO79]) who considered the combination of theories with disjoint signatures. Since that time the search was on to extend that result to non-disjoint theories. This proved to be rather difficult. Only recently has some headway been made (cf. [BT02, Ghi03a, Ghi03b, Ghi04, BGT04, BG05, GNZ05, SS07]).

In this chapter we will look at two of these approaches. After laying some necessary groundwork in Section 5.1, we will first consider Silvio Ghilardi's work on information exchange in Section 5.2. We offer a new, and – we believe – much simpler proof of Theorem 3.2 in [Ghi04].

After some model-theoretic background in Section 5.3 we will offer some new results on the combination of local theories in Section 5.4. Finally, we will consider the case of combining Ψ-local theories in Section 5.5.

5.1 Model Completeness and Quantifier Elimination

An important element of this section is the notion of model-completeness. This warrants to reiterate the definition (cf. Definition 2.1.18).

Definition 5.1.1 (Model complete theory) *An $\mathcal{L}$-theory T is called* model complete *or m.c. for short, if every embedding between its models is elementary (Definition 2.1.4). With our nota-*

tion, whenever we have two models $\mathcal{A}, \mathcal{B} \models T$ and an embedding $\varphi : \mathcal{A} \to \mathcal{B}$ it already holds that $\varphi : \mathcal{A} \preccurlyeq \mathcal{B}$.

We also give a standard characterization of model completeness, following [CK90], 3.5.1 and [Hod97], 7.3.1.

Theorem 5.1.2 *Let T be a consistent $\mathcal{L}$-theory. Then the following are equivalent.*

(1) T is model complete.

(2) If $\mathcal{A} \models T$ then $T \cup \Delta_\mathcal{A}$ is a complete theory (in $\mathcal{L}_A$), where $\Delta_\mathcal{A}$ is the diagram of $\mathcal{A}$.

(3) (Robinson's Test). If $\mathcal{A}, \mathcal{B} \models T$ with $\mathcal{A} \subseteq \mathcal{B}$ then every existential sentence which holds in $(\mathcal{B}, A)$ also holds in $(\mathcal{A}, A)$.

(4) For every existential formula $\varphi(x_1, ..., x_n)$ there is a universal formula $\psi(x_1, ..., x_n)$ with $T \models \varphi \leftrightarrow \psi$.

(5) For every formula $\varphi(x_1, ..., x_n)$ there is a universal formula $\psi(x_1, ..., x_n)$ with $T \models \varphi \leftrightarrow \psi$.

Recall form Definition 2.1.19 that a theory T is said to admit the elimination of quantifiers if every formula is equivalent modulo T to a quantifier-free formula with (at most) the same free variables. The above characterization therefore immediately gives us that every theory which admits elimination of quantifiers is model complete. The reverse does not hold, however.

Example 5.1.3 *Consider the theory T of real closed fields where we have no symbol for $<$ in the signature. The theory is model complete but, without order as a primitive notion, the theory does not enjoy quantifier elimination ([ES71]), e.g., $\exists x. \ x \cdot x \approx y$ ($= y$ is non-negative) is not expressible by an open formula ([CK90], 3.5.19; Remark).*

A further useful fact is the following (cf. [CK90], 3.5.10 and [Hod97], 7.3.3), which is an immediate consequence of the Chang-Łos-Suszko theorem and the elementary chain theorem (Theorems 2.1.16 and 2.1.17).

Corollary 5.1.4 *Let T be a model complete theory. Then T has a set of $\forall \exists$ axioms.*

Example 5.1.5 *Here are some examples of model complete theories from algebra.*

(1) The theory of the model $(\mathbb{Z}, +, -, 0, 1, \leq)$ ([CK90], Example 3.5.2).

(2) The theory of divisible torsion-free Abelian groups (Ibid.).

(3) The theory of divisible ordered Abelian groups (Ibid.).

(4) The theory of infinite Abelian groups with all elements of order p ([CK90], Example 3.5.9).

Example 5.1.6 *The following theories have quantifier-elimination and are therefore model complete by the above remark.*

(1) Presburger arithmetic with congruence modulo n ($\equiv_n$), $n = 2, 3, ...$ ([End02], page 197).

(2) Rational linear arithmetic in the signature $\{+, 0, \leq\}$ ([Wei88]).

(3) Real closed ordered fields ([Hod97], 7.4.4). Examples are

    (a) the real algebraic numbers,

    (b) the computable numbers,

(c) the definable numbers (i.e., definable in set theory),

(d) the real numbers.

(4) Dense linear orders without endpoints ([CK90], chapter 1.5).

(5) Algebraically closed fields ([CK90], Example 3.5.2, [Hod97], chapter 7.4).

(6) Finite fields ([Hod97], chapter 7.4).

(7) Infinite (left) vector spaces over a field (Ibid.).

(8) Atomless Boolean algebras (cf. [CK90] 3.5.19 and Remark).

(9) $\mathrm{Th}(\omega, 0, s)$, the theory of the natural number with successor ([End02], page 191).

(10) The theory of acyclic lists in the signature $\{\mathrm{car}, \mathrm{cdr}, \mathrm{cons}\}$ ([Mal71, Ghi03b, Ghi04]).

Remark 5.1.7 (Complete v Model complete) *Neither one of model completeness and completeness implies the other. For example, we saw in Example 5.1.6.(5) that the theory of algebraically closed field is model complete. That theory is certainly not complete, however, because fields of different characteristic are not elementarily equivalent (cf. [CK90], page 188). On the other hand, the theory of dense linear orders with endpoints is complete but not model complete (cf. [CK90], page 187).*

Of particular interest to us are theories that share the same universal fragment.

Definition 5.1.8 (Cotheories) *Let T, U be $\mathcal{L}$-theories. T, U are called* cotheories *if $T_\forall = U_\forall$. Also, we say about two theories T and U that T* embeds *into U (Notation: $T \hookrightarrow U$) if every model of T embeds into a model of U.*

We collect some straightforward yet useful facts about cotheories.

Observation 5.1.9 (cf. [CK90], Remark 3.5.6)

(1) $\mathcal{A}$ is a model of $T_\forall$ if and only if $\mathcal{A}$ is a submodel of some model of T.

(2) $T \hookrightarrow U$ if and only if $U_\forall \subseteq T_\forall$.

(3) T and U are cotheories if and only if any model of T can be extended to a model of U, and vice versa.

(4) $T_\forall$ is a cotheory of T, and it is the unique cotheory which has a set of universal axioms.

We now turn to the important question when two models of a theory can be fused.

Definition 5.1.10 (Joint embedding/Amalgamation property) *A theory T has the* joint embedding property *(JEP) if for any two models $\mathcal{A}, \mathcal{B}$ of T there is a third model $\mathcal{C}$ of T such that $\mathcal{A}$ and $\mathcal{B}$ are both embeddable in $\mathcal{C}$.*

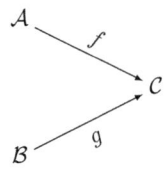

T has the amalgamation property (AP) *if for any three models*, $\mathcal{A}, \mathcal{B}$ *and* $\mathcal{C}$ *of* T *and embeddings* $f : \mathcal{C} \to \mathcal{A}$, $g : \mathcal{C} \to \mathcal{B}$ *there is a model* $\mathcal{C}'$ *and embeddings* $f' : \mathcal{A} \to \mathcal{C}'$, $g' : \mathcal{B} \to \mathcal{C}'$ *such that the diagram commutes.* $\mathcal{C}'$ *is said to* amalgamate $\mathcal{A}$ *and* $\mathcal{B}$ *over* $\mathcal{C}$.

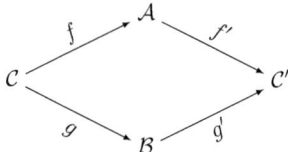

Although the two properties look similar neither one implies the other. For instance, fields have the amalgamation property but not the joint embedding property. Embeddings preserve the characteristic of a field and so it is impossible two embed two fields of different characteristic into a third one ([CK90], page 196). An example of a theory which has (JEP) but not (AP) is the theory of equivalence relations with at most one equivalence relation having more than one element (Ibid.).

Using Robinson's diagram lemma we can observe connections between these two properties.

Observation 5.1.11

(1) T has the amalgamation property if and only if for all models $\mathcal{A}$ of T, it holds that $T \cup \Delta_{\mathcal{A}}$ has the joint embedding property where $\Delta_{\mathcal{A}}$ is the diagram of $\mathcal{A}$ ([CK90], page 196).

(2) If T is complete, then the analogues of the joint embedding property and the amalgamation property hold for elementary embeddings. In particular, T has the joint embedding property (Ibid.).

(3) If T is model complete it has the amalgamation property (Ibid.).

(4) Let T be a model complete theory. Then T is complete if and only if T has the joint embedding property ([CK90], Proposition 3.5.11.(ii)).

The next definition brings together model complete theories with cotheories.

Definition 5.1.12 (Model completion) *An $\mathcal{L}$-theory T^* is called a* model companion *of T if T and T^* are cotheories and T^* is model complete. T^* is a* model completion *of T if it additionally holds that for every model $\mathcal{A}$ of T we already have that $T^* \cup \Delta_{\mathcal{A}}$ is complete, where $\Delta_{\mathcal{A}}$ is the diagram of $\mathcal{A}$.*

A theory has at most one model companion up to logical equivalence and the condition of model completeness adds uniqueness in the sense that if $\mathcal{A}$ is a model of T and $\mathcal{B}, \mathcal{C}$ are two extensions of $\mathcal{A}$ satisfying T^* then they satisfy the same $\mathcal{L}_{\mathcal{A}}$-sentences.

Example 5.1.13

(1) The theory of algebraically closed fields is the model completion of the theory of fields. This was the motivating example for developing the theory of model completions ([CK90], Example 3.5.2, Example 3.5.12 and following Remark 3.5.6; [Hod97], 7.3).

(2) The theory of dense total orders without endpoints is the model completion of the theory of total orders ([Ghi03a, Ghi04], without proof). According to [CK90], Example 3.5.12, the theory of dense linear orders without endpoints T^* is a model companion of the theory T of linear orders. We can see that it is also its model completion as follows. Assume towards a contradiction that $\mathcal{A}$ were a linear order such that $T^* \cup \Delta_\mathcal{A}$ were not a complete theory. This means that there would be a sentence $\varphi(\bar{a})$ of $\mathcal{L}_\mathcal{A}$ such that neither $T^* \cup \Delta_\mathcal{A} \vdash \varphi(\bar{a})$ nor $T^* \cup \Delta_\mathcal{A} \vdash \neg\varphi(\bar{a})$. From the diagram lemma it follows that there are two models $\mathcal{B}, \mathcal{C}$ of T^* such that $\mathcal{A} \subseteq \mathcal{B}$, $\mathcal{A} \subseteq \mathcal{C}$, $\mathcal{B} \models \varphi(\bar{a})$ and $\mathcal{C} \models \neg\varphi(\bar{a})$. From Example 5.1.6.(4) we know that there is a quantifier-free formula φ_0 such that $T^* \vdash \forall \bar{x}.(\varphi(\bar{x}) \leftrightarrow \varphi_0(\bar{x}))$. In particular, $\mathcal{B} \models \varphi_0(\bar{a})$ and $\mathcal{C} \models \neg\varphi_0(\bar{a})$. But since quantifier-free formulas are reflected in substructures this implies $\mathcal{A} \models \varphi_0(\bar{a})$ and $\mathcal{A} \models \neg\varphi_0(\bar{a})$. A distinct impossibility.

(3) The theory of atomless Boolean algebras is the model-completion of Boolean algebras ([CK90], Example 3.5.9; [Mac77], §3, Example 4).

(4) Universal Horn theories in finite signatures have a model completion if they are locally finite and have the amalgamation property (e.g., graphs, posets) ([Whe76]).

Here is another characterization of the difference between model companions and model completions.

Proposition 5.1.14 ([CK90], 3.5.18) *Let T^* be a model companion of T. Then the following are equivalent:*

(1) T^* is a model completion of T.

(2) T has the amalgamation property.

A theory T is always a cotheory of $T_\forall$ and, hence, a model complete theory T is automatically a model companion of $T_\forall$. Thus we get

Corollary 5.1.15 *Let T be a model complete theory. Then T is a model completion of $T_\forall$ if and only if $T_\forall$ has the amalgamation property.*

We already saw that quantifier elimination is a property strictly stronger than model completeness. We are interested in the exact relation between these two properties, particularly for the case of universal theories.

Proposition 5.1.16 ([CK90], 3.5.19) *Let T be a model complete theory in $\mathcal{L}$. Then the following are equivalent.*

(1) T is the model completion of its universal fragment $T_\forall$.

(2) $T_\forall$ has (AP).

(3) T admits elimination of quantifiers.

(4) If $\mathcal{A}$ is a submodel of a model $\mathcal{B}$ of T then $T \cup \Delta_\mathcal{A}$ is a complete theory in $\mathcal{L}_\mathcal{A}$. (This is sometimes called submodel completeness, cf. [CK90], page 203.)

It will be convenient for the next section to formulate the case for universal theories explicitly. Note that if T is universal we have $\mathcal{A} \models T \Leftrightarrow \mathcal{A} \models T_\forall$.

Corollary 5.1.17 *Let T be a universal theory. Then the following are equivalent.*

(1) T^* is the model completion of T.

(2) It holds that $T_\forall = (T^*)_\forall$ and T^* eliminates quantifiers.

Proof. Assume (1). Since T^* is the model completion of T it holds in particular that $T_\forall = (T^*)_\forall$. We need to show that T^* eliminates quantifiers. By Proposition 5.1.16 this is the same as establishing that T^* is the model completion of its universal fragment. It is clear that T^* is a model companion of $T_\forall^*$. To show the rest, consider $\mathcal{A} \models T_\forall^*$. We have to show that $T^* \cup \Delta_\mathcal{A}$ is complete. Because $T_\forall^* = T_\forall$ and Observation 5.1.9.(3) we have that $\mathcal{A}$ extends to a model $\mathcal{B}$ of T. Since T is universal, $\mathcal{A}$ is itself a model of T and the claim follows from the fact that T^* was a model completion of T.

Assume (2). We immediately get that T^* is a model companion of T. The only thing left to show is that $\mathcal{A} \models T$ implies that $T^* \cup \Delta_\mathcal{A}$ is a complete theory. In particular we have $\mathcal{A} \models T_\forall$. By assumption, this is the same as $\mathcal{A} \models (T^*)_\forall$. As T^* admits the elimination of quantifiers, we know from Proposition 5.1.16 that T^* is the model completion of its universal fragment. This implies the claim. □

5.2 Combinations of Theories

In an important paper [Ghi03a, Ghi04], Silvio Ghilardi used model completions of universal theories as an essential tool for the combination of theories over non-disjoint signatures. The approach taken there towards detecting the inconsistency of two (non-disjoint) theories T_1, T_2 is to ask how much information needs to be shared between them. More concretely, assuming that a given proof task φ is already purified into the languages of the theories T_1, T_2 as well, we know from Craig's interpolation lemma (Lemma 2.1.12), that the joint unsatisfiability of T_1, φ_1 with T_2, φ_2 implies the existence of a formula ψ *in the shared language* of the two theories which separates T_1, φ_1 from T_2, φ_2, i.e, $T_1, \varphi_1 \models \psi$ but $T_2, \varphi_2 \models \neg\psi$. Isolating the source of the joint unsatisfiability like this is helpful, but from a verificational standpoint it is still not enough.[1] At the very least, we would like the separating formula ψ to be quantifier-free or, better still, positive.

Silvio Ghilardi showed that the repeated exchange of positive ground clauses between T_1, φ_1 and T_2, φ_2 is enough to establish their joint unsatisfiability. As a corollary, it follows that the exchange of a single quantifier-free formula is enough. In this section we will give a direct proof of that corollary, circumventing more complicated techniques. The key notion is the following.

Definition 5.2.1 (Compatibility, [Ghi03a, Ghi04]) *Let T be a Σ-theory, $\Sigma_0 \subseteq \Sigma$ and let T_0 be a Σ_0-theory. T is T_0-compatible if*

(1) T_0 is a universal theory.

(2) $T_0^+ \subseteq T^+$.

(3) T_0 has a model completion T_0^*.

(4) $T \hookrightarrow T \cup T_0^*$. (Equivalently, $(T \cup T_0^*)_\forall \subseteq T_\forall$.)

---

[1] We thank Cesare Tinelli for his clear exposition of the problem (cf. [Tin07]).

Here is the main result of this section.

Lemma 5.2.2 *Let T_i be $\mathcal{L}_i$-theories, $i = 1, 2$, which are T_0-compatible for an $\mathcal{L}_0$-theory T_0 where $\mathcal{L}_0 = \mathcal{L}_1 \cap \mathcal{L}_2$. Let $\bar{a}, \bar{b}, \bar{c}$ be mutually disjoint sets of fresh constants and let $\varphi(\bar{a}, \bar{b})$, $\psi(\bar{a}, \bar{c})$ be quantifier-free ground $\mathcal{L}_1(\bar{a}, \bar{b})$- or $\mathcal{L}_2(\bar{a}, \bar{c})$-sentences, respectively. Suppose that $T_1, \varphi(\bar{a}, \bar{b}), T_2, \psi(\bar{a}, \bar{c}) \vdash \bot$. Then there is a quantifier-free $\mathcal{L}_0(\bar{a})$-sentence χ such that $T_1, \varphi(\bar{a}, \bar{b}) \vdash \chi(\bar{a})$ and $T_2, \psi(\bar{a}, \bar{c}) \vdash \neg \chi(\bar{a})$.*

Proof. Using Craig's interpolation theorem and compactness, it follows from $T_1, \varphi(\bar{a}, \bar{b}), T_2, \psi(\bar{a}, \bar{c}) \vdash \bot$ that there is a $\mathcal{L}_0(\bar{a})$-sentence $\chi(\bar{a})$ with $T_1, \varphi(\bar{a}, \bar{b}) \vdash \chi(\bar{a})$ and $T_2, \psi(\bar{a}, \bar{c}) \vdash \neg \chi(\bar{a})$. However, χ will normally contain quantifiers. By Corollary 5.1.17, we can use T_0^* to obtain a quantifier-free $\mathcal{L}_0$-sentence χ' such that $T_0^* \vdash \forall \bar{x}.(\chi(\bar{x}) \leftrightarrow \chi'(\bar{x}))$. In particular $T_1 \cup T_0^* \vdash \forall \bar{x}.(\chi(\bar{x}) \leftrightarrow \chi'(\bar{x}))$ and therefore $T_1 \cup T_0^*, \varphi(\bar{a}, \bar{b}) \vdash \chi'(\bar{a})$. This is logically equivalent to $T_1 \cup T_0^* \vdash \forall \bar{x}, \bar{y}.\varphi(\bar{x}, \bar{y}) \to \chi'(\bar{x})$. Because φ was quantifier-free, $\forall \bar{x}, \bar{y}.\varphi(\bar{x}, \bar{y}) \to \chi'(\bar{x})$ is universal. It follows from T_0^*-compatibility that $T_1 \vdash \forall \bar{x}, \bar{y}.\varphi(\bar{x}, \bar{y}) \to \chi'(\bar{x})$. Hence, $T_1, \varphi(\bar{a}, \bar{b}) \vdash \chi'(\bar{a})$. By the same token we get $T_2, \psi(\bar{a}, \bar{c}) \vdash \neg \chi'(\bar{a})$. Thus $\chi'(\bar{a})$ is as desired. □

Remark 5.2.3 *As mentioned in the introduction to this section, Ghilardi obtained this lemma as a corollary of a different result. There is also a direct proof of the lemma given in [GNRZ07] which uses elementary amalgamation instead of quantifier elimination (cf. Theorem 5.3.2 and Remark 5.3.4).*

5.3 Elementary Amalgamation

Before turning our attention to the combination of local and Ψ-local theories, we need to introduce another important technique: elementary amalgamation. The following two theorems (and their proofs) will be the cornerstone of the remainder of the chapter. We demonstrate the proof technique of elementary amalgamation (which we will need later) on the following lemma. The main results of this and the following sections are published in [ISS10a, ISS10b].

Lemma 5.3.1 (Simple elementary amalgamation; [Hod97], 5.3.1) *Let $\mathcal{L}$ be a first-order language, $\mathcal{B}$ and $\mathcal{C}$ $\mathcal{L}$-structures, $\bar{a}$ some elements of $\mathcal{B}$ and suppose there are some elements $\bar{c}$ of $\mathcal{C}$ such that $(\mathcal{B}, \bar{a}) \equiv (\mathcal{C}, \bar{c})$. Let $f : \langle \bar{a} \rangle \to \mathcal{C}$ be the unique embedding taking $\bar{a}$ to $\bar{c}$ then there exists an elementary extension $\mathcal{D}$ of $\mathcal{B}$ and an elementary embedding $g : \mathcal{C} \to \mathcal{D}$ such that $gf\bar{a} = \bar{a}$.*

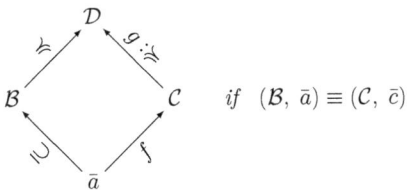

Proof. Replacing $\mathcal{B}$ and $\mathcal{C}$ with isomorphic copies if necessary, we might as well assume that f is the identity and that $\bar{a}$ is the intersection of $\mathcal{B}$ and $\mathcal{C}$. It suffices to show that $\Delta_{\mathcal{B}}^{el} \cup \Delta_{\mathcal{C}}^{el}$ is consistent according to the elementary diagram lemma (Corollary 2.1.9). Assume it were not. By compactness, there then would be a $\varphi(\bar{a},\bar{b}) \in \mathcal{L}_B$ and a $\psi(\bar{a},\bar{c}) \in \mathcal{L}_C$ such that $\varphi(\bar{a},\bar{b}),\psi(\bar{a},\bar{c}) \vdash \bot$. By the lemma on constants (Lemma 2.1.11), this is logically equivalent to $\exists \bar{x}.\psi(\bar{a},\bar{x}) \vdash \forall \bar{y}.\neg\varphi(\bar{a},\bar{y})$. Now, $\exists \bar{x}.\psi(\bar{a},\bar{x})$ is a sentence of $\mathcal{L}_A$ which $\mathcal{C}$ satisfies and, hence, which is also satisfied by $\mathcal{B}$. But this would imply $\mathcal{B} \models \forall \bar{y}.\neg\varphi(\bar{a},\bar{y})$. Contradiction. □

By using this theorem repeatedly we arrive at a slight abstraction of Robinson's joint consistency theorem. We give the proof in full because we want to reemploy the same technique later.

Theorem 5.3.2 ([Hod97], 5.5.1) *Let Π_1, Π_2 be signatures, $\Pi_0 = \Pi_1 \cap \Pi_2$, $\mathcal{B}$ a Π_1-structure, $\mathcal{C}$ a Π_2-structure and $\bar{a}$ some elements in both $\mathcal{B}$ and $\mathcal{C}$ such that $(\mathcal{B}\restriction_{\Pi_0}, \bar{a}) \equiv (\mathcal{C}\restriction_{\Pi_0}, \bar{a})$. Then there is a $(\Pi_1 \cup \Pi_2)$-structure $\mathcal{D}$ such that $\mathcal{B} \preccurlyeq \mathcal{D}\restriction_{\Pi_1}$ and an elementary embedding $g : \mathcal{C} \to \mathcal{D}\restriction_{\Pi_2}$ with $g\bar{a} = \bar{a}$.*

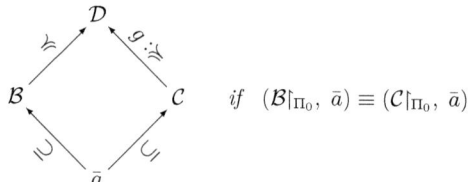

if $(\mathcal{B}\restriction_{\Pi_0}, \bar{a}) \equiv (\mathcal{C}\restriction_{\Pi_0}, \bar{a})$

Proof. Set $\mathcal{C}_0 := \mathcal{C}$ and $\mathcal{B}_0 := \mathcal{B}$. We may assume that $\mathcal{B}$ and $\mathcal{C}$ have no elements other than $\bar{a}$ in common. First, we get an elementary extension $\mathcal{B}_1$ of $\mathcal{B}_0$ and an elementary embedding $f_0 : \mathcal{C}_0\restriction_{\Pi_0} \to \mathcal{B}_1\restriction_{\Pi_0}$ by showing that $\Delta^{el}_\mathcal{B} \cup \Delta^{el}_{\mathcal{C}\restriction \mathcal{L}}$ is consistent. Suppose $\Delta^{el}_\mathcal{B} \cup \Delta^{el}_{\mathcal{C}\restriction \mathcal{L}}$ were inconsistent. By compactness, there then would be a $\varphi(\bar{a},\bar{b}) \in \mathcal{L}_B$ and a $\psi(\bar{a},\bar{c}) \in \mathcal{L}_A$ such that $\varphi(\bar{a},\bar{b}),\psi(\bar{a},\bar{c}) \vdash \bot$. This is equivalent to $\psi(\bar{a},\bar{x}) \vdash \neg\varphi(\bar{a},\bar{y})$. By logic (cf. Lemmas 2.1.10 and 2.1.11), this in turn is equivalent to $\exists \bar{x}.\psi(\bar{a},\bar{x}) \vdash \forall \bar{y}.\neg\varphi(\bar{a},\bar{y})$. Now, $\exists \bar{x}.\psi(\bar{a},\bar{x})$ is a sentence of $\mathcal{L}_A$ which $\mathcal{C}\restriction_{\Pi_0}$ satisfies and, hence, which is also satisfied by $\mathcal{B}$. But this would imply $\mathcal{B} \models \forall \bar{y}.\neg\varphi(\bar{a},\bar{y})$. Contradiction.

We employ the same argument to get an elementary extension $\mathcal{C}_1$ of $\mathcal{C}_0$ and an elementary embedding $g_1 : (\mathcal{B}_1\restriction_{\Pi_0}, (f_0 c \,|\, c \in C_0)) \preccurlyeq (\mathcal{C}_1\restriction_{\Pi_0}, (c \,|\, c \in C_0))$.
We may do so because it holds that $(\mathcal{B}_1\restriction_{\Pi_0}, (f_0 c \,|\, c \in C_0)) \equiv (\mathcal{C}_1\restriction_{\Pi_0}, (c \,|\, c \in C_0))$. Symmetrically, we get an elementary extension $\mathcal{B}_2$ of $\mathcal{B}_1$ and an elementary embedding $f_1 : (\mathcal{C}_1\restriction_{\Pi_0}, (g_1 b \,|\, b \in B_1)) \preccurlyeq (\mathcal{B}_2\restriction_{\Pi_0}, (b \,|\, b \in B_1))$, because of
$(\mathcal{B}_1\restriction_{\Pi_0}, (b \,|\, b \in B_1)) \equiv (\mathcal{C}_1\restriction_{\Pi_0}, (g_1 b \,|\, b \in B_1))$. Continuing in this fashion, we get a tower

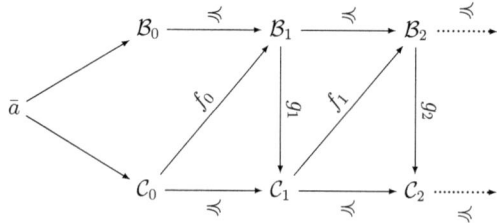

such that for each i we have $f_i \circ g_{i+1} = \mathrm{id}_{C_i}$, $g_i \circ f_i = \mathrm{id}_{B_i}$ and $f_i \subseteq f_{i+1}$.

Define $\hat{\mathcal{B}} := \bigcup_{i<\omega} \mathcal{B}_i$, $\hat{\mathcal{C}} := \bigcup_{i<\omega} \mathcal{C}_i$ and $\hat{f} := \bigcup_{i<\omega} f_i$. Then $\hat{f}$ is an isomorphism $\hat{\mathcal{C}}\restriction_{\Pi_0} \to \hat{\mathcal{B}}\restriction_{\Pi_0}$. Hence, there is a structure $\mathcal{C}'$ isomorphic to $\hat{\mathcal{C}}$ such that $\mathcal{C}'\restriction_{\Pi_0} = \hat{\mathcal{B}}\restriction_{\Pi_0}$. Using the interpretations of $\mathcal{C}'$ for the symbols in $\Pi_2 \setminus \Pi_0$ and those of $\hat{\mathcal{B}}$ for the symbols in $\Pi_1 \setminus \Pi_0$ we thus obtain a $\Pi_1 \cup \Pi_2$-structure $\mathcal{D}$ with $\mathcal{D}\!\upharpoonright_{\Pi_1} = \hat{\mathcal{B}}$ and $\mathcal{D}\!\upharpoonright_{\Pi_2} = \mathcal{C}'$. Finally, by the elementary chain theorem we get $\mathcal{B} \preccurlyeq \hat{\mathcal{B}}$ and $\mathcal{C} \preccurlyeq \hat{\mathcal{C}} \cong \mathcal{C}'$. □

Choosing $\bar{a}$ to be empty gives us Robinson's theorem back saying that two structures that are elementarily equivalent w.r.t. some shared language can be elementarily embedded together into some structure.

Corollary 5.3.3 *Let Π_1, Π_2 be signatures, $\Pi_0 = \Pi_1 \cap \Pi_2$, $\mathcal{B}$ a Π_1-structure, $\mathcal{C}$ a Π_2-structure with $\mathcal{B}\!\upharpoonright_{\Pi_0} \equiv \mathcal{C}\!\upharpoonright_{\Pi_0}$. Then there is a $(\Pi_1 \cup \Pi_2)$-structure $\mathcal{D}$ such that $\mathcal{B} \preccurlyeq \mathcal{D}\!\upharpoonright_{\Pi_1}$ and an elementary embedding $g : \mathcal{C} \to \mathcal{D}\!\upharpoonright_{\Pi_2}$.*

Remark 5.3.4 *Theorem 5.3.2 gives us a direct proof of the modularity of T_0-compatibility (Ghilardi's Proposition 3.3 [Ghi03b]): If we have two theories T_1 and T_2 which are compatible with a theory T_0 in the shared signature, then $T_1 \cup T_2$ is T_0-compatible too. For this, we need to embed a model of $\mathcal{A}$ of $T_1 \cup T_2$ into a model of $T_1 \cup T_2 \cup T_0^*$. We can extend the respective reducts of $\mathcal{A}$ into models $\mathcal{B}_i$ of $T_i \cup T_0^*$. In particular, the $\mathcal{B}_i$'s are models of T_0 and because its model completion was T_0^*, they are elementarily equivalent as $\mathcal{L}_0^A$-models. Hence, they can be elementarily embedded into a model of $T_1 \cup T_2 \cup T_0^*$ which is also an extension of $\mathcal{A}$.*

As already pointed out by Ghilardi[2], this is also the same argument as in his Lemma 5.2 which he uses to prove the above theorem. It states, assuming that we have two theories T_1, T_2 which are compatible with T_0^*, and two models $\mathcal{M}_i$ of the theories T_i, $i = 1, 2$ which share a substructure $\mathcal{A}$ in the common signature, that those two models can then be embedded into a model $\mathcal{M}$ of $T_1 \cup T_2$. This is a direct consequence of Theorem 5.3.2. By compatibility, $T_0^* \cup \Delta_\mathcal{A}$ is a complete theory because T_0^* is the model completion of T_0. In particular $(\mathcal{M}_1\!\upharpoonright_{\Pi_0}, \bar{a}) \equiv (\mathcal{M}_2\!\upharpoonright_{\Pi_0}, \bar{a})$ and Theorem 5.3.2 applies.

The amalgamation result also gives us an easy proof of Craig's interpolation theorem, demonstrating further the power of this technique.

Corollary 5.3.5 ([Hod97], 5.5.3) *Let T_1 be an Π_1-theory, T_2 an Π_2-theory such that $T_1 \cup T_2$ is inconsistent. Then there's a sentence φ in the common signature $\Pi_0 := \Pi_1 \cap \Pi_2$ such that $T_1 \vdash \varphi$ and $T_2 \vdash \neg\varphi$.*

Proof. Let us write $(T_2)_{\Pi_0}$ for the Π_0-sentences which are deducible from T_2. It suffices to show that $T_1 \cup (T_2)_{\Pi_0}$ is inconsistent. Assume towards a contradiction that it had a model $\mathcal{A}$. Now consider the set Γ of Π_0-sentences true in $\mathcal{A}$. We claim that T_2, Γ is consistent. Suppose it were not. By the compactness theorem, there then would be an Π_0-sentence $\varphi \in \Gamma$ with $T_2 \vdash \neg\varphi$, contradicting $\mathcal{A} \models (T_2)_{\Pi_0}$.

Let $\mathcal{B}$ be a model of T_2, Γ. By construction it holds that $\mathcal{A}\!\upharpoonright_{\Pi_0} \equiv \mathcal{B}\!\upharpoonright_{\Pi_0}$. But this means that we can jointly embed $\mathcal{A}$ and $\mathcal{B}$ into a model $\mathcal{C}$ of $T_1 \cup T_2$. Contradiction. □

The following two corollaries are joint work with Viorica Sofronie-Stokkermans.

---

[2]cf. [Ghi03b], p. 14.

Corollary 5.3.6 ((EEmb) transfer) *Let Π_0 be a signature, T_0 a theory in Π_0, Σ_1 and Σ_2 two disjoint sets of fresh function symbols, $\Pi_i := \Pi_0 \cup \Sigma_i$, $i = 1, 2$, $T_2 \supseteq T_0$ an Π_2-theory and $\mathcal{K}$ a set of universally closed clauses in Π_1.*

(1) If the extension $T_0 \subseteq T_0 \cup \mathcal{K}$ enjoys (EEmb$_w$) then so does $T_2 \subseteq T_2 \cup \mathcal{K}$.
(2) If the extension $T_0 \subseteq T_0 \cup \mathcal{K}$ enjoys (EEmb$_w^f$) then so does $T_2 \subseteq T_2 \cup \mathcal{K}$.
(3) If the extension $T_0 \subseteq T_0 \cup \mathcal{K}$ enjoys (EEmb$_w^{fd}$) then so does $T_2 \subseteq T_2 \cup \mathcal{K}$.

In particular, if all the Σ_2-terms are linear then extension $T_2 \subseteq T_2 \cup \mathcal{K}$ is local in case (1) or finitely local in case (3).

Proof. The argument is the same for all three cases. Suppose that $\mathcal{A} \in \mathsf{PMod}_w(\Sigma_1, T_2 \cup \mathcal{K})$ with possibly (2) $\mathcal{A}$ is finite or (3) all functions $f \in \Sigma_1$ have a finite definition domain. We need to show that $\mathcal{A}$ embeds into a total model $\mathcal{D}$ of $T_2 \cup \mathcal{K}$ such that $\mathcal{A}\!\restriction_{\Pi_2}$ is elementarily embedded into $\mathcal{D}\!\restriction_{\Pi_2}$.

By assumption, $\mathcal{A}$ is a total model of T_2 and therefore of T_0. It follows by (1) (EEmb$_w$), (2) (EEmb$_w^f$) or (3) (EEmb$_w^{fd}$) respectively, that there is a (total) model $\mathcal{B}$ of $T_0 \cup \mathcal{K}$ such that $\mathcal{A}$ is a weak substructure of $\mathcal{B}$ and $\mathcal{A}\!\restriction_{\Pi_0} \preccurlyeq \mathcal{B}\!\restriction_{\Pi_0}$. Let $\bar{a}$ list all the elements of $\mathcal{A}$, then it holds that $(\mathcal{A}\!\restriction_{\Pi_0}, \bar{a}) \equiv (\mathcal{B}\!\restriction_{\Pi_0}, \bar{a})$. We use Theorem 5.3.2 to get an $\mathcal{L}_1 \cup \mathcal{L}_2$-structure $\mathcal{D}$ such that $\mathcal{A}\!\restriction_{\Pi_2} \preccurlyeq \mathcal{D}\!\restriction_{\Pi_2}$ (in particular $\mathcal{D} \models T_2$) and an elementary embedding $g : \mathcal{B} \to \mathcal{D}\!\restriction_{\Pi_1}$ with $g(a) = a$ for all elements $a \in A$.

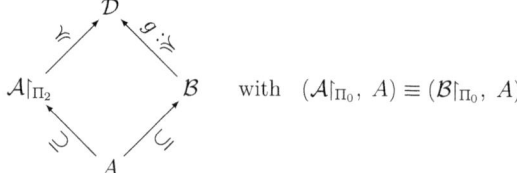

with $(\mathcal{A}\!\restriction_{\Pi_0}, A) \equiv (\mathcal{B}\!\restriction_{\Pi_0}, A)$

The only thing left to show is that $\mathcal{A}$ is a weak substructure of $\mathcal{D}$. Let $f \in \Sigma_1$ be an extension function such that $f^\mathcal{A}(\bar{a})$ is defined and equal to $b \in A$, say. It follows that $f^\mathcal{A}(\bar{a}) = f^\mathcal{B}(\bar{a}) = b$ because $\mathcal{A}\!\restriction_{\Pi_1}$ is a weak substructure of $\mathcal{B}$. Because the diagram commutes and $g(a) = a$, for all $a \in A$, we have

$$f^\mathcal{D}(\bar{a}) = f^\mathcal{D}(g\bar{a}) = g(f^\mathcal{B}(\bar{a})) = g(b) = b = f^\mathcal{A}(\bar{a}).$$

□

Corollary 5.3.7 *Let Π_0 be a signature, T_0 a model complete theory in Π_0, Σ_1 and Σ_2 two disjoint sets of fresh function symbols, $\Pi_i := \Pi_0 \cup \Sigma_i$, $i = 1, 2$, $\mathcal{K}$ a set of linear, universally closed clauses in Σ_1 and T_2 an arbitrary Π_2-theory with $T_0 \subseteq T_2$. Suppose the extension $T_0 \subseteq T_0 \cup \mathcal{K}$ is local. Then the extension $T_2 \subseteq T_2 \cup \mathcal{K}$ is local as well.*

Example 5.3.8 (Sofronie-Stokkermans) *According to Lemma 3.6.6 and consequent remark, extensions of lattices, join-semilattices with 0 and meet-semilattices with 1 by a monotone functions enjoy (Comp$_w^{fd}$). They therefore enjoy (EEmb$_w^{fd}$) in particular, which implies (ELoc^f) according to 4.6.10.(1). Hence, for any extension Lat^* of the theory of lattices or semi-lattices of the above* variety, e.g., distributive lattices or Boolean algebras, it holds that the extension $\mathsf{Lat}^* \subseteq \mathsf{Lat}^* \cup \mathsf{Mon}_g^\sigma$ enjoys (ELoc^f), where Mon_g^σ is a monotonicity axiom for an extension function g.

There is also a connection between the techniques of this section and the notion of compatibility of Section 5.2.

Corollary 5.3.9 (Sofronie-Stokkermans) *Let T_0 be a theory. Assume that T_0 has a model completion T_0^* such that $T_0 \subseteq T_0^*$. Let $T = T_0 \cup \mathcal{K}$ be an extension of T_0 with new function symbols Σ_1 whose properties are axiomatized by a set of flat and linear clauses $\mathcal{K}$ (all of which contain symbols in Σ_1).*

(1) Assume that:
  (a) Every model of $T_0 \cup \mathcal{K}$ embeds into a model of $T_0^* \cup \mathcal{K}$.[3]
  (b) $T_0 \cup \mathcal{K}$ is a local extension of T_0.

  Then $T_0^* \cup \mathcal{K}$ satisfies condition (EEmb_w), hence, if $\mathcal{K}$ is a set of quasi-flat and linear augmented clauses, then the extension $T_0^* \subseteq T_0^* \cup \mathcal{K}$ is local.

(2) If all variables in $\mathcal{K}$ occur below an extension function and $T_0^* \cup \mathcal{K}$ is a local extension of T_0^*, then $T_0 \cup \mathcal{K}$ is a local extension of T_0.

5.4 Combinations of Local Theories

In this section we consider two theory extensions over a common base theory. A natural question to ask is whether the union of the theories is local given that each extension was local on its own. This question was first studied by Viorica Sofronie-Stokkermans in [SS10] and [SS07].

Recall the following definition for a theory extension $T_0 \subseteq T_0 \cup \mathcal{K} =: T_1$.

(Comp_w) Every $\mathcal{A} \in \mathsf{PMod}_w(\Sigma_1, T_1)$ weakly embeds into a total model $\mathcal{B}$
         of T_1 such that $\mathcal{A}|_{\Pi_0}$ and $\mathcal{B}|_{\Pi_0}$ are isomorphic.

where $\mathsf{PMod}_w(\Sigma_1, T_1)$ denoted the class of all weak partial models of $T_0 \cup \mathcal{K}$ with total Σ_0-functions.

(EEmb_w) For every $\mathcal{A} \in \mathsf{PMod}_w(\Sigma_1, T_1)$ there is a total model $\mathcal{B}$ of T_1
         and a weak embedding $\varphi : \mathcal{A} \to \mathcal{B}$
         such that $(\mathcal{A}|_{\Pi_0}, (\bar{a} \,|\, \bar{a} \in A)) \equiv (\mathcal{B}|_{\Pi_0}, (\varphi\bar{a} \,|\, \bar{a} \in A))$.

In other words, the embedding $\varphi : \mathcal{A}|_{\Pi_0} \to \mathcal{B}|_{\Pi_0}$ is elementary.

Since every isomorphism is an elementary embedding we have the implications (Comp_w) $\to$ (EEmb_w) $\to$ (Emb_w).

Lemma 5.4.1 *Let Π_0 be a signature, T_0 a theory in Π_0, Σ_1 and Σ_2 two disjoint sets of fresh function symbols and $\mathcal{K}_i$ a set of universally closed clauses in $\Pi_i := \Pi_0 \cup \Sigma_i$, for $i = 1, 2$. If both extensions $T_0 \subseteq T_0 \cup \mathcal{K}_i$, $i = 1, 2$, satisfy (EEmb_w) then so does the extension $T_0 \subseteq T_0 \cup \mathcal{K}_1 \cup \mathcal{K}_2$. In particular, if all the extension terms are linear then the extension $T_0 \subseteq T_0 \cup \mathcal{K}_1 \cup \mathcal{K}_2$ is local.*

---

[3] If T_0 is universal, this is the notion of compatibility from Definition 5.2.1.

Proof. Let $\mathcal{A} \in \mathsf{PMod}_w(\Sigma_1, T_0 \cup \mathcal{K}_1 \cup \mathcal{K}_2)$. By assumption there are (total) models $\mathcal{B}, \mathcal{C}$ of $T_0 \cup \mathcal{K}_1$ and $T_0 \cup \mathcal{K}_2$ respectively into which $\mathcal{A}$ weakly embeds. We lose nothing in assuming that $\mathcal{A}$ is a weak substructure of both $\mathcal{B}$ and $\mathcal{C}$. By assumption we have $(\mathcal{A}|_{\Pi_0}, \bar{a}) \equiv (\mathcal{B}|_{\Pi_0}, \bar{a}) \equiv (\mathcal{C}|_{\Pi_0}, \bar{a})$.

We use Theorem 5.3.2 to get an $\Pi_1 \cup \Pi_2$-structure $\mathcal{D}$ such that $\mathcal{B} \preccurlyeq \mathcal{D}|_{\Pi_1}$ and an elementary embedding $\psi : \mathcal{C} \to \mathcal{D}|_{\Pi_2}$ with $\psi(a) = a$ for all elements $a \in A$. Now $\mathcal{A}$ is a weak substructure of $\mathcal{D}$: Let f be an extension function such that $f^{\mathcal{A}}(\bar{a})$ is defined. If f is in Σ_1 we have $f^{\mathcal{A}}(\bar{a}) = f^{\mathcal{B}}(\bar{a}) = f^{\mathcal{D}}(\bar{a})$. If f is an Σ_2-function it follows that $f^{\mathcal{A}}(\bar{a}) = \psi(f^{\mathcal{A}}(\bar{a})) = \psi(f^{\mathcal{C}}(\bar{a})) = f^{\mathcal{D}}(\psi\bar{a}) = f^{\mathcal{D}}(\bar{a})$. Obviously, $\mathcal{D}$ is a model of $T_1 \cup T_2$ and $(\mathcal{A}|_{\Pi_0}, \bar{a}) \equiv (\mathcal{D}|_{\Pi_0}, \bar{a})$. So $\mathcal{D}$ is as desired. □

The defining feature of model completeness for a theory is that every embedding between its models is elementary. So if we choose a model complete base theory (**EEmb**$_w$) and (**Emb**$_w$) coincide.

Corollary 5.4.2 *Let T_0 be a model complete theory in Σ_0, Σ_1 and Σ_2 two disjoint sets of fresh function symbols and $\mathcal{K}_i$ a set of universally closed clauses in $\Sigma_0 \cup \Sigma_i$, for $i = 1, 2$. If both extensions $T_0 \subseteq T_0 \cup \mathcal{K}_i$, $i = 1, 2$, satisfy (**Emb**$_w$) then so does the extension $T_0 \subseteq T_0 \cup \mathcal{K}_1 \cup \mathcal{K}_2$. In particular, if all the extension terms are linear then the above extension is local.*

Recall that every theory which allows quantifier elimination is model complete. We gave some examples of this in Example 5.1.6. Consider these examples again.

Example 5.4.3

(1) Presburger arithmetic with $\equiv_2, \equiv_3, \dots$.

(2) Real closed fields (e.g., real numbers).

(3) Linear arithmetic in $(+, -, 0, 1, \leq)$ (= divisible, torsion-free ordered abelian groups with 1).

A theory is called κ-*categorical for some cardinal κ if all its models of size κ are isomorphic. The above theories are not categorical in any cardinality. Thus, to consider elementary equivalence was expedient in order to deal with them. Consider 3). Since models are torsion-free the theory is not locally finite. This rules out* $\aleph_0$-*categoricity [Hod97], 6.3.2. To rule out categoricity for uncountable cardinals it suffices to rule it out for one. Take the cardinality of* $\mathbb{R}$. *It is easy to check that* $\mathbb{R}$ *and* $\mathbb{R} \times \mathbb{R}$ *with a lexicographical order are both models of the theory. However, the former is Archimedean, i.e., for all $y > x > 0$ there is some n with $nx > y$, while the latter is not (Take $(0, 1) < (1, 0)$. Then, still, $(0, n) < (1, 0)$).*[4]

Next we generalize Theorem 19 of [SS07] to elementary embeddability.

Theorem 5.4.4 *Let T_0 be a theory in the signature Π_0, Σ_1 and Σ_2 two disjoint sets of fresh function symbols and $\mathcal{K}_i$ a set of universally closed clauses in $\Pi_0 \cup \Sigma_i$ for $i = 1, 2$. Let $T_i := T_0 \cup \mathcal{K}_i$, $i = 1, 2$. Suppose that*

*(1) $T_0 \subseteq T_1$ satisfies (**EEmb**$_w$),*

*(2) $T_0 \subseteq T_2$ satisfies (**Emb**$_w$) and*

(3) $\mathcal{K}_1$ is Σ_1-flat in which all variables are shielded, i.e., all variables occur below some Σ_1-function.

---
[4]This counterexample is due to Uwe Waldmann.

Then the extension $T_0 \subseteq T_0 \cup \mathcal{K}_1 \cup \mathcal{K}_2$ satisfies (Emb$_w$). In particular, if all the extension terms are linear then the above extension is local.

Crucial for the proof is Viorica Sofronie-Stokkermans' insight that a model of the base theory can be extended to a partial model of the extended theory provided it has a weak substructure which is a partial model of the extension and the extension clauses are flat and shield all variables.

Recall that given two signatures $\Pi \subseteq \Pi'$ and a Π-structure $\mathcal{A}$ we call a corresponding Π'-structure $\mathcal{A}'$ with $\mathcal{A}'|_\Pi = \mathcal{A}|_\Pi$ a Π'-expansion of $\mathcal{A}$.

Lemma 5.4.5 ([SS10], Lemma 5) *Let T_0 be a theory in Σ_0, Σ_1 a set of fresh function symbols and $\mathcal{K}$ a (Σ_1)-flat set of clauses in $\Pi_0 := \Sigma_0 \cup \Sigma_1$. Let $T_1 := T_0 \cup \mathcal{K}$ and assume that for each clause C of $\mathcal{K}$ it holds that each variable appears below a Σ_1-function. Let $\mathcal{A} \in \mathsf{PMod}_w(\Sigma_1, T_1)$ and let $\mathcal{B}$ be a (total) model of T_0 such that $\chi : \mathcal{A}|_{\Pi_0} \to \mathcal{B}$ is a (Π_0)-embedding. Then χ and $\mathcal{B}$ can be expanded such that $\hat{\chi} : \mathcal{A} \to \hat{\mathcal{B}}$ is a weak Π_1-embedding and $\hat{\mathcal{B}} \in \mathsf{PMod}_w(\Sigma_1, T_1)$. Schematically:*

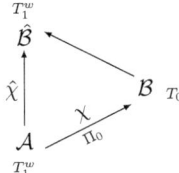

where T_1^w indicates that we have a weak partial model of T_1.

Proof of Theorem 5.4.4. We start in exactly the same way as in the proof of the lemma in [SS10]. Let $\mathcal{A}$ be a weak partial model of $T_0 \cup \mathcal{K}_1 \cup \mathcal{K}_2$ with total Π_0-functions. Then $\mathcal{A}|_{\Pi_2}$ is a partial model of T_2. By assumption $\mathcal{A}|_{\Pi_2}$ weakly embeds into a total model $\mathcal{B}$ of T_2. By Lemma 5.4.5, we can extend $\mathcal{B}|_{\Pi_0}$ to a weak partial model $\mathcal{C}^-$ of T_1. Since Σ_1 and Σ_2 are disjoint and $\mathcal{B}$ and $\mathcal{C}^-$ have the same carrier, we may reattach $\mathcal{B}$'s (total) Σ_2-functions to $\mathcal{C}^-$, yielding a (total) model $\mathcal{C}$ of T_2, which is also a partial model of T_1, and some weak embedding $\varphi : \mathcal{A} \to \mathcal{C}$. Now we use (EEmb$_w$) to get an ($\Pi_0$)-elementary extension $\mathcal{D}$ of $\mathcal{C}$ which is a total model of T_1. In a picture:

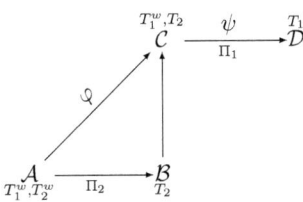

where $(\mathcal{C}|_{\Pi_0}, \bar{c})_{\bar{c}\in C} \equiv (\mathcal{D}|_{\Pi_0}, \psi\bar{c})_{\bar{c}\in C}$. We may further assume that ψ is the identity. Now we use Theorem 5.3.2 on $\mathcal{C}|_{\Pi_2}$ and $\mathcal{D}$ (choose some listing $\bar{c}$ of $\mathcal{C}$'s elements) to obtain a ($\Pi_1 \cup \Pi_2$)-structure $\mathcal{E}$ such that $\mathcal{C}|_{\Pi_2} \preccurlyeq \mathcal{E}|_{\Pi_2}$ and some elementary embedding $\chi : \mathcal{D} \to \mathcal{E}|_{\Pi_1}$.

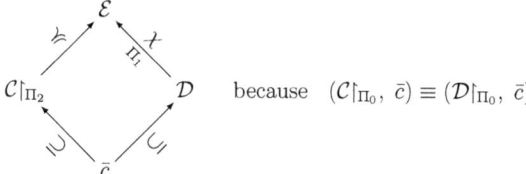

In particular, $\mathcal{C}\restriction_{\Pi_2} \equiv \mathcal{E}\restriction_{\Pi_2}$ and $\mathcal{E}\restriction_{\Pi_1} \equiv \mathcal{D}$. Hence, $\mathcal{E}$ is a model of $T_1 \cup T_2$ and φ can be extended to a weak embedding from $\mathcal{A}$ into $\mathcal{E}$: Suppose $f^\mathcal{A}(\bar{a})$ is defined. We need to show that $\varphi(f^\mathcal{A}(\bar{a})) = f^\mathcal{E}(\varphi\bar{a})$. If $f \in \Sigma_2$ we have $\varphi(f^\mathcal{A}(\bar{a})) = f^\mathcal{C}(\varphi\bar{a}) = f^\mathcal{E}(\varphi\bar{a})$. If $f \in \Sigma_1$ we have

$$\varphi(f^\mathcal{A}(\bar{a})) = f^\mathcal{C}(\varphi\bar{a}) = f^\mathcal{D}(\varphi\bar{a})$$

because $\mathcal{C}$ was a weak substructure of $\mathcal{D}$ as an Π_1-structure. On the other hand, χ is the identity on C, thus,

$$f^\mathcal{C}(\varphi\bar{a}) = \chi(f^\mathcal{C}(\varphi\bar{a})) = \chi(f^\mathcal{D}(\varphi\bar{a})) = f^\mathcal{E}(\chi\varphi\bar{a}) = f^\mathcal{E}(\varphi\bar{a}).$$

This establishes the claim. □

5.5 Combinations of Ψ-Local Theories

We also want to address the question of how combinations of different Ψ-local extensions over a common base theory fare. For a partial algebra $\mathcal{A}$ and a term operator Ψ let us write $\Psi_\mathcal{K}(\mathcal{A})$ for the set $\Psi_\mathcal{K}(\mathcal{D}(\mathcal{A}))$ where $\mathcal{D}(\mathcal{A})$ is the table of $\mathcal{A}$ (cf. Definition 4.6.4). The following lemma lifts the argument in [SS07] to Ψ-locality.

Lemma 5.5.1 *Let T_0 be a theory in Π_0, Σ_1 and Σ_2 two disjoint sets of fresh function symbols and $\mathcal{K}_i$ a set of universally closed clauses in $\Pi_i := (\Sigma_0 \cup \Sigma_i, \text{Pred})$, for $i = 1, 2$. Let $T_i := T_0 \cup \mathcal{K}_i$, $i = 1, 2$. Let Ψ be a term closure operator w.r.t. $(\Sigma_1^\mathcal{C})$- ground terms, $\mathcal{A}$ be a partial $(\Pi_1 \cup \Pi_2)$-structure such that $\mathcal{A}\restriction_{\Pi_1} \in \mathsf{PMod}_w(\Sigma_1, T_1)$ and let $\mathcal{B}$ be a (total) model of T_2 such that $\chi : \mathcal{A}\restriction_{\Pi_2} \to \mathcal{B}$ is a weak Π_2-embedding. Suppose that*

(1) $\mathcal{K}_1$ is a set of universally closed Σ_1-flat clauses,

(2) all variables of $\mathcal{K}_1$ appear below an extension function,

(3) all terms in $\Psi_{\mathcal{K}_1}(\mathcal{A}\restriction_{\Pi_1})$ are defined in $\mathcal{A}$.

Then $\mathcal{B}$ can be expanded to a partial $(\Pi_1 \cup \Pi_2)$-structure and χ can be expanded such that $\hat{\chi} : \mathcal{A} \to \hat{\mathcal{B}}$ is a weak $(\Pi_1 \cup \Pi_2)$-embedding with $\hat{\mathcal{B}}\restriction_{\Pi_1} \in \mathsf{PMod}_w(\Sigma_1, T_1)$, $\hat{\mathcal{B}}\restriction_{\Pi_2}$ is a total model of T_2 and all terms of $\Psi_{\mathcal{K}_1}(\mathcal{B}\restriction_{\Pi_1})$ are defined in $\mathcal{B}$. Schematically:

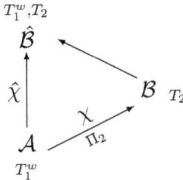

where T_1^w indicates that we have a weak partial model of T_1 and T_2 indicates that we have a total model of T_2

Proof. We need to add the Σ_1-functions to $\mathcal{B}$. For $f \in \Sigma_1$ set

$$f^{\hat{\mathcal{B}}}(b_1, ..., b_n) := \begin{cases} \chi(f^{\mathcal{A}}(a_1, ..., a_n)) & \exists a_i \in A \text{ s. t. } \chi(a_i) = b_i \\ & \text{and } f^{\mathcal{A}}(a_1, ..., a_n) \text{ is defined.} \\ \text{undefined} & \text{otherwise.} \end{cases}$$

Since χ is 1–1 this is well-defined and $\hat{\chi}$ is a weak embedding by construction. Also, because the Σ_1-functions of $\hat{\mathcal{B}}$ are defined in terms of the Σ_1-functions of $\mathcal{A}$, we have $\mathcal{D}(\hat{\mathcal{B}}\!\restriction_{\Pi_1}) = \bar{h}(\mathcal{D}(\mathcal{A}\!\restriction_{\Pi_1}))$, where h maps a name a of an element $a \in A$ to the name b with $\chi(a) = b$ and leaves all other base terms unchanged. In particular, $\Psi_{\mathcal{K}_1}(\mathcal{B}\!\restriction_{\Pi_1}) = \bar{h}\Psi_{\mathcal{K}_1}(\mathcal{A}\!\restriction_{\Pi_1})$ by 4.6.1.(5). It follows that all terms in $\Psi_{\mathcal{K}_1}(\mathcal{B}\!\restriction_{\Pi_1})$ are defined in $\hat{\mathcal{B}}$.

Since $\hat{\mathcal{B}}$ and $\mathcal{B}$ are the same as Π_2-structures we trivially have $\hat{\mathcal{B}} \models T_2$, so the only thing left to show is $\hat{\mathcal{B}} \models_w T_1$. To do this, fix on a clause $D \in \mathcal{K}_1$ and a valuation $\beta : X \to B$. We may assume that all terms t of D are defined in $(\hat{\mathcal{B}}, \beta)$ (otherwise there is nothing to show). We will construct a valuation for $\mathcal{A}$ from this. Consider an extension term t in D. By assumption, $\mathcal{K}_1$ was flat. This means that t has the form $f(x_1, ..., x_n)$ for some variables x_i. Because t was defined it follows that there are elements $a_{x_1}, ..., a_{x_n}$ of A such that $\chi(a_{x_i}) = \beta(x_i)$ and

$$\beta(t) = f^{\hat{\mathcal{B}}}(\beta(x_1), ..., \beta(x_n)) = \chi(f^{\mathcal{A}}(a_{x_1}, ..., a_{x_n})).$$

Note that since χ was $1-1$ the choice of the element a_x for a variable x is unique. Hence, we may define a map $\alpha : x \mapsto a_x$. As all terms in D were defined in $(\hat{\mathcal{B}}, \beta)$ so they are in $(\mathcal{A}, \alpha)$ and we have $\mathcal{A}, \alpha \models D$ as well as $\chi(\alpha(t)) = \beta(t)$ for all terms t in D. The claim now follows from the fact that weak embeddings preserve quantifier-free formulas in which all terms are defined. $\square$

Union of chain of partial models. As we saw in Section 2.1, the technique of building up a model step-by-step, is always admissible provided the theory is $\forall\exists$. Then the limit will also be a model of T (Chang-Łos-Suszko theorem).

We want to employ this powerful tool on partial structures as well. Let $\mathcal{B}_i$ be partial Σ_1-models such that $\mathcal{B}_i \subseteq_w \mathcal{B}_{i+1}$, $i = 0, 1, 2, \ldots$. We want to construct the union $\mathcal{B}_\omega$ of this chain. As carrier, we simply take the union of the carriers B_i just as we would for the union of a chain of total models. Now we have to say what the functions of $\mathcal{B}_\omega$ should be. Note that if a partial function $f^{\mathcal{B}_i}$ is defined on a tuple $\bar{b}$ it will remained defined on $\bar{b}$ and will have the same value in any model

$\mathcal{B}_j$ with $j \geq i$. This is because we are dealing with weak inclusions. Thus we may define

$$f^{\mathcal{B}_\omega}(\bar{b}) := \begin{cases} f^{\mathcal{B}_i}(\bar{b}) & \text{if there is an } i \text{ such that } f^{\mathcal{B}_i}(\bar{b}) \text{ is defined.} \\ \text{undefined} & \text{otherwise.} \end{cases}$$

and we now get our structure $\mathcal{B}_\omega := \bigcup_{i<\omega} \mathcal{B}_i$.

The following theorem lifts a theorem of [SS10] from locality to Ψ-locality.

Theorem 5.5.2 *Let T_0 be a theory in the signature Π_0, Σ_1 and Σ_2 two disjoint sets of fresh function symbols and $\mathcal{K}_i$ a set of universally closed clauses in $\Pi_i := \Pi_0 \cup \Sigma_i$, for $i = 1, 2$. Let $T_i := T_0 \cup \mathcal{K}_i$, $i = 1, 2$. Let Ψ_i be term closure operators w.r.t. ground $(\Sigma_i^\mathcal{C})$-terms, $i = 1, 2$. Suppose that*

(1) T_0 is $\forall \exists$,

(2) $\mathcal{K}_i$ is Σ_i-flat and $T_0 \subseteq T_i$ has $(\mathsf{Emb}_w^{\Psi_i})$, for $i = 1, 2$,

(3) all variables are shielded in $\mathcal{K}_i$, i.e., all variables occur below an extension function, $i = 1, 2$.

Then $T_0 \subseteq T_0 \cup \mathcal{K}_1 \cup \mathcal{K}_2$ has $(\mathsf{Emb}_w^{\Psi_1 \cup \Psi_2})$ where $(\Psi_1 \cup \Psi_2)(\Gamma) := \Psi_1(\Gamma) \cup \Psi_2(\Gamma)$.

Proof. To reduce clutter, let us drop the subscript $\mathcal{K}$ for the term operators Ψ_i in this proof and say '$\Psi_i(\mathcal{A})$ is defined' to mean '$\Psi_i(\mathcal{A}\restriction_{\Pi_i})$ is defined in $\mathcal{A}\restriction_{\Pi_i}$'.

Let $\mathcal{A}$ be a partial model of $T_0 \cup \mathcal{K}_1 \cup \mathcal{K}_2$ with total Σ_0-functions such that the terms in $(\Psi_1 \cup \Psi_2)(\mathcal{A})$ are all defined. We need to embed $\mathcal{A}$ into a total model of $T_0 \cup \mathcal{K}_1 \cup \mathcal{K}_2$. We will build up this total model inductively by repeatedly using the above lemma and embeddability to get a diagram

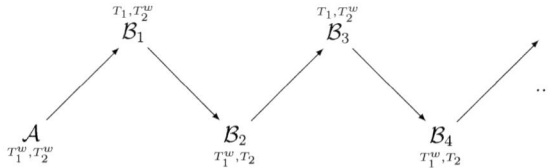

where all the arrows are weak $(\Pi_1 \cup \Pi_2)$-inclusions, $\mathcal{B}_{2k} \models T_2$, $\mathcal{B}_{2k} \models_w T_1$, and all terms in $\Psi_1(\mathcal{B}_{2k})$ are defined; and $\mathcal{B}_{2k+1} \models T_1$, $\mathcal{B}_{2k+1} \models_w T_2$, and all terms in $\Psi_2(\mathcal{B}_{2k+1})$ are defined.

We begin by using $(\mathsf{Emb}_w^{\Psi_1})$ to get a total model $\mathcal{C}_1$ of T_1 into which $\mathcal{A}\restriction_{\Pi_1}$ weakly embeds ($\Psi_1(\mathcal{A})$ is defined). Here and hereafter we may assume that the (weak) embedding is the identity. We then use Lemma 5.5.1 to extend $\mathcal{C}_1$ to a partial model $\mathcal{B}_1$ of T_2. We may do so because $\Psi_2(\mathcal{A})$ was also defined, hence it follows from Lemma 5.5.1 that $\Psi_2(\mathcal{B}_1)$ is defined as well. Hence, we may (weakly) embed $\mathcal{B}_1$ into a total model $\mathcal{C}_2$ of T_2. Trivially, all terms of $\Psi_1(\mathcal{B}_1)$ are defined. We may therefore extend $\mathcal{C}_2$ to a partial model $\mathcal{B}_2$ of T_1 (which is still a model of T_2) in which all terms of $\Psi_1(\mathcal{B}_2)$ are defined.

Continuing in this manner we obtain a chain of partial models. Now consider its union $\mathcal{B}_\omega$. $\mathcal{B}_\omega$ is a model of T_0 because T_0 was $\forall\exists$. Now note that $\mathcal{B}_\omega$ is in fact a total structure. Suppose $f^{\mathcal{B}_\omega}(\bar{b})$ was undefined for $f \in \Sigma_1$, say. Then we could choose i big enough such that $\bar{b} \in B_i$. Now, i cannot be odd because $\mathcal{B}_{2k+1}$ has total Σ_1-functions. Hence, i is even. For the same reason, $f^{\mathcal{B}_{i+1}}(\bar{b})$ will be defined. But then it will stay defined thereafter. Contradiction.

We claim that $\mathcal{B}_\omega$ is also a (total) model of $T_1 \cup T_2$. Let's do this for $\mathcal{K}_1$, the other case is similar. Fix a valuation $\beta : X \to \mathcal{B}_\omega$ and a clause $D \in \mathcal{K}_1$ in the variables $\bar{x}$. Let $\bar{b} := \beta(\bar{x})$. Now, choose k big enough such that $\bar{b} \in \mathcal{B}_{2k+1}$. We have $\mathcal{B}_{2k+1} \models D[\bar{b}]$. And because $\mathcal{B}_{2k+1}$ is a substructure of $\mathcal{B}_\omega$ (considered as Π_1-models) and quantifier-free formulas are preserved under embeddings we get $\mathcal{B}_\omega \models D[\bar{b}]$ as desired. $\square$

Corollary 5.5.3 *With the above notations, suppose that the $\mathcal{K}_i$ are additionally Σ_i-linear for $i = 1, 2$. Then for any closure operator such that $\Psi_3 \supseteq (\Psi_1 \cup \Psi_2)$ it holds that $T_0 \subseteq T_0 \cup \mathcal{K}_1 \cup \mathcal{K}_2$ is a Ψ_3-local extension.*

Chapter 6

Implementation: H-PILoT

We developed and implemented the software system H-PILoT (Hierarchical Proving by Instantiation in Local Theory extensions) for hierarchical reasoning in local theory extensions: A given proof task (set of ground clauses), over the extension of a theory with functions axiomatized by a set of clauses, is reduced to an equi-satisfiable ground problem over the base theory (cf. Lemma 2.5.1).

After H-PILoT has carried out this reduction, it hands over the transformed problem to a dedicated prover for the base theory. This reduction is always sound. For local theory extensions the hierarchical reduction is sound and complete. If the formulas obtained in this way belong to a fragment decidable in the base theory, H-PILoT thus provides a decision procedure for testing satisfiability of ground formulas. In case the reduced formulas are satisfiable (modulo the base theory), H-PILoT can be used for model generation, which is of great help in detecting and localizing errors.

H-PILoT is implemented in Ocaml[1]. The system, together with a manual and examples, can be downloaded from www.mpi-inf.mpg.de/~ihlemann/software/. There is both a 32-bit and a 64-bit Linux version available, the current version is 1.92.

H-PILoT has been used in large case studies and the system has been presented at CADE 2009 ([ISS09]). For complex case studies H-PILoT's ability to handle *chains* of extensions has been crucial. H-PILoT has advanced abilities to handle the common data structures of *arrays* (Section 6.5) and *pointers* (Section 6.8): H-PILoT automatically detects whether a given specification falls within the local fragment of these theories. To improve user-friendliness, a clausifier has also been integrated into H-PILoT (Section 6.10). On request, H-PILoT provides an extensive step-by-step trace of the reduction process, making its results verifiable (Section 6.15).

The provers integrated with H-PILoT are the general-purpose prover SPASS ([WDF$^+$09]); the SMT-solvers Yices ([DdM06]), CVC3 ([BT07]) and Z3 ([dMB08]); and the prover Redlog ([DS97]), for non-linear real problems.

State-of-the-art SMT provers, such as the ones above, are very efficient for testing the satisfiability of ground formulas over standard theories, such as linear arithmetic (real, rational or integer), but use heuristics in the presence of universally quantified formulas, hence, cannot reliably detect satisfiability of such formulas. However, if SMT solvers are used for finding software bugs, their being able to detect the actual satisfiability of satisfiable sets of formulas is crucial

---
[1]http://caml.inria.fr/ocaml/index.en.html

(cf. [dM09, dMB08, GdM09, BdM09]).

H-PILoT recognizes a class of local axiomatizations, performs the instantiation and hands in a ground problem to the SMT provers or other specialized provers, for which they are known to terminate with a yes/no answer, so it can be used as a tool for steering standard SMT provers, in order to provide decision procedures in the case of local theory extensions.

6.1 Structure of the Program

The main algorithm which hierarchically reduces a decision problem in a theory extension to a decision problem in the base theory can be divided into a preprocessing part, the main loop and a post-processing part; see Figure 6.1.

Preprocessing

The input is read and parsed. If it is detected to be in SMT format, we set the options to "use arithmetic" (e.g., $+$, $-$,... are predefined). If the input is not in clause normal form (CNF), it is translated to CNF, then the input is flattened and linearized. The program then checks if the clauses in the axiomatization given are local extensions and sets the flag -local to true/false. This ends the preprocessing phase.

Main Algorithm

The main loop proceeds as follows: We consider chains of extensions $T_0 \subseteq T_1 \subseteq \cdots \subseteq T_n$, where $T_i = T_0 \cup \bigcup_{j=1}^{i} \mathcal{K}_j$ of T_0 with function symbols in a set Σ_i (extension functions) whose properties are axiomatized by a set $\mathcal{K}_i$ of $(\Pi_0 \cup \bigcup_{j=1}^{i} \Sigma_j)$-clauses.

Let $i = n$. As long as the extension level i is greater than 0, we compute $\mathcal{K}_i[G]$ ($\mathcal{K}_i[\Psi]$ for arrays). If no separation of the extension symbols is required, we stop here (the result will be passed to an external prover that can reason about the extension of the theory T_0 with free function symbols in Σ_n). Otherwise, we perform the hierarchical reduction by purifying $\mathcal{K}_i$ and G (to $\mathcal{K}_i^0$, G^0 respectively) and by adding corresponding instances of the congruence axioms Con_i. To prepare for the next iteration, we transform the clauses into the form $\forall \bar{x}.\Phi \vee \mathcal{K}_i$ (compute prenex form, skolemize). If $\mathcal{K}_i[G]$ ($i > 1$) is not ground, we quit with a corresponding message. Otherwise we set $G' := \mathcal{K}_i^0 \wedge G^0 \wedge \mathsf{Con}_i$ and $T' := T \setminus \{\mathcal{K}_i\}$. We flatten and linearize $\mathcal{K}'$ and decrease i. If level $i = 0$ is reached G' is handed to an external prover.

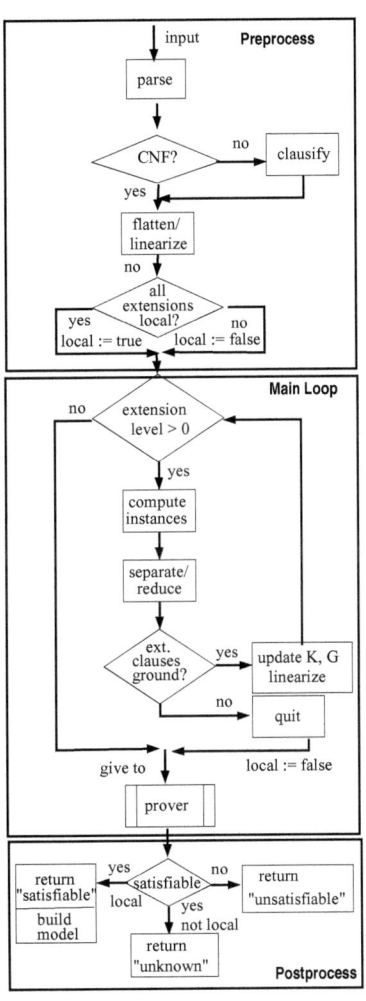

Figure 6.1: H-PILoT Structure

Post-processing

If the answer is "unsatisfiable" then $G \models_{T_n} \bot$. If the answer is "satisfiable" and all extensions were local, then G is satisfiable w.r.t. T_n and we know how to build a model. If the answer is satisfiable but we do not know that all extensions are local, or if the instantiated clauses (of level > 1) were not ground, we answer "unknown".

6.2 Modules of H-PILoT

We present the different parts of H-PILoT in more detail.

Preprocessing

H-PILoT receives as input a many-sorted specification of the signature; a specification of the hierarchy of local extensions to be considered; an axiomatization $\mathcal{K}$ of the theory extension(s); a set G of ground clauses containing possibly additional constants. H-PILoT allows the following preprocessing functionality.

Translation to Clause Form. H-PILoT provides a translator to clause normal form (CNF) for ease of use. First-order formulas can be given as input; H-PILoT translates them into CNF. In the present implementation, the CNF translator does not provide the full functionality of FLOTTER ([NW01]) – it has only restricted subformula renaming – but is powerful enough for most applications.

Flattening/Linearization. Methods for recognizing local theory extensions usually require that the clauses in the set $\mathcal{K}$ extending the base theory are *flat* and *linear*, which does nothing to improve readability. If the flags -linearize and/or -flatten are used then the input is flattened and/or linearized (the general purpose flag -preprocess may also be used). H-PILoT allows the user to enter a more intelligible non-flattened version and will perform the flattening and linearization of $\mathcal{K}$.

Recognizing Syntactic Criteria which Imply Locality. Examples of local extensions include (the fragments of) the theories of data structures discussed in Section 4.2 and Section 4.8, respectively (and also iterations and combinations thereof). In the preprocessing phase H-PILoT analyzes the input clauses to check whether they are in one of these fragments.

- If the flag -array is on, H-PILoT checks if the input is in the array property fragment (cf. Definition 4.2.1).

- If the keyword "pointer" is detected, H-PILoT checks if the input is in the pointer fragment (cf. Definition 4.8.1) and adds missing "nullability" terms, i.e., it adds premises of the form "$t \neq \text{null}$", in order to relieve the user of this clerical labor.

If the answer to either of these questions is "yes", we know that the extensions we consider are local, i.e., that H-PILoT can be used as a decision procedure.

Main Algorithm

The main algorithm hierarchically reduces a decision problem in a theory extension to a decision problem in the base theory.

Given a set of clauses $\mathcal{K}$ and a set of ground clauses G, the algorithm we use carries out a hierarchical reduction of G to a set of formulas in the base theory. It then hands over the new problem to a dedicated prover such as Yices, CVC3 or Z3. H-PILoT is also coupled with Redlog (for handling non-linear real arithmetic) and with SPASS[2].

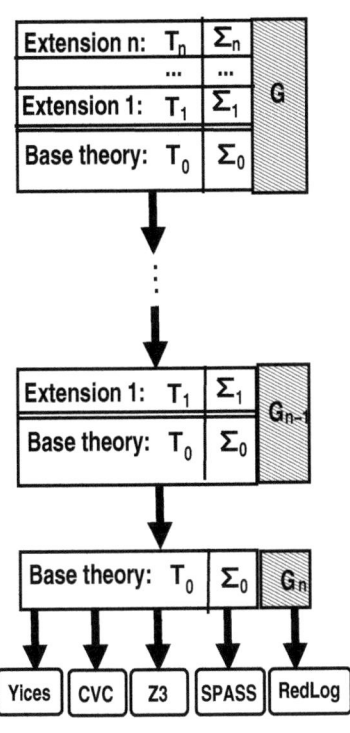

Loop. For a chain of local extensions:

$$T_0 \subseteq T_1 = T_0 \cup \mathcal{K}_1 \subseteq T_2 = T_0 \cup \mathcal{K}_1 \cup \mathcal{K}_2$$
$$\subseteq \ldots \subseteq T_n = T_0 \cup \mathcal{K}_1 \cup \ldots \cup \mathcal{K}_n.$$

a satisfiability check w.r.t. the last extension can be reduced (in n steps) to a satisfiability check w.r.t. T_0. The only caveat is that at each step the reduced clauses $\mathcal{K}_i^0 \cup G^0 \cup \mathsf{Con}^0$ need to be ground. Groundness is assured if each variable in a clause appears at least once under an extension function. In that case, we know that at each reduction step the total clause size only grows polynomially in the size of G ([SS05]). H-PILoT allows the user to specify a chain of extensions by tagging the extension functions with their place in the chain (e.g., if f belongs to $\mathcal{K}_3$ but not to $\mathcal{K}_1 \cup \mathcal{K}_2$ it is declared as level 3).

Let $i = n$. As long as the extension level i is bigger than 0, we compute $\mathcal{K}_i[G]$ ($\mathcal{K}_i[\Psi(G)]$ in case of arrays). If no separation of the extension symbols is required, we stop here (the result will be passed to an external prover). Otherwise, we perform the hierarchical reduction in Lemma 2.5.1 by purifying $\mathcal{K}_i$ and G (to $\mathcal{K}_i^0, G^0$ respectively) and by adding corresponding instances of the congruence axioms Con_i. To prepare for the next iteration, we transform the clauses into the form $\forall x. \Phi \vee \mathcal{K}_i$ (compute prenex form, skolemize). If $\mathcal{K}_i[G]/\mathcal{K}_i^0$ is not ground, we quit with a corresponding message. Otherwise our new proof task G' becomes $G' := \mathcal{K}_i^0 \wedge G^0 \wedge \mathsf{Con}_i$, our new extension clauses are $\mathcal{K}' := \mathcal{K}_{i-1}$ and our new base theory becomes $T' := T_{i-1} \setminus \{\mathcal{K}_{i-1}\}$. We flatten and linearize $\mathcal{K}'$ and decrease i. If level $i = 0$ is reached, we exit the main loop and G' is handed to an external prover. Completeness is guaranteed if all extensions are known to be local and if each reduction step produces a set of ground clauses for the next step.

Post-processing

Depending on the answer of the external provers to the satisfiability problem G_n, we can infer whether the initial set G of clauses was satisfiable or not.

- If G_n is unsatisfiable w.r.t. T_0 then we know that G is unsatisfiable.

- If G_n is satisfiable, but H-PILoT failed to detect this, and the user did not assert the locality of the sets of clauses used in the axiomatization, its answer is "unknown".

---

[2]H-PILoT only calls one of these solvers once.

- If G_n is satisfiable and H-PILoT detected the locality of the axiomatization, then the answer is "satisfiable". In this case, H-PILoT takes advantage of the ability of SMT-solvers to provide counterexamples for the satisfiable set G_n of ground clauses and specifies a counterexample of G by translating the basic SMT-model of the reduced query to a model of the original query. This improves readability greatly, especially when we have a chain of extensions. The counterexamples can be graphically displayed using Mathematica (cf. Section 6.16). This is currently done separately; an integration with Mathematica is planned for the future.

6.3 Application Areas

H-PILoT has applications in *mathematics, multiple-valued logics, data- structures* and *reasoning in complex systems*.

Mathematics. In Section 3.6.2 we have discussed the locality of theory extensions of *monotone functions* over partially ordered sets. We will give an example of how to use H-PILoT on problems involving monotonicity in Section 6.4 below. Another example from mathematics is an extension with *free functions*, i.e., we have an empty set of extension clauses $\mathcal{K}$ but the proof task G contains new function symbols. Even in this simple case, local and hierarchical reasoning is useful, because expanding the signature might already derail a back-end prover. For instance, consider real arithmetic. Linear arithmetic is tractable and can be handled quite efficiently by state-of-the-art SMT-solvers. Non-linear arithmetic is another matter, however (cf. [FHT+07, BPT07]). Here the options are more limited. To handle non-linear real arithmetic, H-PILoT is integrated with the prover *Redlog* ([DS97]). Since Redlog uses quantifier elimination for real closed fields, it relies on a fixed signature. In a case like this, H-PILoT can be employed as a preprocessor that eliminates the new function symbols in the proof task, allowing the user to employ free function symbols together with (non-linear) real arithmetic. Another example from mathematics, taken from [SS05], is that of a *Lipschitz function* (roughly, smooth continuity at a given point). There it was shown that any extension of the real numbers with a Lipschitz function is local.

Multiple-valued logics. Another important application area of local reasoning and, by the same token, H-PILoT is reasoning in multiple-valued logics. This was discussed in Section 3.6.1. These logics have more than two truth values, in fact they allow as truth values the whole real interval of $[0, 1]$. The semantics are often given algebraically. For example, the class $\mathcal{MV}$ of all MV-algebras is the quasi-variety generated by the real unit interval $[0, 1]$ with connectives $\{\vee, \wedge, \circ, \Rightarrow\}$, defined as explained in Section 3.6.1.[3] The connectives for these algebras can be defined in terms of real functions and relations. Hence, these connectives can be seen as the extension functions of a definitional extension over the reals, which is local (cf. Theorem 3.6.2 on page 39). One may, therefore, reduce universal validity problems over the class of $\mathcal{MV}$-algebras, say, to a constraint satisfiability problem over the unit interval $[0, 1]$ (cf. [SSI07a, SSI07b]). This allows one to use solvers for the real numbers to discharge proof tasks over multiple-valued logics. We will give an example of this in Section 6.6.

Data structures. The ubiquitous data structures of arrays and lists satisfy locality conditions as

---
[3]Other examples are Gödel or product algebras.

we saw in Sections 4.2 and 4.8, respectively, if we confine ourselves to appropriate fragments of these theories. This matters in particular if we have satisfiable problems. In order to have a full decision procedure - one that is also able to give the correct answer for satisfiable problems - one has to stay inside of these fragments. H-PILoT automates this task: it will check whether a given problem lies inside the appropriate fragment of the theory of arrays or pointers, respectively, and give the answer "satisfiable" only if this is the case. Otherwise, H-PILoT will give the answer "unknown" and warn the user that the problem did not fall inside the local fragment. (For unsatisfiable problems this never matters. If we can derive a contradiction from the local instances alone, we can derive one from the universal extension axioms a fortiori.)

Reasoning in complex systems. In order to be able to handle complex real life systems which mix many theories, a stratified approach is expedient: we consider *chains of local extensions* (cf. [JSS07]). This feature is supported in H-PILoT. The user simply has to tag extension functions with their respective level in the chain. A reduction is then carried out iteratively by the program. A full-fledged reduction is possible provided the reduced theory clauses are ground at each level of the extension chain. H-PILoT has been part of a vertically integrated tool chain, checking invariants of a transition system modeling a European train controller system (see Section 6.12). The correctness of the model was shown automatically ([FIJSS10]). The underlying track topology was complex and dynamic, making H-PILoT's ability to decide the pointer fragment essential. It was also a great help in practice, due to its ability to provide (readable) counterexamples in the cases where the problem together with the axiomatization was satisfiable. This aided the modeler in finding gaps in the specification.

6.4 Examples

We illustrate the way H-PILoT is implemented and can be used on some examples. First, let us consider monotone functions over some partially ordered set.

Monotone functions. We consider two monotone functions f and g as extension over the base theory of a partial order. That is, our base theory consists of the axioms for reflexivity, transitivity and anti-symmetry.

(1) $\forall x.\ x \leq x$.
(2) $\forall x, y.\ x \leq y \wedge y \leq x \rightarrow x = y$.
(3) $\forall x, y, z.\ x \leq y \wedge y \leq z \rightarrow x \leq z$.

Our extension consists of the two new function symbols together with the clauses expressing monotonicity.

(1) $\forall x, y.\ x \leq y \rightarrow f(x) \leq f(y)$.
(2) $\forall x, y.\ x \leq y \rightarrow g(x) \leq g(y)$.

Let us call our base theory T_0, the extension clauses $\mathcal{K}$ and our proof task G as before. That is, we want to know whether $T_0 \cup \mathcal{K} \cup G \models \bot$.

In this case, we want to show that $c_0 \leq c_1 \leq d_1 \wedge c_2 \leq d_1 \wedge d_2 \leq c_3 \wedge d_2 \leq c_4 \wedge f(d_1) \leq g(d_2)$ implies $f(c_0) \leq g(c_4)$. Expressed as a satisfiability problem, this gives us the following problem G:

$$c_0 \leq c_1 \leq d_1 \wedge c_2 \leq d_1 \wedge d_2 \leq c_3 \wedge d_2 \leq c_4 \wedge f(d_1) \leq g(d_2) \wedge \neg f(c_0) \leq g(c_4).$$

As an input file for H-PILoT this looks as follows (we use "R" as order relation because $\leq$ is reserved).

```
% Two monotone functions over a poset.
% Status: unsatisfiable

Base_functions:={}
Extension_functions:={(f, 1), (g, 1)}
Relations:={(R, 2)}

% R is partial order
Base := (FORALL x).        R[x, x];
        (FORALL x,y,z).    R[x, y], R[y, z] --> R[x, z];
        (FORALL x,y).      R[x, y], R[y, x] --> x = y;

Clauses := (FORALL x,y).   R[x, y] --> R[f(x), f(y)];
           (FORALL x,y).   R[x, y] --> R[g(x), g(y)];

Query := R[c0, c1];
         R[c1, d1];
         R[c2, d1];
         R[d2, c3];
         R[d2, c4];
         R[f(d1), g(d2)];
         NOT(R[f(c0), g(c4)]);
```

In this case we have no function symbols at all in our base theory and two functions symbols f and g of arity 1 in our extension clauses. This is expressed by:

`Base_functions:={}`
`Extension_functions:={(f, 1), (g, 1)}`

We have only one relation in our (base) clauses, viz. 'R'. It has arity 2 of course. This we express by

`Relations:={(R, 2)}`.

For technical reasons, relations require square brackets for their arguments in H-PILoT as seen above. The symbols <=, <, >= and > are reserved for arithmetic over the integers or over the reals. They may be written infix and there are provers (e.g., Yices, CVC) that "understand" arithmetic and orderings. We wouldn't have needed to axiomatize '$\leq$' at all.

However, the above problem is more general. It concerns every partial order not only orderings of numbers. By default, H-PILoT calls SPASS. SPASS has no in-built understanding of orderings and, thus, <= would be just an arbitrary symbol. For clarity we used the letter 'R'.

As for the syntax of clauses, one should note that the syntax of H-PILoT requires that each clause must end with a semicolon, be in prenex normal form and all names meant to be (universal) variables must be explicitly quantified.

> Every name which is not explicitly quantified will be considered a constant!

As we can see in our query.

```
Query := R[c0, c1];
        R[c1, d1];
        R[c2, d1];
        R[d2, c3];
        R[d2, c4];
        R[f(d1), g(d2)];
        NOT(R[f(c0), g(c4)]);
```

Note further that because the background theory, extension theory and the query must all be clauses[4], we need to break up the conjunction in our original query into a set of unit clauses. A non-unit clause may be written as above in a "sorted" manner $\varphi_1, ..., \varphi_n \rightarrow \psi_1, ..., \psi_k$ for $\varphi_1 \wedge ... \wedge \varphi_n \rightarrow \psi_1 \vee ... \vee \psi_k$, i.e., as an implication with the negated atoms of the clause in the antecedent and the (positive) atoms in the consequent (the operator --> is reserved for sorted clauses) or as an arbitrary disjunctions of literals.

The name of the input files for H-PILoT can be freely chosen, although it is customary to have them have the suffix ".loc". Suppose we have put the above problem in a file named mono_for_poset.loc, then we can run H-PILoT by calling

hpilot.opt mono_for_poset.loc

H-PILoT will parse the input file, carry out the reduction and then will hand over the reduced problem to SPASS (using the same name but with the suffix ".dfg"). SPASS terminates quickly with the result that a proof exists

---

SPASS beiseite: Proof found.
Problem: mono_for_poset.dfg
SPASS derived 35 clauses, backtracked 0 clauses and kept 41 clauses.
SPASS allocated 496 KBytes.
SPASS spent   0:00:02.32 on the problem.
                 0:00:00.00 for the input.
                 0:00:00.00 for the FLOTTER CNF translation.
                 0:00:00.00 for inferences.
                 0:00:00.00 for the backtracking.
                 0:00:00.10 for the reduction.

---

[4]In fact, the extension clauses might be more general as we will see later.

meaning that the set of clauses is inconsistent. Just what we wanted to show.

One can see the full reduction process by using the option `-prClauses`. The reduction performed is that of Lemma 2.5.1.

Arrays. For a more complicated example, let us consider an algorithm for inserting an element x into a sorted array a with the bounds l and u. We want to check that the algorithm is correct, i.e., that the updated array a' remains sorted. This could be an invariant being checked in a verification task. There are three different cases. First, x could be smaller than any element in a (equivalently, $x < a[l]$), x could be greater than any element of a ($x > a[u]$) or, thirdly, there is a position p ($l < p \leq u$) such that $a[p-1] < x$ and $x \leq a[p]$. In the first two cases we put x at the first respectively last position of the array. In the third case, we insert x at position p and shift the other elements to the right, i.e., $a'[i+1] = a[i]$ for $i > p$. We have to take care to cover aberrant cases where the array contains only 1 or 2 elements. As input it will look as follows.

```
Clauses :=
  % case 1
  (FORALL i). i = l, x <= a(i) --> a'(i) = x;
  (FORALL i). x <= a(l), l < i, i <= u + _1 --> a'(i) = a(i - _1);

  % case 2
  (FORALL i). i = u, a(i) <= x --> x <= a(l), a'(i + _1) = x;
  (FORALL i). a(u) <= x, l - _1 <= i, i < u
              --> x <= a(l), a'(i + _1) = a(i + _1);

  % case 3
  (FORALL i). x < a(u), l <= i, i < u, a(i) < x, x <= a(i + _1)
              --> a'(i + _1) = x;
  (FORALL i). a(l) < x, x < a(u), l <= i, i < u, x <= a(i),
              x <= a(i + _1) --> a'(i + _1) = a(i);
  (FORALL i). a(l) < x, x < a(u), i = u + _1 --> a'(i) = a(i - _1);
  (FORALL i). a(l) < x, x < a(u), l - _1 <= i, i < u, a(i + _1) < x
              --> a'(i + _1) = a(i + _1);

  (FORALL i,j). l <= i, i <= j, j <= u --> a(i) <= a(j);
```

with the last clause saying that a was sorted at the beginning.

There are several things to note. Most importantly, we now have a two-step extension. First, an array can be simply seen as a partial function. This gives us the first extension $T_0 \subseteq T_1$. T_0 here is the theory of indices (integers, say) which we extend by the function a and the axiom for monotonicity of a. Now we update a, giving us a second extension $T_2 \supseteq T_1$ where our extension clauses $\mathcal{K}_2$ are given by the three cases above.

Of course, we need to make sure that the last extension is also local. This is easy to establish, however, because $\mathcal{K}_2$ is a *definitional extension* or case distinction, (cf. Definition 3.6.2). A definitional extension is one where extension functions f only appear in the form $\varphi_i(\bar{x}) \to f(\bar{x}) =$

$t_i(\bar{x})$ with t_i being a base theory term and the φ_i are mutually exclusive base theory clauses. This is the reason that we have written $\forall i.i = l, x \leq a(i) \to a'(i) = x$ instead of the shorter $x \leq a(l) \to a'(l) = x$: to ensure that the antecedents of the clauses are all mutually exclusive. Now we know that we are dealing with a definitional and therefore local extension. (Remember that for assessing if $T_2 \supseteq T_1$ is a local extension, T_1 is our base theory, that T_1 is itself an extension is of no moment.)

We need to tell the program that we are dealing with a chain of extensions instead of a single one. We do this by the simple expedient of declaring to which level of the chain an extension function belongs, like thus $(f, arity, level)$.

In our example that would be

`Extension_functions:={(a', 1, 2), (a, 1, 1)}`

The program will now automatically determine the level of each extension clause. In our example, an extension clause will have level 2 if and only if a' occurs in it and level 1 otherwise (level 0 means base clause).

Also note that numerals (names for integers) must be preceded by an underscore such as `_1` and that $+$ and $-$ may be written infix for readability; $(=, +, -, *, /)$ are the only functions for which this is allowed[5].

Our declarations, therefore should look like this.

```
Base_functions:={(+,2), (-, 2)}
Extension_functions:={(a', 1, 2), (a, 1, 1)}
Relations:={(<=, 2), (<, 2)}
```

All that is left to do now is add our query – the negation of

$$\forall i, j.\, l \leq i \leq j \leq u \to a'(i) \leq a'(j)$$

– to the mix and hand it over. The entire file looks like this.

```
% ai.loc
% Arrays for definitional extensions;

Base_functions:={(+,2), (-, 2)}
Extension_functions:={(a', 1, 2), (a, 1, 1)}
Relations:={(<=, 2), (<, 2)}

% K
Clauses :=
  % case 1
  (FORALL i). i = 1, x <= a(i) --> a'(i) = x;
  (FORALL i). x <= a(1), 1 < i, i <= u + _1 --> a'(i) = a(i - _1);
```

---

[5]When using SPASS, they may also be written infix but nevertheless they are just free functions for SPASS.

```
% case 2
(FORALL i). i = u, a(i) <= x --> x <= a(1), a'(i + _1) = x;
(FORALL i). a(u) <= x, 1 - _1 <= i, i < u
                 --> x <= a(1), a'(i + _1) = a(i + _1);

% case 3
(FORALL i). x < a(u), 1 <= i, i < u, a(i) < x, x <= a(i + _1)
                 --> a'(i + _1) = x;
(FORALL i). a(1) < x, x < a(u), 1 <= i, i < u, x <= a(i),
                 x <= a(i + _1) --> a'(i + _1) = a(i);
(FORALL i). a(1) < x, x < a(u), i = u + _1 --> a'(i) = a(i - _1);
(FORALL i). a(1) < x, x < a(u), 1 - _1 <= i, i < u, a(i + _1) < x
                 --> a'(i + _1) = a(i + _1);

(FORALL i,j). 1 <= i, i <= j, j <= u --> a(i) <= a(j);

Query := 1 <= m;
         m <= n;
         n <= u + _1;
         NOT( a'(m) <= a'(n) );
```

We do not need to declare a base theory here because we will be using Yices and Yices already "knows" integer arithmetic. We call H-PILoT thus.

`hpilot.opt -yices -preprocess ai.loc`

H-PILoT will produce a reduction, put it in a file name *ai.ys* and pass it over to Yices which will say unsat or sat. A note on the flag -preprocess: Establishing that some extension is local, presupposes that the extension clauses $\mathcal{K}$ be *flat* and *linear*. Recall that flatness simply means that we have no nesting of extension functions and linearity means first, that we have no variable occurring twice in any extension term and, further, that if any variable occurs in two extension terms, the terms are the same. In this example, we have non-flat clauses such as

`(FORALL i). i = u, a(i) <= x --> x <= a(1), a'(i + _1) = x;`

We rectify matters by a *flattening* operation - rewriting the above clause to

```
(FORALL i,j). j = i + _1, i = u, a(i) <= x -->
                 x <= a(1), a'(j) = x;
```

This will not affect consistency of any query w.r.t. $\mathcal{K}$ (Corollary 2.3.3). It hardly improves readability however. Therefore the program will do it for you if you tell it to -preprocess the input.

6.5 Arrays

We pick up the example from Section 4.3 to show how it can be dealt with by H-PILoT. Recall that for the *array property fragment* the following syntactical restrictions were imposed.

(1) An *index guard* is a positive Boolean combination of atoms of the form $t \leq u$ or $t = u$ where t and u are either a variable or a ground term of linear arithmetic.

(2) A universal formula of the form $(\forall \bar{x})(\varphi_I(\bar{x}) \to \varphi_V(\bar{x}))$ is an *array property* if it is flat, if φ_I is an index guard and if all occurrences of the variables are shielded by extension functions in φ_V, i.e., variables x only occur as direct array reads $a[x]$ in φ_V.

In this section we will only consider extensions by clauses of the above form. Our base theory will always be linear integer arithmetic (Presburger). We will have to use minimal local in order to be able to handle this fragment.
In H-PILoT minimal locality is also implemented. Call

```
hpilot.opt -arrays k.loc
```

to use this feature.

Let us again consider the example of inserting into a sorted array a from Section 4.3. Arrays are modeled as free functions and array updates are dealt with by introducing new array names. In this fashion, Let d be just like a but for position k which is w and let e be just like d except maybe at position l where we have written x and similarly for c,b and a. Our set $\mathcal{K}$ of extension clauses looks as follows.

$$\left. \begin{array}{ll} (\forall i,j)(0 \leq i \leq j \leq n-1 \to c[i] \leq c[j]), & (1) \\ (\forall i,j)(0 \leq i \leq j \leq n-1 \to e[i] \leq e[j]), & (2) \\ (\forall i)(i \neq l \to b[i] = c[i]), & (3) \\ (\forall i)(i \neq k \to a[i] = b[i]), & (4) \\ (\forall i)(i \neq l \to d[i] = e[i]), & (5) \\ (\forall i)(i \neq k \to a[i] = d[i]). & (6) \end{array} \right\} \mathcal{K}$$

Our query (with additional constraints) is

$$\left. \begin{array}{l} w < x < y < z, \\ 0 < k < l < n, \\ k + 3 < l, \\ c[l] = x, \\ b[k] = w, \\ e[l] = z, \\ d[k] = y. \end{array} \right\} G$$

The input file looks just like this. (The operators are written prefix here which requires the names plus and minus, because + and - are reserved for infix.)

```
% Arrays for minimal locality
Base_functions:={(plus,2), (minus, 2)}
Extension_functions:={(a, 1), (b, 1), (c, 1), (d, 1), (e, 1)}
Relations:={(<=, 2)}

% K
Clauses := (FORALL i,j). _0 <= i, i <= j,
                        j <= minus(n, _1) --> c(i) <= c(j);
           (FORALL i,j). _0 <= i, i <= j,
                        j <= minus(n, _1) --> e(i) <= e(j);
           (FORALL i).  --> i=1, b(i) =  c(i);
           (FORALL i).  --> i=k, a(i) =  b(i);
           (FORALL i).  --> i=1, d(i) =  e(i);
           (FORALL i).  --> i=k, a(i) =  d(i);


Query := plus(w, _1)  <= x;
         plus(x, _1)  <= y;
         plus(y, _1)  <= z;
         plus(_0, _1) <= k;
         plus(k, _1)  <= l;
         plus(l, _1)  <= n;
         plus(k, _3)  <= l;
         c(1) = x;
         b(k) = w;
         e(1) = z;
         d(k) = y;
```

$\mathcal{K}$ does not yet fulfill the syntactic requirements (index guards must be positive!). We must rewrite $\mathcal{K}$ in a suitable fashion. We change an expression $i \neq l$ where i is the (universally quantified) variable to $i \leq l - 1 \lor l + 1 \leq i$. We have to rewrite it like this because the universally quantified variable i must appear unshielded in the index guard. This gives us the following set of clauses.

H-PILoT performs this and the following rewrite steps automatically to spare the user this tedious labor.

$$
\left.\begin{array}{ll}
(\forall i,j)(0 \leq i \leq j \leq n-1 \rightarrow c[i] \leq c[j]), & (1) \\
(\forall i,j)(0 \leq i \leq j \leq n-1 \rightarrow e[i] \leq e[j]), & (2) \\
(\forall i)(i \leq l-1 \rightarrow b[i] = c[i]), & (3) \\
(\forall i)(l+1 \leq i \rightarrow b[i] = c[i]), & (4) \\
(\forall i)(i \leq k-1 \rightarrow a[i] = b[i]), & (5) \\
(\forall i)(k+1 \leq i \rightarrow a[i] = b[i]), & (6) \\
(\forall i)(i \leq l-1 \rightarrow d[i] = e[i]), & (7) \\
(\forall i)(l+1 \leq i \rightarrow d[i] = e[i]), & (8) \\
(\forall i)(i \leq k-1 \rightarrow a[i] = d[i]), & (9) \\
(\forall i)(k+1 \leq i \rightarrow a[i] = d[i]). & (10)
\end{array}\right\} \mathcal{K}'
$$

Also, $\mathcal{K}$ is not linear, this must also be taken care of. H-PILoT will carry out all these necessary rewrite steps for the user. He can simply input the above file to deal with this example.

Instead of using a cluster of free functions to specify array updates, H-PILoT allows the user to *model array updates directly* by using a "write" function. For example, use write(a, i, x) to denote a new array which is just like a except (possibly) at position i where the value of the new array is set to x. In this way we could have specified our problem above as

```
% Arrays for minimal locality with 'write'function.
Base_functions:={(+, 2), (-, 2)}
Extension_functions:={(a, 1)}
Relations:={(<=, 2)}

% K
Clauses :=
  (FORALL i,j). _0 <= i, i <= j, j <= n - _1 -->
     write(write(a,k,w), l, x)(i) <= write(write(a,k,w), l, x)(j);

  (FORALL i,j). _0 <= i, i <= j, j <= n - _1 -->
     write(write(a,k,y), l, z)(i) <= write(write(a,k,y), l, z)(j);

Query := w + _1  <= x;
         x + _1  <= y;
         y + _1  <= z;
         _0 + _1 <= k;
         k + _1  <= l;
         l + _1  <= n;
         k + _3  <= l;
```

As above, H-PILoT will also automatically split on disequations in the antecedent. Note also that since we assume that indices of arrays are integers, it makes no difference whether we write `w + _1` or `plus(w, _1)` in the input file. Linear integer arithmetic will be used (Yices is default).

6.6 Global Constraints[6]

Sometimes we want to restrict the domain of the problem, e.g., we want to consider natural numbers instead of integers or we are interested in a real interval $[a,b]$ only. Yices and CVC support the definition of subtypes. When using one of these it is possible to state a global constraint on the domain of the models in the preamble like thus.

```
Interval := 0 <= x <= 1;
```

This will restrict the domain of the models of the theory to the unit interval $[0,1]$. It is equivalent to adding the antecedent $0 \leq x \wedge x \leq 1$, for every variable x, to each formula in the clauses and the query.

The bounds of the interval can also be exclusive or mixed as in

```
Interval := 0 < x <= 1;
```

or one-sided as in

```
Interval := 2 <= x;
```

Consider again the example from Section 3.6.1, concerning multiple-valued logic. The class $\mathcal{MV}$ of all MV-algebras is the quasi-variety generated by the real unit interval $[0,1]$ with the Łukasiewicz connectives $\{\vee, \wedge, \circ, \Rightarrow\}$, i.e., the algebra $[0,1]_L = ([0,1], \vee, \wedge, \circ, \Rightarrow)$. Further the Łukasiewicz connectives can be defined in terms of the real functions '$+, -$' and the relation '$\leq$', giving us a local extension over the real unit interval.

Therefore, the following are equivalent:

(1) $\mathcal{MV} \models \forall \overline{x} \bigwedge_{i=1}^{n} s_i(\overline{x}) = t_i(\overline{x}) \rightarrow s(\overline{x}) = t(\overline{x})$

(2) $[0,1]_L \models \forall \overline{x} \bigwedge_{i=1}^{n} s_i(\overline{x}) = t_i(\overline{x}) \rightarrow s(\overline{x}) = t(\overline{x})$

(3) $T_0 \cup \mathsf{Def}_L \wedge \bigwedge_{i=1}^{n} s_i(\overline{c}) = t_i(\overline{c}) \wedge s(\overline{c}) \neq t(\overline{c}) \models \perp$,

where T_0 consists of the real unit interval $[0,1]$ with the operations $+, -$ and predicate symbol $\leq$.

For instance, we might want to establish that linearity $x \Rightarrow y. \vee .y \Rightarrow x = 1$ follows from the axioms. As an input file for H-PILoT it looks like this.

```
% file mv1.loc
% Example for MV-algebras
% The Lukasiewicz connectives can be defined
% in terms of the (real) connectives +,-,<=
```

---

[6]This feature is not supported for Z3.

```
Base_functions:={(+, 2), (-, 2)}
Extension_functions:={(V, 1), (M, 1), (o, 1), (r, 1)}
Relations:={(<=, 2), (<, 2), (>, 2), (>=, 2)}

Interval := 0 <= x <= 1;

% K
Clauses := % definition of \/
           (FORALL x,y). x <= y --> V(x, y) = y;
           (FORALL x,y). x >  y --> V(x, y) = x;

           % definition of /\
           (FORALL x,y). x <= y --> M(x, y) = x;
           (FORALL x,y). x >  y --> M(x, y) = y;

           % definition of o
           (FORALL x,y). x + y <  _1 --> o(x, y) = _0;
           (FORALL x,y). x + y >= _1 --> o(x, y) = (x + y) - _1;

           % definition of =>
           (FORALL x,y). x <= y --> r(x, y) = _1;
           (FORALL x,y). x >  y --> r(x, y) = (_1 - x) + y;

Query := % linearity: x => y . \/ . y => x = 1
         NOT(V(r(a, b), r(b, a)) = _1);
```

6.7 Types

In default mode using SPASS, H-PILoT hands over a set of general first-order formulas without types. However, H-PILoT also provides support for the standard types int, real, bool and for free types. When using CVC or Yices the default type is int, for Redlog it is real. The default type does not need to be specified in the input file. One can also use the -real flag to set the default type to real for Yices and CVC.

Free types are specified as free#i, $i = 1, 2..$ or simply as free if there is only one free type. When using free types the flag -freeType must be set. Only Yices and CVC are able to handle free types (Yices is default when the flag is set). When using mixed type in one input file, the types of the functions and the constants need to be declared. If the domain of a function is the same as the range it is enough to specify the domain as in

   $(foo, arity, level, domainType)$

if they differ say

   $(foo, arity, level, domainType, rangeType)$.

Constants are simply declared as

($name, type$).

We offer the following example taken from [SS06b].

```
% Pointers
% status unsatisfiable
Base_functions:={(+,2), (-, 2)}
Extension_functions:={(next, 1, 1, free#1), (prev, 1, 1, free#1),
                      (priority, 1, 1, free#1, real),
                      (state, 1, 1, free#1, free#2)}
Relations:={(>=, 2)}
Constants:={(null, free#1), (eps, real), (a, free#1), (b, free#1),
            (RUN, free#2), (WAIT, free#2), (IDLE, free#2)}

% K
Clauses :=
  (FORALL x). OR(state(x) = RUN, state(x) = WAIT, state(x) = IDLE);
  % prev and next are inverse
  (FORALL p). OR(p = null, prev(next(p)) = null, prev(next(p)) = p);
  (FORALL p). --> p = null, next(prev(p)) = null, next(prev(p)) = p;
  (FORALL p, q). next(q) = next(p) --> p = null, q = null, p = q;
  (FORALL p, q). prev(q) = prev(p) --> p = null, q = null, p = q;
  (FORALL p). --> p = null, next(p) = null, state(p) = IDLE,
                  state(next(p)) = IDLE, state(p) = state(next(p));
  (FORALL p). OR(p = null, next(p) = null, NOT(state(p) = RUN),
                 priority(p) >= priority(next(p)));


Query := NOT(eps = _5);
         NOT(eps = _6);
         priority(a) = _5;
         priority(b) = _6;
         a = prev(b);
         state(a) = RUN;
         NOT(next(a) = null);
         NOT(a = null);
         NOT(b = null);
```

6.8 Pointers

The local fragment of the theory of pointers of Section 4.8 is also implemented in H-PILoT. We consider pointer problems over a two-typed language. One of which is the type pointer and the other is some scalar type. The scalar type can be concrete like real, say, or kept abstract in which case it is written as scalar. There are two function types involving pointers, viz. pointer →

`pointer` and `pointer` → *scalar*, where *scalar* is either a concrete scalar type (e.g., `real`) or an abstract scalar type. The axioms considered are all of the form

$$\forall \bar{p}. \; \mathcal{E} \vee \mathcal{C}$$

where $\bar{p}$ is a set of pointer variables containing all the pointer variables occurring in $\mathcal{E} \vee \mathcal{C}$, $\mathcal{E}$ contains disjunctions of pointer equalities and $\mathcal{C}$ is a disjunction of scalar constraints (i.e., literals of scalar type). $\mathcal{E} \vee \mathcal{C}$ may also contain free variables of scalar type or, equivalently, free scalar constants.

As in Section 4.8, we demand that pointer terms appearing below a function should not be null in order to rule out null pointer errors. That is, for all terms $f_1(f_2(\ldots f_n(p)))$, $i = 1, .., n$, occurring in the axiom, the axiom also contains the disjunction $p = \mathsf{null} \vee f_n(p) = \mathsf{null} \vee \cdots \vee f_2(\ldots f_n(p)) = \mathsf{null}$.

Pointer/scalar formulas complying with this restriction were called *nullable*. The locality result of Theorem 4.8.2 allows the integration of pointer reasoning with the above features into H-PILoT. The example given by Necula and McPeak ([MN05]), quoted in Section 4.8, looks like this as input for H-PILoT. (We have added an appropriate proof task.)

```
Base_functions:={(+,2), (-, 2)}
Extension_functions:={(next, 1, 1, pointer),
                      (prev, 1, 1, pointer),
                      (priority, 1, 1, pointer, real)}
Relations:={(>=, 2)}
Constants:={(a, pointer), (b, pointer)}

Clauses :=
    (FORALL p). prev(next(p)) = p;
    (FORALL p). --> next(prev(p)) = p;
    (FORALL p). --> q = null, priority(p) >= priority(next(p));

Query := priority(a) = _5;
         priority(b) = _6;
         a = prev(b);
         NOT(a = null);
         NOT(b = null);
```

H-PILoT can be called without any parameters because the keyword `pointer` is present. This will trigger H-PILoT's pointer mode so that it will add all the nullable terms to the axioms and use the specific (stable) locality required.

Because the scalar type is concrete here (`real`), H-PILoT will use Yices as the back-end prover (its default for arithmetic). If we want to leave the scalar type abstract we could write something like

```
%psiPointers.scalar.loc
Base_functions:={}
Extension_functions:={(next, 1, 1, pointer),
                      (prev, 1, 1, pointer),
                      (priority, 1, 1, pointer, scalar)}
Relations:={}
Constants:={(a, pointer), (b, pointer), (c5, scalar), (c6, scalar)}

Clauses := (FORALL p). prev(next(p)) = p;
           (FORALL p). next(prev(p)) = p;
           (FORALL p). NOT(priority(p) = priority(next(p)));


Query := priority(a) = c5;
         priority(b) = c6;
         a = prev(b);
         c5 = c6;
         NOT(a = null);
         NOT(b = null);
```

We again can simply type

```
hpilot.opt -preprocess psiPointers.scalar.loc
```

without any parameters. H-PILoT will recognize this as a pointer problem and use Yices as default, this time because of the free type `scalar`. There can also be more than one pointer type and pointer extensions can be fused with other types of extensions in a hierarchy. However, due to the different types of locality that need to be employed, the user must specify which levels are pointer extensions. He does this by using the keyword `Stable`.

For example, the header of a more complicated verification task which mixes different pointer types might look like this.

```
Base_functions:={(-, 2), (+, 2)}
Extension_functions:=
   { % level 4
     (next',1,4, pointer#2,pointer#2), (pos',1,4,pointer#2,real)
     % level 3
     (next,1,3,pointer#2,pointer#2), (pos,1,3,pointer#2,real),
     (spd,1,3,pointer#2,real), (segm,1,3,pointer#2,pointer#1),
     % level 2
     (bd,1,2,real,real),
     % level 1
     (lmax,1,1,pointer#1,real), (length,1,1,pointer#1,real),
     (nexts,1,1,pointer#1,pointer#1), (alloc,1,1,pointer#1,int)}
```

```
Relations :={(<=, 2), (>=, 2), (>, 2), (<, 2)}

Constants:= {(t3,pointer#2), (t2,pointer#2), (t1,pointer#2),
             (d,real), (State0,int), (s,pointer#1), (State1,int)}

Stable := 1, 3;
```

Note that the type `pointer#2` must be declared higher than `pointer#1` because `pointer#2` refers to `pointer#1` but not vice versa.

6.9 Extended Locality

H-PILoT is also able to handle extensions with augmented clauses as in Section 4.6. For some applications we would like to allow more complicated extension clauses, say we want them to be inductive ($\forall\exists$) instead of universal. Consider the following example, taken from [IJSS08] and introduced as Example 3.6.1.

Suppose there is a parametric number m of processes. The priorities associated with the processes (non-negative real numbers) are stored in an array p. The states of the process – enabled (1) or disabled (0) – are stored in an array a. At each step only the process with maximal priority is enabled, its priority is set to x and the priorities of the waiting processes are increased by y. This can be expressed by the following set of axioms which we denote as $\mathsf{Update}(p, p', a, a')$.

$\forall i (1 \leq i \leq m \wedge (\forall j (1 \leq j \leq m \wedge j \neq i \rightarrow p(i) > p(j))) \rightarrow a'(i) = 1)$
$\forall i (1 \leq i \leq m \wedge (\forall j (1 \leq j \leq m \wedge j \neq i \rightarrow p(i) > p(j))) \rightarrow p'(i) = x)$
$\forall i (1 \leq i \leq m \wedge \neg(\forall j (1 \leq j \leq m \wedge j \neq i \rightarrow p(i) > p(j))) \rightarrow a'(i) = 0)$
$\forall i (1 \leq i \leq m \wedge \neg(\forall j (1 \leq j \leq m \wedge j \neq i \rightarrow p(i) > p(j))) \rightarrow p'(i) = p(i) + y)$,

where x and y are considered to be parameters. We may need to check whether, given that at the beginning the priority list is injective, i.e., formula $(\mathsf{Inj})(p)$ holds:

$(\mathsf{Inj})(p) \quad \forall i, j (1 \leq i \leq m \wedge 1 \leq j \leq m \wedge i \neq j \rightarrow p(i) \neq p(j))$,

then it remains injective after the update, i.e., check whether

$(\mathsf{Inj})(p) \wedge \mathsf{Update}(p, p', a, a') \wedge (1 \leq c \leq m \wedge 1 \leq d \leq m \wedge c \neq d \wedge p'(c) = p'(d)) \models \bot$.

We need to deal with alternations of quantifiers in the extension. The extension formulas $\mathcal{K}$ are augmented clauses of the form

$$\forall x_1, ..., x_n. (\Phi(x_1, \ldots, x_n) \vee C(x_1, \ldots, x_n)),$$

where $\Phi(x_1, \ldots, x_n)$ is an *arbitrary first-order formula* in the base signature with free variables $x_1, \ldots, x_n$ and $C(x_1, \ldots, x_n)$ is a *clause* in the extended signature. As input for H-PILoT, extended clauses may be either written as $\forall \bar{x}. (\Phi(\bar{x}) \vee C(\bar{x}))$ or as $\forall \bar{x}. (\Phi(\bar{x}) \rightarrow C'(\bar{x}))$. The input file for H-PILoT looks as follows.

```
% Updating of priorities of processes
% File update_AE.loc
Base_functions:={(+,2), (-, 2)}
Extension_functions:={(a', 1, 2, bool), (a, 1, 1, bool),
                      (p', 1, 2, real), (p, 1, 1, real)}
Relations:={(<=, 2), (<, 2), (>, 2)}
Constants:={(x, real), (y, real)}

% K
Clauses :=
  (FORALL i). _1 <= i, i <= m --> _0 <= p(i);
  (FORALL i). { AND(_1 <= i, i <= m,
    (FORALL j). (AND(_1 <= j, j <= m, NOT(j = i))
                                  --> p(i) > p(j)))}
                                  --> a'(i) = _1;

  (FORALL i). { AND(_1 <= i, i <= m,
    (FORALL j). (AND(_1 <= j, j <= m, NOT(j = i))
                                  --> p(i) > p(j)))}
                                  --> p'(i) = x;
  (FORALL i). { AND(_1 <= i, i <= m,
    NOT((FORALL j,i).(AND(_1 <= j, j <= m, NOT(j = i))
                                  --> p(i) > p(j))))}
                                  --> a'(i) = _0;
  (FORALL i). { AND(_1 <= i, i <= m,
    NOT((FORALL j).(AND(_1 <= j, j <= m, NOT(j = i))
                                  --> p(i) > p(j))))}
                                  --> p'(i) = p(i) + y;

  (FORALL i,j). _1 <= i, i <= m, _1 <= j, j <= m, p(i) = p(j)
                                  --> i = j;

Query := _1 <= c;
         c <= m;
         _1 <= d;
         d <= m;
         x <= _0;
         y > _0;
         NOT(c=d);
         p'(c) = p'(d);
```

The curly braces '{', '}' are required to demarcate the beginning and the end of the base formula Φ.

6.10 Clausification

H-PILoT also provides a clausifier for ease of use. First-order formulas can be given as input and H-PILoT will translate them into clausal normal form (CNF). The CNF-translator does not provide the full functionality of FLOTTER. It uses structural formula renaming ([PG86]) and standard Skolemization, not the more exotic variants thereof (cf. [NW01]). Nevertheless, it should be quite powerful enough for most applications. As a simple example consider the following.

```
% cnf.fol
Base_functions:={(delta, 2), (abs, 1), (-, 2)}
Extension_functions:={(f, 1)}
Relations:={}


Formulas :=
    (FORALL eps, a, x). (_0 < eps -->
            AND( _0 < delta(eps, a),
                    (abs(x - a) < delta(eps, a)
                        --> abs(f(x) - f(a)) < eps)));

Query :=
```

H-PILoT will clausify the **Formulas** for us. To see the output let us use

> hpilot.opt -preprocess -prClauses cnf.fol

We will see an output like

```
!- Adding formula:
    (FORALL eps, a, x).
        (_0 < eps -->
            AND( _0 < delta(eps, a), (abs(-(x, a)) < delta(eps, a)
                --> abs(-(f(x), f(a))) < eps)))
!- add_formulas
!- We have 1 levels.
!- done
!- Our base theory is:
!- empty.
!- Clausifying formulas...
!- (FORALL z_1, z_3). OR( _0 < delta(z_1, z_3), NOT(_0 < z_1))
!- (FORALL z_1, z_2, z_3).
                OR( NOT(abs(-(z_2, z_3)) < delta(z_1, z_3)),
                    abs(-(f(z_2), f(z_3))) < z_1, NOT(_0 < z_1))
!- Yielding 2 new clauses:
!- [z_1, z_2, z_3] abs(-(z_2, z_3)) < delta(z_1, z_3), _0 < z_1
```

```
                     ---> abs(-(f(z_2), f(z_3))) < z_1
!- [z_1, z_3] _0 < z_1 ---> _0 < delta(z_1, z_3)
!- After rewriting we have as clauses K:
!- [z_1, z_2, z_3] abs(-(z_2, z_3)) < delta(z_1, z_3), _0 < z_1
                     ---> abs(-(f(z_2), f(z_3))) < z_1
!- [z_1, z_3] _0 < z_1 ---> _0 < delta(z_1, z_3)
```

telling us that the above formula resulted in two new clauses (in addition to those given outright under Clauses, viz.

$$\forall z_1, z_3.\ 0 < delta(z_1, z_3) \vee \neg(0 < z_1)$$

and

$$\forall z_1, z_2, z_3.\ \neg(abs(z_2 - z_3) < delta(z_1, z_3)) \vee abs(f(z_2) - f(z_3)) < z_1 \vee \neg(0 < z_1).$$

In this case no ground clause resulted and H-PILoT stops.

6.11 System Evaluation

We have used H-PILoT on a variety of local extensions and on chains of local extensions. An overview of the tests we made is given below. For these tests, we have used Yices as the back-end solver for H-PILoT. We distinguish between satisfiable and unsatisfiable problems.

Unsatisfiable Problems. For simple unsatisfiable problems, there hardly is any difference in run-time whether one uses H-PILoT or an SMT-solver directly. This is due to the fact that a good SMT-solver uses the heuristic of trying out all the occurring ground terms as instantiations of universal quantifiers. For local extensions this is always sufficient to derive a contradiction.

When we consider chains of extensions the picture changes dramatically. On one test example – the array insertion of Section 6.4 which used a chain of two local extensions – Yices performed considerably slower than H-PILoT: The original problem took Yices over 5 minutes to solve. The hierarchical reduction yielded 113 clauses of the background theory (integers) which were proved to be unsatisfiable by Yices in a mere 0.07s.

Satisfiable Problems. For satisfiable problems over local theory extensions, H-PILoT always provides the right answer. In local extensions, H-PILoT is a decision procedure whereas completeness of other SMT-solvers is not guaranteed. In the test runs, Yices either ran out of memory or took more than 6 hours when given any of the unreduced problems. This even was the case for small problems, e.g., problems over the reals with less than ten clauses. With H-PILoT as a front end, Yices solved all the satisfiable problems in less than a second with the single exception of monotone functions over posets/distributive lattices.

Test runs for H-PILoT

We analyzed the following examples. The satisfiable variant of a problem carries the suffix ".sat".

array insert. Insertion of an element into a sorted integer array. This is the example from Section 6.4. Arrays are definitional extensions here.

array insert (∃). Insertion of an element into a sorted integer array. Arrays are definitional extensions here. Alternate version with (implicit) existential quantifier.

array insert (linear). Linear version of array insert.

array insert real. Like array insert but with an array of reals.

array insert real (linear). Linear version of array insert real.

update process priorities (∀∃). Updating of priorities of processes. This is the example from Section 6.9. We have an ∀∃-clause.

list1. Made-up example of integer lists. Some arithmetic is required

chain1. Simple test for chains of extensions (plus transitivity).

chain2. Simple test for chains of extensions (plus transitivity and arithmetic).

double array insert. A sorted array is updated twice. This is our running example from the Sections 4.3 and 6.5. Inside the array property fragment.

mono. Two monotone functions over integers/reals for SMT solver.

mono for distributive lattices.R. Two monotone functions over a distributive lattice. The axioms for a distributive lattice are stated together with the definition of a relation R: $R(x,y) :\Leftrightarrow x \wedge y = x$. Monotonicity of f (respectively of g) is given in terms of R: $R(x,y) \rightarrow R(f(x), f(y))$. Flag `-freeType` must be used.

mono for distributive lattices. Same as mono for distributive lattices.R except that no relation R is defined. Monotonicity of the two functions f, g is directly given: $x \wedge y = x \rightarrow f(x) \wedge f(y) = f(x)$. (Much harder than defining R.) Flag `-freeType` must be used.

mono for poset. Two monotone functions over a poset with poset axioms as in Section 6.4. Same as mono, except the order is modeled by a relation R.

mono for total order. Same as mono except linearity is an axiom. This makes no difference unless SPASS is used.

own. Simple test for monotone function.

mvLogic/mv1. The example for MV-algebras from Section 6.6. The Łukasiewicz connectives can be defined in terms of the (real) operations $+, -, \leq$. Linearity is deducible from axioms.

mvLogic/mv2. Example for MV-algebras. The Łukasiewicz connectives can be defined in terms of $+, -, \leq$. The BL axiom is deducible.

mvLogic/bl1. Example for MV-algebras with BL axiom (redundantly) included. The Łukasiewicz connectives can be defined in terms of $+, -, \leq$.

mvLogic/example_6.1. Example for MV-algebras with monotone and bounded function. The Łukasiewicz connectives can be defined in terms of $+, -, \leq$.

RBC_simple. Example with train controller.

RBC_variable2. Example with train controller.

Test results

The running times are given in User + sys times (in s). Run on an Intel Xeon 3 GHz, 512 kB cache; median of 100 runs (entries marked with [1]: 10 runs; marked with [2]: 3 runs). The third column lists the number of clauses produced; "unknown" means Yices answer was unknown, "out. mem." means out of memory and time out was set at 6h. Yices version 1.0.19 was used.

The answer "unknown*" for the satisfiable examples with monotone functions over distributive lattices/posets (H-PILoT followed by Yices) is due to the fact that Yices cannot handle the universal axioms of distributive lattices/posets. A translation of such problems to SAT provides a decision procedure (cf. [SS05] and also [SS03]).

Name	status	#cl.	H-PILoT + yices	H-PILoT + yices stop at $\mathcal{K}[G]$	yices
array insert (implicit ∃)	Unsat	310	0.29	0.06	0.36
array insert (implicit ∃).sat	Sat	196	0.13	0.04	time out
array insert	Unsat	113	0.07	0.03	318.22[1]
array insert (linear version)	Unsat	113	0.07	0.03	7970.53[2]
array insert.sat	Sat	111	0.07	0.03	time out
array insert real	Unsat	113	0.07	0.03	360.00[1]
array insert real (linear)	Unsat	113	0.07	0.03	7930.00[2]
array insert real.sat	Sat	111	0.07	0.03	time out
update process priorities	Unsat	45	0.02	0.02	0.03
update process priorities.sat	Sat	37	0.02	0.02	unknown
list1	Unsat	18	0.02	0.01	0.02
list1.sat	Sat	16	0.02	0.01	unknown
chain1	Unsat	22	0.01	0.01	0.02
chain2	Unsat	46	0.02	0.02	0.02
mono	Unsat	20	0.01	0.01	0.01
mono.sat	Sat	20	0.01	0.01	unknown
mono for distributive lattices.R	Unsat	27	0.22	0.06	0.03
mono for distributive lattices.R.sat	Sat	26	unknown*	unknown*	unknown
mono for distributive lattices	Unsat	17	0.01	0.01	0.02
mono for distributive lattices.sat	Sat	17	0.01	0.01	unknown
mono for poset	Unsat	20	0.02	0.02	0.02
mono for poset.sat	Sat	19	unknown*	unknown*	unknown
mono for total order	Unsat	20	0.02	0.02	0.02
own	Unsat	16	0.01	0.01	0.01
mvLogic/mv1	Unsat	10	0.01	0.01	0.02
mvLogic/mv1.sat	Sat	8	0.01	0.01	unknown
mvLogic/mv2	Unsat	8	0.01	0.01	0.06
mvLogic/bl1	Unsat	22	0.02	0.01	0.03
mvLogic/example_6.1	Unsat	10	0.01	0.01	0.03
mvLogic/example_6.1.sat	Sat	10	0.01	0.01	unknown
RBC_simple	Unsat	42	0.03	0.02	0.03
double array insert	Unsat	791	1.16	0.20	0.07
double array insert	Sat	790	1.10	0.20	unknown
RBC_simple.sat	Sat	40	0.03	0.02	out. mem.
RBC_variable2	Unsat	137	0.08	0.04	0.04
RBC_variable2.sat	Sat	136	0.08	0.04	out. mem.

6.12 A Case Study

Recently ([FIJSS10]), H-PILoT's ability to decide the pointer fragment of Section 6.8 has been used in the verification of real-time systems which exhibit rich and dynamic data structures. There H-PILoT was part of a tool chain employed for the verification of a case study from the European Train Control System standard. The tool chain ranged from high level specification to the automatic verification of proof obligations which was done by H-PILoT (with Yices).

For the verification of real-life examples with complex topologies such as this one, efficient verification techniques are of the essence. The verification problem considered is expressed as a satisfiability problems for universally quantified formulas, hence cannot be solved by SMT-solvers alone. The experimental results show H-PILoT to be a very efficient tool for the discharging of all the proof tasks of the case study. The full type system implemented in H-PILoT increased the efficiency considerably by blocking unnecessary instantiations. The tool chain used in the case study range from a specification language for real-time systems called COD to the translation of such a specification via phase-event automata (Syspect/PEA) to transition constraint systems (TCS) which can then be exported to H-PILoT.

We checked the invariant for every transition in two parts yielding 92 proof obligations. Additional tests were used to ensure that the specifications are consistent. The overall time to verify all transition updates with Yices and H-PILoT in the unsatisfiable case (when the invariant is correct) does not differ much. However, there is one example (the speed update) where H-PILoT was 5 times faster than Yices on its own. In the case where a set of conditions was not inductive over all transitions, H-PILoT was able to provide a model after 8s whereas Yices detected unsatisfiability for 17 problems, returned "unknown" for 28 and timed out once.

During the development of the case study H-PILoT ability to provide (readable) counterexamples was useful in two ways. First, this helped the modelers to fine-tune the specification by identifying additional constraints which were needed but not included at first. Second, this helped us finding the correct transition invariants by providing models for satisfiable sets of clauses which allowed us to refine the candidate formula.

6.13 Parameters of H-PILoT

H-PILoT has several input parameters controlling its behavior. They can be listed by calling `hpilot.opt -help`.

-min	Use minimal Locality. This is only relevant for the array property fragment right now.
-prClauses	Produce output: print all the clauses calculated and used.
-noProver	Do not hand over to prover, just produce output.
-arith	Use arithmetic. 'plus','+','-' etc. are predefined. Numerals can be used, e.g., '_3'.
-yices	Use Yices as background solver: 'plus', '+' etc. are predefined as are the order relations $\leq, \geq, <, >$. Numbers can also be given in the input. Numbers are integers by default (use '-real' for real numbers).
-cvc	Use CVC as background solver. Arithmetic is predefined as with '-yices'.
-z3	Use Z3 as background solver. Arithmetic is predefined as with '-yices'.
-flatten	Flatten clauses first.
-linearize	Linearize clauses first.
-flattenQuery	Flattens the query first.
-preprocess	Preprocess input: flatten/linearize clauses, flatten query. In array-context: split clauses which contain inequalities like $i \neq j$ into two clauses.
-noSeparation	Stop at calculating the instances $\mathcal{K}[G]$. Don't introduce names for extension terms and don't reduce to base theory.
-unPseudofy	Eliminate pseudo-quantifiers like $\forall i.i = 3...$ before handing over to a prover.[7]
-noProcessing	No computation. Just translate into prover syntax and hand over. Overrides '-preprocess'. When using this flag one should provide the domains of functions too. When used in combination with CVC there may arise problems with boolean types.[8]
-clausification	Toggle clausification (true/false). Default is 'true'. 'false' implies '-noProcessing'.
-real	Use reals instead of integers as the default type.
-redlog	Call Redlog for base prover. Assumes '-real'.
-version	Print version number.

[6]This is automatically carried out if we have a multiple-step extension. This is because the next step can only be carried out if the current step resulted in ground clauses.

[8]This is because CVC only provides booleans as bit-vectors of length 1. The type 'BOOLEAN' is the type of formulas.

-freeType	Enables the use of an unspecified type 'free' in addition to 'real' and 'int'. Only CVC, Z3 and Yices accept free types. Yices is default.
-renameSubformulas	Toggles the renaming of subformulas during clausification (true/false). Subformula renaming avoids exponential growth. Default is "true".
-verbosity	Verbosity level (0,1,2). From taciturn to garrulous. To be used in conjunction with '-prClauses'. Default is 0
-arrays	Use settings for array. This combines '-preprocess', '-min' and '-arith'; It also splits clauses on negative equalities.
-model	Gives a counter-model for satisfiable queries. Needs Yices or CVC (implies Yices by default).
-smt	Produce SMT-LIB output without calling a prover.
-isLocal	Use this flag (true/false) to tell the program whether all the extensions are local or not. This matters only if H-PILoT cannot derive a contradiction. In that case this means that there really is none only if the extensions are local. Default is false.
-help	Display list of options

6.14 Error Handling

In case there is a parsing error one can use

`export OCAMLRUNPARAM='p'` (in *bash* syntax).

This will give you a walk-through of the parsing process. This is of great help in localizing syntax errors. To turn it back off use

`export OCAMLRUNPARAM=''`.

6.15 A Run Example of H-PILoT

We consider an example taken from [BM07] (Example 11.10). The input file looks as follows.

```
% arrays_from_book.loc
Base_functions:={(+, 2), (-, 2)}
Extension_functions:={(a, 1, 1, int, int), (b, 1, 1, int, int)}
Relations:={(<=, 2)}

% K
Formulas :=
  AND( (FORALL i). (AND(1 <= i, i <= u) --> a(i) = b(i)),
       NOT((FORALL i). (AND(1 <= i, i <= u + _1) -->
                       write(a, u + _1, b(u +_1))(i) = b(i))));
```

The arrays a and b are considered to be equal between the constants l and u. We prove that if we update a at $u+1$ to $b(u+1)$ then a and b should be equal between l and $u+1$. The formula above denies this and should therefore be inconsistent. We call H-PILoT with

   hpilot.opt -preprocess -prClauses arrays_from_book.loc

-preprocess is needed as usual; we use -prClauses to get a trace of the program. (Because the array keyword write appears in the input we don't have to use the flag -arrays: it is implicit.) The trace looks like this (to improve readability we aligned the level labels and will often leave out the listing of the extension ground terms due to space constraints).

First, H-PILoT reads the input and clausifies the formula.

```
************************************************ Starting hpilot************************************************
arrays_from_book.loc
Adding formula:
AND( (FORALL i). (AND( 1 <= i, i <= u) --> a(i) = b(i)),
     NOT((FORALL i). (AND(1 <= i, i <= +(u, _1)) --> read(write(a, +(u, _1),b(+(u, _1))), i) = b(i))))
done.
Clausifying formulas...
(FORALL z_1). OR( NOT(1 <= z_1), NOT(z_1 <= u), a(z_1) = b(z_1))
1 <= sk_1
sk_1 <= +(u, _1)
NOT(read(write(a, +(u, _1), b(+(u, _1))), sk_1) = b(sk_1))
Yielding 4 new clauses:
read(write(a, +(u, _1), b(+(u, _1))), sk_1) = b(sk_1) --->    L: 0; Extension ground terms: b(sk_1), b(+(u, _1))
---> sk_1 <= +(u, _1)                                         L: 0; Extension ground terms:
---> 1 <= sk_1                                                L: 0; Extension ground terms:
[z_1] 1 <= z_1, z_1 <= u ---> a(z_1) = b(z_1)                 L: 0; Extension ground terms:
```

H-PILoT then replaces array writes by introducing new arrays: $write(a, u+1, b(u+1))$ is replaced by: $\forall i. i \neq u+1 \rightarrow a_{w1}(i) = a(i)$ and $a_{w1}(u+1) = b(u+1)$. To remain in the decidable fragment, H-PILoT replaces $\forall i. i \neq u+1 \rightarrow a_{w1}(i) = a(i)$ with $\forall i. i \leq u+1-1 \rightarrow a_{w1}(i) = a(i)$ and $\forall i. u+1+1 \leq i \rightarrow a_{w1}(i) = a(i)$.

```
Replacing writes...
We have 1 levels.
Our base theory is:
empty.
Splitting clause [i]   ---> i = +(u, _1), a_w1(i) = a(i)                L: 1;
terms:   on eq i = +(u, _1)
Checking APF for clause [i] i <= -(+(u, _1), _1) ---> a_w1(i) = a(i)    L: 0;
Extension ground terms: ---> true
Checking APF for clause [i] +(+(u, _1), _1) <= i ---> a_w1(i) = a(i)    L: 0;
Extension ground terms: ---> true
Checking APF for clause [z_1] 1 <= z_1, z_1 <= u ---> a(z_1) = b(z_1)   L: 1;
Extension ground terms: ---> true
Recalculating all levels.
```

H-PILoT then flattens and linearizes the result.

```
After rewriting we have as clauses K:
[i, x_1] x_1 = i, i <= -(+(u, _1), _1) ---> a_w1(i) = a(x_1)   L: 1; Extension ground terms:
[i, x_1] x_1 = i, +(+(u, _1), _1) <= i ---> a_w1(i) = a(x_1)   L: 1; Extension ground terms:
[z_1, x_1] x_1 = z_1, 1 <= z_1, z_1 <= u ---> a(z_1) = b(x_1)  L: 1; Extension ground terms:
and as query:
  ---> 1 <= sk_1                                               L: 0; Extension ground terms:
  ---> sk_1 <= +(u, _1)                                        L: 0; Extension ground terms:
  a_w1(sk_1) = b(sk_1) --->                                    L: 1; Extension ground terms: a_w1(sk_1), b(sk_1)
  ---> a_w1(+(u, _1)) = b(+(u, _1))  L: 1; Extension ground terms: a_w1(+(u, _1)),b(+(u, _1))
Our query G is :
  ---> 1 <= sk_1                                               L: 0; Extension ground terms:
  ---> sk_1 <= +(u, _1)                                        L: 0; Extension ground terms:
  a_w1(sk_1) = b(sk_1) --->                                    L: 1; Extension ground terms: a_w1(sk_1), b(sk_1)
  ---> a_w1(+(u, _1)) = b(+(u, _1))  L: 1; Extension ground terms: a_w1(+(u, _1)),b(+(u, _1))
xxxxxxxxxxx End preprocessing.
```

H-PILoT then calculates the set of instances $\mathcal{K}[\Psi(G)]$ and simplifies the terms to avoid redundant instances of clauses (e.g. $u+1-1$ is replaced by u).

```
We have 5 index terms for minimal locality 1, sk_1, u, +(u, _1), +(u, _2)
K has 3 members.
[i, x_1] x_1 = i, i <= -(+(u, _1), _1) ---> a_w1(i) = a(x_1)                    L: 1;
[i, x_1] x_1 = i, +(+(u, _1), _1) <= i ---> a_w1(i) = a(x_1)                    L: 1;
[z_1, x_1] x_1 = z_1, 1 <= z_1, z_1 <= u ---> a(z_1) = b(x_1)                   L: 1;
Computing K<G>...
K<G> looks as follows:
K_G has 75 members.
[] 1 = 1, 1 <= -(+(u, _1), _1) ---> a_w1(1) = a(1)                              L: 0;
[] 1 = sk_1, sk_1 <= -(+(u, _1), _1) ---> a_w1(sk_1) = a(1)                     L: 0;
[] 1 = u, u <= -(+(u, _1), _1) ---> a_w1(u) = a(1)                              L: 0;
[] 1 = +(u, _1), +(u, _1) <= -(+(u, _1), _1) ---> a_w1(+(u, _1)) = a(1)         L: 0;
[] 1 = +(u, _2), +(u, _2) <= -(+(u, _1), _1) ---> a_w1(+(u, _2)) = a(1)         L: 0;
[] sk_1 = 1, 1 <= -(+(u, _1), _1) ---> a_w1(1) = a(sk_1)                        L: 0;
[] sk_1 = sk_1, sk_1 <= -(+(u, _1), _1) ---> a_w1(sk_1) = a(sk_1)               L: 0;
[] sk_1 = u, u <= -(+(u, _1), _1) ---> a_w1(u) = a(sk_1)                        L: 0;
[] sk_1 = +(u, _1), +(u, _1) <= -(+(u, _1), _1) ---> a_w1(+(u, _1)) = a(sk_1)   L: 0;
[] sk_1 = +(u, _2), +(u, _2) <= -(+(u, _1), _1) ---> a_w1(+(u, _2)) = a(sk_1)   L: 0;
[] u = 1, 1 <= -(+(u, _1), _1) ---> a_w1(1) = a(u)                              L: 0;
[] u = sk_1, sk_1 <= -(+(u, _1), _1) ---> a_w1(sk_1) = a(u)                     L: 0;
[] u = u, u <= -(+(u, _1), _1) ---> a_w1(u) = a(u)                              L: 0;
[] u = +(u, _1), +(u, _1) <= -(+(u, _1), _1) ---> a_w1(+(u, _1)) = a(u)         L: 0;
[] u = +(u, _2), +(u, _2) <= -(+(u, _1), _1) ---> a_w1(+(u, _2)) = a(u)         L: 0;
[] +(u, _1) = 1, 1 <= -(+(u, _1), _1) ---> a_w1(1) = a(+(u, _1))                L: 0;
[] +(u, _1) = sk_1, sk_1 <= -(+(u, _1), _1) ---> a_w1(sk_1) = a(+(u, _1))       L: 0;
[] +(u, _1) = u, u <= -(+(u, _1), _1) ---> a_w1(u) = a(+(u, _1))                L: 0;
[] +(u, _1) = +(u, _1), +(u, _1) <= -(+(u, _1), _1) ---> a_w1(+(u, _1)) = a(+(u,_1))  L: 0;
[] +(u, _1) = +(u, _2), +(u, _2) <= -(+(u, _1), _1) ---> a_w1(+(u, _2)) = a(+(u,_1))  L: 0;
[] +(u, _2) = 1, 1 <= -(+(u, _1), _1) ---> a_w1(1) = a(+(u, _2))                L: 0;
[] +(u, _2) = sk_1, sk_1 <= -(+(u, _1), _1) ---> a_w1(sk_1) = a(+(u, _2))       L: 0;
[] +(u, _2) = u, u <= -(+(u, _1), _1) ---> a_w1(u) = a(+(u, _2))                L: 0;
[] +(u, _2) = +(u, _1), +(u, _1) <= -(+(u, _1), _1) ---> a_w1(+(u, _1)) = a(+(u,_2))  L: 0;
[] +(u, _2) = +(u, _2), +(u, _2) <= -(+(u, _1), _1) ---> a_w1(+(u, _2)) = a(+(u,_2))  L: 0;
[] 1 = 1, +(+(u, _1), _1) <= 1 ---> a_w1(1) = a(1)                              L: 0;
[] 1 = sk_1, +(+(u, _1), _1) <= sk_1 ---> a_w1(sk_1) = a(1)                     L: 0;
[] 1 = u, +(+(u, _1), _1) <= u ---> a_w1(u) = a(1)                              L: 0;
[] 1 = +(u, _1), +(+(u, _1), _1) <= +(u, _1) ---> a_w1(+(u, _1)) = a(1)         L: 0;
[] 1 = +(u, _2), +(+(u, _1), _1) <= +(u, _2) ---> a_w1(+(u, _2)) = a(1)         L: 0;
[] sk_1 = 1, +(+(u, _1), _1) <= 1 ---> a_w1(1) = a(sk_1)                        L: 0;
[] sk_1 = sk_1, +(+(u, _1), _1) <= sk_1 ---> a_w1(sk_1) = a(sk_1)               L: 0;
[] sk_1 = u, +(+(u, _1), _1) <= u ---> a_w1(u) = a(sk_1)                        L: 0;
[] sk_1 = +(u, _1), +(+(u, _1), _1) <= +(u, _1) ---> a_w1(+(u, _1)) = a(sk_1)   L: 0;
[] sk_1 = +(u, _2), +(+(u, _1), _1) <= +(u, _2) ---> a_w1(+(u, _2)) = a(sk_1)   L: 0;
[] u = 1, +(+(u, _1), _1) <= 1 ---> a_w1(1) = a(u)                              L: 0;
[] u = sk_1, +(+(u, _1), _1) <= sk_1 ---> a_w1(sk_1) = a(u)                     L: 0;
[] u = u, +(+(u, _1), _1) <= u ---> a_w1(u) = a(u)                              L: 0;
[] u = +(u, _1), +(+(u, _1), _1) <= +(u, _1) ---> a_w1(+(u, _1)) = a(u)         L: 0;
[] u = +(u, _2), +(+(u, _1), _1) <= +(u, _2) ---> a_w1(+(u, _2)) = a(u)         L: 0;
[] +(u, _1) = 1, +(+(u, _1), _1) <= 1 ---> a_w1(1) = a(+(u, _1))                L: 0;
[] +(u, _1) = sk_1, +(+(u, _1), _1) <= sk_1 ---> a_w1(sk_1) = a(+(u, _1))       L: 0;
[] +(u, _1) = u, +(+(u, _1), _1) <= u ---> a_w1(u) = a(+(u, _1))                L: 0;
[] +(u, _1) = +(u, _1), +(+(u, _1), _1) <= +(u, _1) ---> a_w1(+(u, _1)) = a(+(u,_1))  L: 0;
[] +(u, _1) = +(u, _2), +(+(u, _1), _1) <= +(u, _2) ---> a_w1(+(u, _2)) = a(+(u,_1))  L: 0;
[] +(u, _2) = 1, +(+(u, _1), _1) <= 1 ---> a_w1(1) = a(+(u, _2))                L: 0;
[] +(u, _2) = sk_1, +(+(u, _1), _1) <= sk_1 ---> a_w1(sk_1) = a(+(u, _2))       L: 0;
[] +(u, _2) = u, +(+(u, _1), _1) <= u ---> a_w1(u) = a(+(u, _2))                L: 0;
[] +(u, _2) = +(u, _1), +(+(u, _1), _1) <= +(u, _1) ---> a_w1(+(u, _1)) = a(+(u,_2))  L: 0;
[] +(u, _2) = +(u, _2), +(+(u, _1), _1) <= +(u, _2) ---> a_w1(+(u, _2)) = a(+(u,_2))  L: 0;
[] 1 = 1, 1 <= 1, 1 <= u ---> a(1) = b(1)                                       L: 0;
[] sk_1 = 1, 1 <= 1, 1 <= u ---> a(1) = b(sk_1)                                 L: 0;
[] u = 1, 1 <= 1, 1 <= u ---> a(1) = b(u)                                       L: 0;
[] +(u, _1) = 1, 1 <= 1, 1 <= u ---> a(1) = b(+(u, _1))                         L: 0;
[] +(u, _2) = 1, 1 <= 1, 1 <= u ---> a(1) = b(+(u, _2))                         L: 0;
[] 1 = sk_1, 1 <= sk_1, sk_1 <= u ---> a(sk_1) = b(1)                           L: 0;
[] sk_1 = sk_1, 1 <= sk_1, sk_1 <= u ---> a(sk_1) = b(sk_1)                     L: 0;
```

```
[] u = sk_1, 1 <= sk_1, sk_1 <= u ---> a(sk_1) = b(u)                              L: 0;
[] +(u, _1) = sk_1, 1 <= sk_1, sk_1 <= u ---> a(sk_1) = b(+(u, _1))                L: 0;
[] +(u, _2) = sk_1, 1 <= sk_1, sk_1 <= u ---> a(sk_1) = b(+(u, _2))                L: 0;
[] 1 = u, 1 <= u, u <= u ---> a(u) = b(1)                                          L: 0;
[] sk_1 = u, 1 <= u, u <= u ---> a(u) = b(sk_1)                                    L: 0;
[] u = u, 1 <= u, u <= u ---> a(u) = b(u)                                          L: 0;
[] +(u, _1) = u, 1 <= u, u <= u ---> a(u) = b(+(u, _1))                            L: 0;
[] +(u, _2) = u, 1 <= u, u <= u ---> a(u) = b(+(u, _2))                            L: 0;
[] 1 = +(u, _1), 1 <= +(u, _1), +(u, _1) <= u ---> a(+(u, _1)) = b(1)              L: 0;
[] sk_1 = +(u, _1), 1 <= +(u, _1), +(u, _1) <= u ---> a(+(u, _1)) = b(sk_1)        L: 0;
[] u = +(u, _1), 1 <= +(u, _1), +(u, _1) <= u ---> a(+(u, _1)) = b(u)              L: 0;
[] +(u, _1) = +(u, _1), 1 <= +(u, _1), +(u, _1) <= u ---> a(+(u, _1)) = b(+(u, _1))  L: 0;
[] +(u, _2) = +(u, _1), 1 <= +(u, _1), +(u, _1) <= u ---> a(+(u, _1)) = b(+(u, _2))  L: 0;
[] 1 = +(u, _2), 1 <= +(u, _2), +(u, _2) <= u ---> a(+(u, _2)) = b(1)              L: 0;
[] sk_1 = +(u, _2), 1 <= +(u, _2), +(u, _2) <= u ---> a(+(u, _2)) = b(sk_1)        L: 0;
[] u = +(u, _2), 1 <= +(u, _2), +(u, _2) <= u ---> a(+(u, _2)) = b(u)              L: 0;
[] +(u, _1) = +(u, _2), 1 <= +(u, _2), +(u, _2) <= u ---> a(+(u, _2)) = b(+(u, _1))  L: 0;
[] +(u, _2) = +(u, _2), 1 <= +(u, _2), +(u, _2) <= u ---> a(+(u, _2)) = b(+(u, _2))  L: 0;
```

The result is then purified:

```
computing defs ...
We have the following definitions:
  ---> e_1 = a(1)                          L: 0; Extension ground terms: a(1)
  ---> e_2 = a(sk_1)                       L: 0; Extension ground terms: a(sk_1)
  ---> e_3 = a(u)                          L: 0; Extension ground terms: a(u)
  ---> e_4 = a(+(u, _1))                   L: 0; Extension ground terms: a(+(u, _1))
  ---> e_5 = a(+(u, _2))                   L: 0; Extension ground terms: a(+(u, _2))
  ---> e_6 = a_w1(1)                       L: 0; Extension ground terms: a_w1(1)
  ---> e_7 = a_w1(sk_1)                    L: 0; Extension ground terms: a_w1(sk_1)
  ---> e_8 = a_w1(u)                       L: 0; Extension ground terms: a_w1(u)
  ---> e_9 = a_w1(+(u, _1))                L: 0; Extension ground terms: a_w1(+(u, _1))
  ---> e_10 = a_w1(+(u, _2))               L: 0; Extension ground terms: a_w1(+(u, _2))
  ---> e_11 = b(1)                         L: 0; Extension ground terms: b(1)
  ---> e_12 = b(sk_1)                      L: 0; Extension ground terms: b(sk_1)
  ---> e_13 = b(u)                         L: 0; Extension ground terms: b(u)
  ---> e_14 = b(+(u, _1))                  L: 0; Extension ground terms: b(+(u, _1))
  ---> e_15 = b(+(u, _2))                  L: 0; Extension ground terms: b(+(u, _2))
Purified:
K_G has 75 members.
[] 1 = 1, 1 <= -(+(u, _1), _1) ---> e_6 = e_1                   L: 0; Extension ground terms:
[] 1 = sk_1, sk_1 <= -(+(u, _1), _1) ---> e_7 = e_1             L: 0; Extension ground terms:
[] 1 = u, u <= -(+(u, _1), _1) ---> e_8 = e_1                   L: 0; Extension ground terms:
[] 1 = +(u, _1), +(u, _1) <= -(+(u, _1), _1) ---> e_9 = e_1     L: 0; Extension ground terms:
[] 1 = +(u, _2), +(u, _2) <= -(+(u, _1), _1) ---> e_10 = e_1    L: 0; Extension ground terms:
[] sk_1 = 1, 1 <= -(+(u, _1), _1) ---> e_6 = e_2                L: 0; Extension ground terms:
[] sk_1 = sk_1, sk_1 <= -(+(u, _1), _1) ---> e_7 = e_2          L: 0; Extension ground terms:
[] sk_1 = u, u <= -(+(u, _1), _1) ---> e_8 = e_2                L: 0; Extension ground terms:
[] sk_1 = +(u, _1), +(u, _1) <= -(+(u, _1), _1) ---> e_9 = e_2  L: 0; Extension ground terms:
[] sk_1 = +(u, _2), +(u, _2) <= -(+(u, _1), _1) ---> e_10 = e_2 L: 0; Extension ground terms:
[] u = 1, 1 <= -(+(u, _1), _1) ---> e_6 = e_3                   L: 0; Extension ground terms:
[] u = sk_1, sk_1 <= -(+(u, _1), _1) ---> e_7 = e_3             L: 0; Extension ground terms:
[] u = u, u <= -(+(u, _1), _1) ---> e_8 = e_3                   L: 0; Extension ground terms:
[] u = +(u, _1), +(u, _1) <= -(+(u, _1), _1) ---> e_9 = e_3     L: 0; Extension ground terms:
[] u = +(u, _2), +(u, _2) <= -(+(u, _1), _1) ---> e_10 = e_3    L: 0; Extension ground terms:
[] +(u, _1) = 1, 1 <= -(+(u, _1), _1) ---> e_6 = e_4            L: 0; Extension ground terms:
[] +(u, _1) = sk_1, sk_1 <= -(+(u, _1), _1) ---> e_7 = e_4      L: 0; Extension ground terms:
[] +(u, _1) = u, u <= -(+(u, _1), _1) ---> e_8 = e_4            L: 0; Extension ground terms:
[] +(u, _1) = +(u, _1), +(u, _1) <= -(+(u, _1), _1) ---> e_9 = e_4   L: 0; Extension ground terms:
[] +(u, _1) = +(u, _2), +(u, _2) <= -(+(u, _1), _1) ---> e_10 = e_4  L: 0; Extension ground terms:
[] +(u, _2) = 1, 1 <= -(+(u, _1), _1) ---> e_6 = e_5            L: 0; Extension ground terms:
[] +(u, _2) = sk_1, sk_1 <= -(+(u, _1), _1) ---> e_7 = e_5      L: 0; Extension ground terms:
[] +(u, _2) = u, u <= -(+(u, _1), _1) ---> e_8 = e_5            L: 0; Extension ground terms:
[] +(u, _2) = +(u, _1), +(u, _1) <= -(+(u, _1), _1) ---> e_9 = e_5   L: 0; Extension ground terms:
[] +(u, _2) = +(u, _2), +(u, _2) <= -(+(u, _1), _1) ---> e_10 = e_5  L: 0; Extension ground terms:
[] 1 = 1, +(+(u, _1), _1) <= 1 ---> e_6 = e_1                   L: 0; Extension ground terms:
[] 1 = sk_1, +(+(u, _1), _1) <= sk_1 ---> e_7 = e_1             L: 0; Extension ground terms:
[] 1 = u, +(+(u, _1), _1) <= u ---> e_8 = e_1                   L: 0; Extension ground terms:
[] 1 = +(u, _1), +(+(u, _1), _1) <= +(u, _1) ---> e_9 = e_1     L: 0; Extension ground terms:
[] 1 = +(u, _2), +(+(u, _1), _1) <= +(u, _2) ---> e_10 = e_1    L: 0; Extension ground terms:
[] sk_1 = 1, +(+(u, _1), _1) <= 1 ---> e_6 = e_2                L: 0; Extension ground terms:
[] sk_1 = sk_1, +(+(u, _1), _1) <= sk_1 ---> e_7 = e_2          L: 0; Extension ground terms:
[] sk_1 = u, +(+(u, _1), _1) <= u ---> e_8 = e_2                L: 0; Extension ground terms:
[] sk_1 = +(u, _1), +(+(u, _1), _1) <= +(u, _1) ---> e_9 = e_2  L: 0; Extension ground terms:
[] sk_1 = +(u, _2), +(+(u, _1), _1) <= +(u, _2) ---> e_10 = e_2 L: 0; Extension ground terms:
[] u = 1, +(+(u, _1), _1) <= 1 ---> e_6 = e_3                   L: 0; Extension ground terms:
[] u = sk_1, +(+(u, _1), _1) <= sk_1 ---> e_7 = e_3             L: 0; Extension ground terms:
[] u = u, +(+(u, _1), _1) <= u ---> e_8 = e_3                   L: 0; Extension ground terms:
[] u = +(u, _1), +(+(u, _1), _1) <= +(u, _1) ---> e_9 = e_3     L: 0; Extension ground terms:
[] u = +(u, _2), +(+(u, _1), _1) <= +(u, _2) ---> e_10 = e_3    L: 0; Extension ground terms:
[] +(u, _1) = 1, +(+(u, _1), _1) <= 1 ---> e_6 = e_4            L: 0; Extension ground terms:
[] +(u, _1) = sk_1, +(+(u, _1), _1) <= sk_1 ---> e_7 = e_4      L: 0; Extension ground terms:
[] +(u, _1) = u, +(+(u, _1), _1) <= u ---> e_8 = e_4            L: 0; Extension ground terms:
[] +(u, _1) = +(u, _1), +(+(u, _1), _1) <= +(u, _1) ---> e_9 = e_4   L: 0; Extension ground terms:
[] +(u, _1) = +(u, _2), +(+(u, _1), _1) <= +(u, _2) ---> e_10 = e_4  L: 0; Extension ground terms:
```

```
[] +(u, _2) = 1, +(+(u, _1), _1) <= 1 ---> e_6 = e_5        L: 0; Extension ground terms:
[] +(u, _2) = sk_1, +(+(u, _1), _1) <= sk_1 ---> e_7 = e_5  L: 0; Extension ground terms:
[] +(u, _2) = u, +(+(u, _1), _1) <= u ---> e_8 = e_5         L: 0; Extension ground terms:
[] +(u, _2) = +(u, _1), +(+(u, _1), _1) <= +(u, _1) ---> e_9 = e_5   L: 0; Extension ground terms:
[] +(u, _2) = +(u, _2), +(+(u, _1), _1) <= +(u, _2) ---> e_10 = e_5  L: 0; Extension ground terms:
[] 1 = 1, 1 <= 1, 1 <= u ---> e_1 = e_11                     L: 0; Extension ground terms:
[] sk_1 = 1, 1 <= 1, 1 <= u ---> e_1 = e_12                  L: 0; Extension ground terms:
[] u = 1, 1 <= 1, 1 <= u ---> e_1 = e_13                     L: 0; Extension ground terms:
[] +(u, _1) = 1, 1 <= 1, 1 <= u ---> e_1 = e_14              L: 0; Extension ground terms:
[] +(u, _2) = 1, 1 <= 1, 1 <= u ---> e_1 = e_15              L: 0; Extension ground terms:
[] 1 = sk_1, 1 <= sk_1, sk_1 <= u ---> e_2 = e_11            L: 0; Extension ground terms:
[] sk_1 = sk_1, 1 <= sk_1, sk_1 <= u ---> e_2 = e_12         L: 0; Extension ground terms:
[] u = sk_1, 1 <= sk_1, sk_1 <= u ---> e_2 = e_13            L: 0; Extension ground terms:
[] +(u, _1) = sk_1, 1 <= sk_1, sk_1 <= u ---> e_2 = e_14     L: 0; Extension ground terms:
[] +(u, _2) = sk_1, 1 <= sk_1, sk_1 <= u ---> e_2 = e_15     L: 0; Extension ground terms:
[] 1 = u, 1 <= u, u <= u ---> e_3 = e_11                     L: 0; Extension ground terms:
[] sk_1 = u, 1 <= u, u <= u ---> e_3 = e_12                  L: 0; Extension ground terms:
[] u = u, 1 <= u, u <= u ---> e_3 = e_13                     L: 0; Extension ground terms:
[] +(u, _1) = u, 1 <= u, u <= u ---> e_3 = e_14              L: 0; Extension ground terms:
[] +(u, _2) = u, 1 <= u, u <= u ---> e_3 = e_15              L: 0; Extension ground terms:
[] 1 = +(u, _1), 1 <= +(u, _1), +(u, _1) <= u ---> e_4 = e_11    L: 0; Extension ground terms:
[] sk_1 = +(u, _1), 1 <= +(u, _1), +(u, _1) <= u ---> e_4 = e_12 L: 0; Extension ground terms:
[] u = +(u, _1), 1 <= +(u, _1), +(u, _1) <= u ---> e_4 = e_13    L: 0; Extension ground terms:
[] +(u, _1) = +(u, _1), 1 <= +(u, _1), +(u, _1) <= u ---> e_4 = e_14  L: 0; Extension ground terms:
[] +(u, _2) = +(u, _1), 1 <= +(u, _1), +(u, _1) <= u ---> e_4 = e_15  L: 0; Extension ground terms:
[] 1 = +(u, _2), 1 <= +(u, _2), +(u, _2) <= u ---> e_5 = e_11    L: 0; Extension ground terms:
[] sk_1 = +(u, _2), 1 <= +(u, _2), +(u, _2) <= u ---> e_5 = e_12 L: 0; Extension ground terms:
[] u = +(u, _2), 1 <= +(u, _2), +(u, _2) <= u ---> e_5 = e_13    L: 0; Extension ground terms:
[] +(u, _1) = +(u, _2), 1 <= +(u, _2), +(u, _2) <= u ---> e_5 = e_14 L: 0; Extension ground terms:
[] +(u, _2) = +(u, _2), 1 <= +(u, _2), +(u, _2) <= u ---> e_5 = e_15 L: 0; Extension ground terms:
---> 1 <= sk_1                                              L: 0; Extension ground terms:
---> sk_1 <= +(u, _1)                                       L: 0; Extension ground terms:
e_7 = e_12 --->                                             L: 0; Extension ground terms:
---> e_9 = e_14                                             L: 0; Extension ground terms:
```

The introduced definitions are replaced by the corresponding congruence axioms.

```
Replacing D by NO:
This yields 30 clauses.
+(u, _1) = +(u, _2) ---> e_14 = e_15       L: 0; Extension ground terms:
u = +(u, _2) ---> e_13 = e_15              L: 0; Extension ground terms:
u = +(u, _1) ---> e_13 = e_14              L: 0; Extension ground terms:
sk_1 = +(u, _2) ---> e_12 = e_15           L: 0; Extension ground terms:
sk_1 = +(u, _1) ---> e_12 = e_14           L: 0; Extension ground terms:
sk_1 = u ---> e_12 = e_13                  L: 0; Extension ground terms:
1 = +(u, _2) ---> e_11 = e_15              L: 0; Extension ground terms:
1 = +(u, _1) ---> e_11 = e_14              L: 0; Extension ground terms:
1 = u ---> e_11 = e_13                     L: 0; Extension ground terms:
1 = sk_1 ---> e_11 = e_12                  L: 0; Extension ground terms:
+(u, _1) = +(u, _2) ---> e_9 = e_10        L: 0; Extension ground terms:
u = +(u, _2) ---> e_8 = e_10               L: 0; Extension ground terms:
u = +(u, _1) ---> e_8 = e_9                L: 0; Extension ground terms:
sk_1 = +(u, _2) ---> e_7 = e_10            L: 0; Extension ground terms:
sk_1 = +(u, _1) ---> e_7 = e_9             L: 0; Extension ground terms:
sk_1 = u ---> e_7 = e_8                    L: 0; Extension ground terms:
1 = +(u, _2) ---> e_6 = e_10               L: 0; Extension ground terms:
1 = +(u, _1) ---> e_6 = e_9                L: 0; Extension ground terms:
1 = u ---> e_6 = e_8                       L: 0; Extension ground terms:
1 = sk_1 ---> e_6 = e_7                    L: 0; Extension ground terms:
+(u, _1) = +(u, _2) ---> e_4 = e_5         L: 0; Extension ground terms:
u = +(u, _2) ---> e_3 = e_5                L: 0; Extension ground terms:
u = +(u, _1) ---> e_3 = e_4                L: 0; Extension ground terms:
sk_1 = +(u, _2) ---> e_2 = e_5             L: 0; Extension ground terms:
sk_1 = +(u, _1) ---> e_2 = e_4             L: 0; Extension ground terms:
sk_1 = u ---> e_2 = e_3                    L: 0; Extension ground terms:
1 = +(u, _2) ---> e_1 = e_5                L: 0; Extension ground terms:
1 = +(u, _1) ---> e_1 = e_4                L: 0; Extension ground terms:
1 = u ---> e_1 = e_3                       L: 0; Extension ground terms:
1 = sk_1 ---> e_1 = e_2                    L: 0; Extension ground terms:
```

Finally we hand over to a prover (Yices is default here). The program checked earlier that the problem was in a decidable fragment of the theory of arrays (APF), which is Ψ-local. Hence Yices' answer can always be trusted irrespective of whether the answer is 'satisfiable' or 'unsatisfiable'.

```
The problem is in APF
Handing over to Yices:
Total number of clauses: 109.
```

```
                            unsat
unsat
H-PILoT spent                     0.161975s on the problem.
Of which clausification took      0.006998s.
The prover needed                 0.021996s for the problem.
Total running time:               0.183971s.
```

6.16 Model Generation and Visualization

We illustrate the method for model generation we use on two examples[9] (cf. [ISS10c]).

Example 1: Theory of Pointers

Consider the following problem, specified in H-PILoT input syntax:

```
Base_functions:={(+,2), (-, 2)}
Extension_functions:={(next, 1, 1, pointer), (prev, 1, 1, pointer),
                      (priority, 1, 1, pointer, real)}
Relations:={(>=, 2)}
Constants:={(null, pointer), (a, pointer), (b, pointer)}

% K
Clauses := (FORALL p). prev(next(p)) = p;
           (FORALL p). --> next(prev(p)) = p;
           (FORALL p). priority(p) >= priority(next(p));

Query := priority(a) = _5; priority(b) = _6; a = prev(b);
         %NOT(a = null); % pivotal for satisfiability
         NOT(b = null);
```

We used CVC3 to generate a model for the set of clauses obtained after the hierarchical reduction. A partial model is given below (after preprocessing/deleting repetitions):

```
null = a
prev(b) = a
prev(a) = d_5
next(prev(prev(b))) = e_5
next(prev(b)) = d_1
next(b) = a
prev(prev(b)) = d_5
prev(next(prev(b))) = d_5
```

---

[9]The visualization with Mathematica was done by Viorica Sofronie-Stokkermans.

```
prev(next(b)) = d_5
prev(next(a)) = d_5
next(a) = d_1
priority(next(a)) = 0
priority(next(prev(b))) = 0
priority(prev(b)) = 5
priority(b) = 6
priority(a) = 5
```

We can make this model total by defining $\mathsf{next}(x) := \mathsf{null}$ and $\mathsf{prev}(y) := \mathsf{null}$ whenever $\mathsf{next}(x)$ respectively. $\mathsf{prev}(y)$ are undefined (cf. 6.8). The obtained model can be visualized using Mathematica (this last step is currently performed separately; it is not yet integrated into H-PILoT, but an integration is planned for the next future.). The result is presented below.

```
In[1]:= GraphPlot[{{"null" -> "null", "prev"}, {"b" -> "null", "prev"}, {"b" -> "null", "next"},
        {"null" -> "d1", "next"}, {"d1" -> "null", "prev"}, {"d1" -> "null", "next"}},
        VertexLabeling -> True, DirectedEdges -> True, MultiedgeStyle -> 0.2, SelfLoopStyle -> 0.2]
```

Example 2: Theory of functions over the real numbers

Consider now the following example: decide whether

$$\mathsf{Mon}_f \cup \mathsf{Mon}_g \models_{\mathbb{R}} \forall x,y,z,u,v (x \leq y \wedge z \leq y \wedge f(y) \leq g(u) \wedge u \leq v \wedge u \leq w \rightarrow f(x) \leq g(v)).$$

We formulate a satisfiable version, by replacing the argument x in the conclusion with a new variable x_0. The problem obtained this way can be formulated as follows in the input format of H-PILoT.

```
Base_functions:={}
Extension_functions:={(f, 1), (g, 1)}
Relations:={(<=, 2)}

Clauses := (FORALL x,y). x <= y --> f(x) <= f(y);
           (FORALL x,y). x <= y --> g(x) <= g(y);

Query := c1 <= d1; c2 <= d1; d2 <= c3; d2 <= c4;
         f(d1) <= g(d2); NOT(f(c0) <= g(c4));
```

CVC3 can be used to generate the following model of the query:

```
model:
c0 = 1
```

c1 = 0
d1 = 0
c2 = 0
c3 = 0
c4 = 1
d2 = 0
g(d2) = 0
f(d1) = 0
g(c4) = 1
f(c0) = 2

From this partial model, a total model can be constructed as explained in [SS08]. This model can then be visualized as follows in Mathematica:

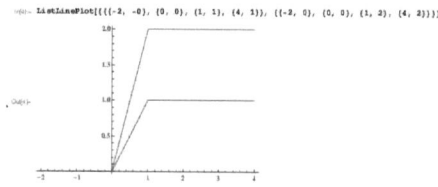

Note that if we require differentiability of f and g then – with the completion described in the previous example – monotonicity of the extensions may not be preserved:

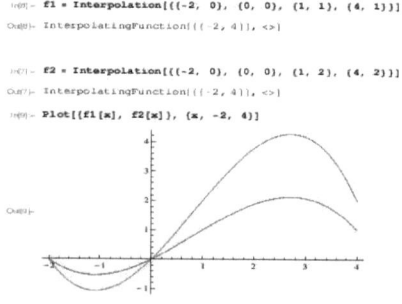

In the example above we can enforce the functions to be linear. A general study of the properties which can be guaranteed when building the models is the topic of work in progress.

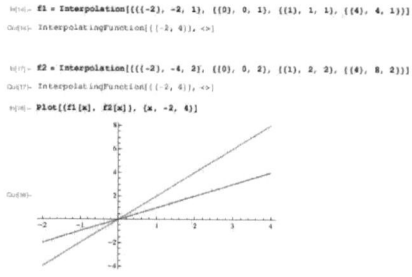

6.17 The Input Grammar

$\langle start \rangle ::= \langle base\_functions \rangle \langle extension\_functions \rangle \langle relations \rangle \langle constants \rangle \langle interval \rangle$
$\qquad \langle baseTheory \rangle \langle formulasOrClauses \rangle \langle groundformulas \rangle \langle query \rangle$

$\langle base\_functions \rangle ::= \texttt{Base\_functions := \{} \langle function\_list \rangle \texttt{\}}$

$\langle extension\_functions \rangle ::= \texttt{Extension\_functions := \{} \langle function\_list \rangle \texttt{\}}$

$\langle relations \rangle ::= \texttt{Relations := \{} \langle relation\_list \rangle \texttt{\}}$

$\langle constants \rangle ::= \epsilon \;|\; \texttt{Constants := \{ constant\_list \}}$

$\langle interval \rangle ::= \epsilon$
$\qquad |\; \texttt{Interval :=} \langle int \rangle \langle sm \rangle \langle identifier \rangle \texttt{;}$
$\qquad |\; \texttt{Interval :=} \langle identifier \rangle \langle sm \rangle \langle int \rangle \texttt{;}$
$\qquad |\; \texttt{Interval :=} \langle int \rangle \langle sm \rangle \langle identifier \rangle \langle sm \rangle \langle int \rangle \texttt{;}$

$\langle base\_theory \rangle ::= \epsilon \;|\; \texttt{Base :=} \langle clause\_list \rangle$

$\langle formulasOrClauses \rangle ::= \epsilon \;|\; \langle formulas \rangle \;|\; \langle clauses \rangle$
$\qquad\qquad\qquad |\; \langle formulas \rangle \langle clauses \rangle \;|\; \langle clauses \rangle \langle formulas \rangle$

$\langle ground\_formulas \rangle ::= \epsilon \;|\; \texttt{Ground\_Formulas :=} \langle formula\_list \rangle$

$\langle query \rangle ::= \texttt{Query :=} \langle ground\_clauses \rangle$

$\langle formulas \rangle ::= \texttt{Formulas :=} \langle formula\_list \rangle$

$\langle clauses \rangle ::= \texttt{Clauses :=} \langle clause\_list \rangle$

$\langle function\_list \rangle ::= \epsilon \;|\; \langle function \rangle \langle additional\_functions \rangle$

$\langle additional\_functions \rangle ::= \epsilon \;|\; \texttt{,} \langle function \rangle \langle additional\_functions \rangle$

$\langle relation\_list \rangle ::= \epsilon \;|\; \langle relation \rangle \langle additional\_relations \rangle$

$\langle additional\_relations \rangle ::= \epsilon \;|\; \texttt{,} \langle relation \rangle \langle additional\_relations \rangle$

$\langle relation \rangle ::= \texttt{(} \langle uneqs \rangle \texttt{,} \langle int \rangle \texttt{)} \;|\; \texttt{(} \langle identifier \rangle \texttt{,} \langle int \rangle \texttt{)}$

$\langle function \rangle ::= \texttt{(} \langle identifier \rangle \texttt{,} \langle int \rangle \texttt{)}$
$\qquad |\; \texttt{(} \langle arithop \rangle \texttt{,} \langle int \rangle \texttt{)}$
$\qquad |\; \texttt{(} \langle arithop \rangle \texttt{,} \langle int \rangle \texttt{,} \langle int \rangle \texttt{,} \texttt{int} \texttt{)}$
$\qquad |\; \texttt{(} \langle arithop \rangle \texttt{,} \langle int \rangle \texttt{,} \langle int \rangle \texttt{,} \texttt{real} \texttt{)}$
$\qquad |\; \texttt{(} \langle identifier \rangle \texttt{,} \langle int \rangle \texttt{,} \langle int \rangle \texttt{)}$
$\qquad |\; \texttt{(} \langle identifier \rangle \texttt{,} \langle int \rangle \texttt{,} \langle int \rangle \texttt{,} \langle domain \rangle \texttt{)}$
$\qquad |\; \texttt{(} \langle identifier \rangle \texttt{,} \langle int \rangle \texttt{,} \langle int \rangle \texttt{,} \langle domain \rangle \texttt{,} \langle domain \rangle \texttt{)}$

$\langle domain \rangle ::= \texttt{bool} \;|\; \texttt{int} \;|\; \texttt{real} \;|\; \texttt{pointer} \;|\; \texttt{pointer\#} \langle int \rangle$
$\qquad |\; \texttt{scalar} \;|\; \texttt{free} \;|\; \texttt{free\#} \langle int \rangle$

⟨base_clause_list⟩ ::= ϵ | ⟨clause⟩ ; ⟨additional_base_clauses⟩
⟨additional_base_clauses⟩ ::= ϵ | ⟨base_clause⟩ ; ⟨additional_base_clauses⟩
⟨constant_list⟩ ::= ⟨constant⟩ ⟨additional_constants⟩
⟨additional_constants⟩ ::= ϵ | , ⟨constant⟩ ⟨additional_constant⟩

⟨constant⟩ ::= (⟨identifier⟩ , bool)
       | (⟨identifier⟩ , int)
       | (⟨identifier⟩ , real)
       | (⟨identifier⟩ , scalar)
       | (⟨identifier⟩ , pointer)
       | (⟨identifier⟩ , pointer# ⟨int⟩)
       | (⟨identifier⟩ , free)
       | (⟨identifier⟩ , free# ⟨int⟩)

⟨base_clause⟩ ::= ⟨clausematrix⟩ | ⟨universalQuantifier⟩ ⟨clausematrix⟩
⟨formula_list⟩ ::= ⟨formula⟩ | ⟨formula⟩ ; ⟨additional_formulas⟩
⟨additional_formulas⟩ ::= ϵ | ⟨formula⟩ ; ⟨additional_formulas⟩
⟨clause_list⟩ ::= ⟨clause⟩ | ⟨clause⟩ ; ⟨additional_clauses⟩
⟨additional_clauses⟩ ::= ϵ | ⟨clause⟩ ; ⟨additional_clauses⟩

⟨clause⟩ ::= ⟨clausematrix⟩
       | ⟨universalQuantifier⟩ ⟨clausematrix⟩
       | { ⟨formula⟩ } OR ⟨clausematrix⟩
       | ⟨universalQuantifier⟩ { ⟨formula⟩ } OR ⟨clausematrix⟩
       | { ⟨formula⟩ } -> ⟨clausematrix⟩
       | ⟨universalQuantifier⟩ { ⟨formula⟩ } -> ⟨clausematrix⟩

⟨universalQuantifier⟩ ::= (FORALL ⟨variables⟩) .
⟨variables⟩ ::= ⟨name⟩ ⟨additional_variable⟩
⟨additional_variables⟩ ::= ϵ | , ⟨name⟩ ⟨additional_variables⟩
⟨ground_clauses⟩ ::= ϵ | ⟨clausematrix⟩ ; ⟨ground_clauses⟩
⟨clausematrix⟩ ::= ⟨literal⟩ | ⟨disjunctive_clause⟩ | ⟨sorted_clause⟩

⟨formula⟩ ::= ⟨atom⟩
       | NOT (⟨formula⟩)
       | OR (⟨formula⟩ ⟨formula_plus⟩)
       | AND (⟨formula⟩ ⟨formula_plus⟩)
       | (⟨formula⟩ -> ⟨formula⟩)
       | (⟨formula⟩ <-> ⟨formula⟩)
       | (FORALL ⟨variables⟩) . ⟨formula⟩
       | (EXISTS ⟨variables⟩) . ⟨formula⟩

$\langle formula\_plus \rangle ::=$, $\langle formula \rangle$ $\langle formula\_star \rangle$

$\langle formula\_star \rangle ::= \epsilon\ |$, $\langle formula \rangle$ $\langle formula\_star \rangle$

$\langle disjunctive\_clause \rangle ::=$ OR ($\langle literal \rangle$ $\langle literal\_plus \rangle$)

$\langle literal\_plus \rangle ::=$, $\langle literal \rangle$ $\langle literal\_star \rangle$

$\langle literal\_star \rangle ::= \epsilon\ |$, $\langle literal \rangle$ $\langle literal\_star \rangle$

$\langle sorted\_clause \rangle ::= \langle atom\_list \rangle$ -> $\langle atom\_list \rangle$

$\langle atom\_list \rangle ::= \epsilon\ |\ \langle atom \rangle\ \langle atom\_star \rangle$

$\langle atom\_star \rangle ::= \epsilon\ |$, $\langle atom \rangle$ $\langle atom\_star \rangle$

$\langle literal \rangle ::= \langle atom \rangle\ |$ NOT ($\langle atom \rangle$)

$\langle atom \rangle ::= \langle equality\_atom \rangle\ |\ \langle ineq\_atom \rangle\ |\ \langle predicate\_atom \rangle$

$\langle equality\_atom \rangle ::= \langle term \rangle$ = $\langle term \rangle$

$\langle ineq\_atom \rangle ::= \langle term \rangle\ \langle uneqs \rangle\ \langle term \rangle$

$\langle predicate\_atom \rangle ::= \langle identifier \rangle$ [$\langle term \rangle$ $\langle additional\_terms \rangle$]

$\langle arguments \rangle ::= \langle term \rangle\ \langle additional\_terms \rangle$

$\langle additional\_terms \rangle ::= \epsilon\ |$, $\langle term \rangle$ $\langle additional\_terms \rangle$

$\langle term \rangle ::= \langle name \rangle$
    $|\ \langle operator \rangle$ ($\langle arguments \rangle$)
    $|\ \langle array \rangle$ ($\langle arguments \rangle$)
    $|\ \langle update \rangle$ ($\langle arguments \rangle$)
    $|\ \langle term\_arith \rangle\ \langle arithop \rangle\ \langle term\_arith \rangle$

$\langle term\_arith \rangle ::= \langle name \rangle$
    $|\ \langle operator \rangle$ ($\langle arguments \rangle$)
    $|\ ($ $\langle term\_arith \rangle\ \langle arithop \rangle\ \langle term\_arith \rangle$)

$\langle sm \rangle ::=$ <= | <

$\langle arithop \rangle ::=$ + | - | * | /

$\langle uneqs \rangle ::=$ <= | >= | < | >

$\langle operator \rangle ::= \langle identifier \rangle$

$\langle array: \rangle ::=$ write ($\langle identifier \rangle$, $\langle term \rangle$, $\langle term \rangle$)
    | write ($\langle array \rangle$, $\langle term \rangle$, $\langle term \rangle$)

$\langle update \rangle ::=$ update ($\langle identifier \rangle$, $\langle term \rangle$, $\langle term \rangle$)
    | update ($\langle update \rangle$, $\langle term \rangle$, $\langle term \rangle$)

$\langle name \rangle ::= \langle identifier \rangle$

$\langle identifier \rangle ::=$ any string consisting of letters and numbers starting with a letter. It may end with "'".

$\langle int \rangle ::=$ any non-negative number.

Chapter 7
Conclusion

In this thesis we have studied efficient reasoning in combinations of first-order theories. The basic case is that of a theory *extension*, where we have a base theory which gets extended by new functions which are axiomatized by clauses. Given that this extension is local, efficient hierarchical reasoning is possible: a ground problem in the extended language can be reduced in polynomial time to an equivalent ground problem in the base language. Because many real-life verification tasks can be considered to be ground problems over combinations of theories, locality is a important technique in verification.

The notion of locality was introduced by Givan and McAllester ([GM92], [McA93]). It was related to a semantical approach by Harald Ganzinger in a seminal paper [Gan01] for the case of Horn clauses. It was lifted to *theory extensions* by Viorica Sofronie-Stokkermans and much developed in a series of papers ([SS05], [SS06a], [SS07]). We have presented the theory of locality in chapter 3 and given some applications. In the following chapter, we have generalized the standard notion of locality to that of Ψ-*locality*. We have shown how to subsume locality results for data structures under this generalized notion, thus giving a unified treatment.

A more complicated case is the union of theories over a common theory in a shared (non-empty) signature which we studied in chapter 5. A key notion in this setting is that of *model completeness* and of *amalgamation*. We gave a simpler proof of a result by Ghilardi ([Ghi03a, Ghi04]) that the joint inconsistency of a ground problem and two theories, which are compatible with their common intersection, can be established by the exchange of a quantifier-free sentence in the shared language. In the subsequent section, we gave new criteria for the locality of the union of local theories. We then considered the combination of Ψ-local theories over a shared theory and gave criteria under which the combination is Ψ-local again, thereby generalizing a result in [SS07].

Finally, we gave an efficient implementation of hierarchical reduction in local theory extensions: the program H-PILoT. It has already proved itself in real-life verification problems, such as the European Train Control System standard, by this means adding to the case for locality as a crucial notion in verification.

In the future, we would like to build on this work by finding new application areas for local reasoning in verification. Theoretically, we would like to research locality in data structures and, practically, provide the necessary decision procedures in H-PILoT. Regarding the implementation, we would also like to enrich H-PILoT in the following ways. First, we would like to enhance H-PILoT's ability to detect the locality of theory extensions automatically. Second, we would like to implement local *theory combinations* over a common theory in H-PILoT. In order to increase user-friendliness, visualizing models and counterexamples using the computer algebra system Mathematica is also on our to-do list.

Another area of interest we would like to study further is that of *interpolation*, whose intimate connection with the satisfiability problem in theory combinations has already been touched upon. This also has an implementation side, as results on how to compute interpolants for local theory extensions already exist ([SS06a]) and should be integrated into H-PILoT.

Bibliography

[ABRS05] A. Armando, M. P. Bonacina, S. Ranise, and S. Schulz. On a rewriting approach to satisfiability procedures: Extension, combination of theories and an experimental appraisal. In B. Gramlich, editor, *Frontiers of Combining Systems, FroCos'05*, volume 3717 of *Lecture Notes in Computer Science*, pages 65–80, 2005.

[ABRS09] A. Armando, M. P. Bonacina, S. Ranise, and S. Schulz. New results on rewrite-based satisfiability procedures. *ACM Transactions on Computational Logic*, 10(1), 2009.

[ARR01] A. Armando, S. Ranise, and M. Rusinowitch. Uniform derivation of decision procedures by superposition. In *Computer Science Logic, CSL-01*, volume 2142 of *Lecture Notes in Computer Science*, pages 513–527. Springer, 2001.

[ARR03] A. Armando, S. Ranise, and M. Rusinowitch. A rewriting approach to satisfiability procedures. *Information and Computation*, 183(2):140–164, 2003.

[Bac75] P. D. Bacsich. Amalgamation properties and interpolation theorems for equational theories. *Algebra Universalis*, 5:45–55, 1975.

[BdM09] N. Bjørner and L. M. de Moura. $Z3^{10}$: Applications, enablers, challenges and directions. In *Constraints in Formal Verification, CFV'09*, 2009. http://research.microsoft.com/en-us/um/people/leonardo/cfv09.pdf.

[BE07a] M. P. Bonacina and M. Echenim. Rewrite-based decision procedures. *Electronic Notes in Theoretical Computer Science*, 174(11):27–45, 2007.

[BE07b] M. P. Bonacina and M. Echenim. Rewrite-based satisfiability procedures for recursive data structures. *Electronic Notes in Theoretical Computer Science*, 174(8):55–70, 2007.

[BG01] D. A. Basin and H. Ganzinger. Automated complexity analysis based on ordered resolution. *Journal of the ACM*, 48(1):70–109, 2001.

[BG05] F. Baader and S. Ghilardi. Connecting many-sorted theories. In R. Nieuwenhuis, editor, *Conference on Automated Deduction, CADE-20*, number 3632 in Lecture Notes in Artificial Intelligence, pages 278–294. Springer, 2005.

[BGN+06a] M. P. Bonacina, S. Ghilardi, E. Nicolini, S. Ranise, and D. Zucchelli. Decidability and undecidability results for Nelson-Oppen and rewrite-based decision procedures. In U. Furbach and N. Shankar, editors, *International Joint Conference on Automated*

Reasoning, IJCAR'06, volume 4130 of Lecture Notes in Artificial Intelligence, pages 513–527. Springer, 2006.

[BGN+06b] M. P. Bonacina, S. Ghilardi, E. Nicolini, S. Ranise, and D. Zucchelli. Decidability and undecidability results for Nelson-Oppen and rewrite-based decision procedures. In U. Furbach and N. Shankar, editors, *International Joint Conference on Automated Reasoning, IJCAR'06*, volume 4130 of *Lecture Notes in Artificial Intelligence*, pages 235–250. Springer, 2006.

[BGT04] F. Baader, S. Ghilardi, and C. Tinelli. A new combination procedure for the word problem that generalizes fusion decidability results in modal logics. In *International Joint Conference on Automated Reasoning, IJCAR'04*, volume 3097 of *Lecture Notes in Artificial Intelligence*, pages 183–197. Springer, 2004.

[BM07] A. R. Bradley and Z. Manna. *The Calculus of Computation*. Springer, 1st edition, 2007.

[BMS06] A. R. Bradley, Z. Manna, and H.B. Sipma. What's decidable about arrays? In E. A. Emerson and K. S. Namjoshi, editors, *Verification, Model Checking and Abstract Interpretation, VMCAI'06*, volume 3855 of *Lecture Notes in Computer Science*, 2006.

[BPT07] A. Bauer, M. Pister, and M. Tautschnig. Tool-support for the analysis of hybrid systems and models. In R. Lauwereins and J. Madsen, editors, *Design, Automation, and Test in Europe, DATE'07*, pages 924–929. ACM, 2007.

[BS81] S. Burris and H.P. Sankappanavar. *A Course in Universal Algebra*. Springer, 1981.

[BT02] F. Baader and C. Tinelli. Deciding the word problem in the union of equational theories. *Information and Computation*, 178(2):346–390, 2002.

[BT07] C. Barrett and C. Tinelli. CVC3. In W. Damm and H. Hermanns, editors, *Computer Aided Verification, CAV'07*, volume 4590 of *Lecture Notes in Computer Science*, pages 298–302. Springer, 2007.

[Bur86] P. Burmeister. *A Model Theoretic Approach to Partial Algebras. Introduction to Theory and Application of Partial Algebras, Part 1*, volume 31 of *Mathematical Research*. Akademie-Verlag, Berlin, 1986.

[Bur95] S. Burris. Polynomial time uniform word problems. *Mathematical Logic Quarterly*, 41:173–182, 1995.

[CK90] C. C. Chang and J. J. Keisler. *Model Theory*. North-Holland, Amsterdam, 1990.

[Cra57] W. Craig. Three uses of the Herbrand-Gentzen theorem in relating model theory and proof theory. *The Journal of Symbolic Logic*, 22(3):269–285, 1957.

[Dal04] D. van Dalen. *Logic and Structure*. Springer, 4th edition, 2004.

[DdM06] B. Dutertre and L. M. de Moura. A fast linear-arithmetic solver for DPLL(T). In T. Ball and R. B. Jones, editors, *Computer Aided Verification, CAV'06*, volume 4144 of *Lecture Notes in Computer Science*, pages 81–94. Springer, 2006.

[dM09] L. M. de Moura. SMT@Microsoft. Talk given at the Max-Planck-Institut für Informatik, Saarbrücken, Germany, 2009. Slides available at http://research.microsoft.com/en-us/um/people/leonardo/mpi2009.pdf.

[dMB08] L. M. de Moura and N. Bjørner. Z3: An efficient SMT solver. In C. R. Ramakrishnan and J. Rehof, editors, *Tools and Algorithms for the Construction and Analysis of Systems, TACAS'08*, volume 4963 of *Lecture Notes in Computer Science*, pages 337–340. Springer, 2008.

[DP90] B. A. Davey and H. A. Priestly. *Introduction to Lattices and Order*. Cambridge University Press, 1990.

[DS97] A. Dolzmann and T. Sturm. Redlog: computer algebra meets computer logic. *SIGSAM Bulletin*, 31(2):2–9, 1997.

[EFT96] H. D. Ebbinghaus, J. Flum, and W. Thomas. *Einführung in die mathematische Logik*. HochschulTaschenbuch. Spektrum-Akademie Verlag, Heidelberg, 1996.

[End02] H. B. Enderton. *A Mathematical Introduction to Logic*. Harcourt Academic press, 2nd edition, 2002.

[ES71] P. Eklof and G. Sabbagh. Model completions and modules. *Annals of Mathematical Logic*, (2):251–295, 1971.

[Eva51] T. Evans. The word problem for abstract algebras. *Journal of the London Mathematical Society*, 26:64–71, 1951.

[FHT+07] M. Fränzle, C. Herde, T. Teige, S. Ratschan, and T. Schubert. Efficient solving of large non-linear arithmetic constraint systems with complex boolean structure. *Journal on Satisfiability, Boolean Modeling and Computation*, 1(3-4):209–236, 2007.

[FIJSS10] J. Faber, C. Ihlemann, S. Jacobs, and V. Sofronie-Stokkermans. Automatic verification of parametric specifications with complex topologies. In *Integrated Formal Methods, iFM'10*, Lecture Notes in Computer Science. Springer, 2010. To appear.

[FRZ04] P. Fontaine, S. Ranise, and C. G. Zarba. Combining lists with non-stably infinite theories. In F. Baader and A. Voronkov, editors, *Logic for Programming, Artificial Intelligence, and Reasoning, LPAR'04*, volume 3452 of *Lecture Notes in Computer Science*, pages 51–66. Springer, 2004.

[Gan01] H. Ganzinger. Relating semantic and proof-theoretic concepts for polynomial time decidability of uniform word problems. In *Logic in Computer Science, LICS'01*, pages 81–92. IEEE Computer Society Press, 2001.

[Gan02]   H. Ganzinger. Shostak light. In A. Voronkov, editor, *Conference on Automated Deduction, CADE-18*, volume 2392 of *Lecture Notes in Computer Science*, pages 332–346. Springer, 2002.

[GdM09]   Y. Ge and L. M. de Moura. Complete instantiation for quantified formulas in satisfiability modulo theories. In A. Bouajjani and O. Maler, editors, *Computer Aided Verification, CAV'09*, volume 5643 of *Lecture Notes in Computer Science*, pages 306–320. Springer, 2009.

[Ghi03a] S. Ghilardi. Quantifier elimination and provers integration. In *First Order Theorem Proving (FTP'03)*, volume 86 of *Electronic Notes in Theoretical Computer Science*, 2003.

[Ghi03b] S. Ghilardi. Reasoners' cooperation and quantifier elimination. Rapporto Interno 288-03, Dipartimento di Scienze dell'Informazione, Università degli Studi di Milano, 2003.

[Ghi04]   S. Ghilardi. Model-theoretic methods in combined constraint satisfiability. *Journal of Automated Reasoning*, 33(3-4):221–249, 2004.

[GM92]   R. Givan and D. A. McAllester. New results on local inference relations. In B. Nebel, C. Rich, and W. R. Swartout, editors, *Knowledge Representation and Reasoning, KR'92*, pages 403–412, 1992.

[GM05]   J. Gispert and D. Mundici. MV-algebras: A variety for magnitudes with archimedean units. *Algebra Universalis*, 53:7–43, 2005.

[GNRZ06] S. Ghilardi, E. Nicolini, S. Ranise, and D. Zucchelli. Deciding extensions of the theory of arrays by integrating decision procedures and instantiation strategies. In M. Fisher, W. van der Hoek, B. Konev, and A. Lisitsa, editors, *European Conference on Logic in Artificial Intelligence, JELIA'06*, volume 4160 of *Lecture Notes in Artificial Intelligence*, pages 177–189. Springer, 2006.

[GNRZ07] S. Ghilardi, E. Nicolini, S. Ranise, and D. Zucchelli. Combination methods for satisfiability and model-checking of infinite-state systems. Rapporto Interno 313-07, Dipartimento di Scienze dell'Informazione, Università degli Studi di Milano, 2007.

[GNRZ08] S. Ghilardi, E. Nicolini, S. Ranise, and D. Zucchelli. Towards SMT model checking of array-based systems. In A. Armando, P. Baumgartner, and G. Dowek, editors, *International Joint Conference on Automated Reasoning, IJCAR'08*, volume 5195 of *Lecture Notes in Computer Science*, pages 67–82. Springer, 2008.

[GNZ05]   S. Ghilardi, E. Nicolini, and D. Zucchelli. A comprehensive framework for combined decision procedures. In *Frontiers of Combining Systems, FroCos'05*, volume 3717 of *Lecture Notes in Computer Science*, pages 1–30. Springer, 2005.

[GSSW04] H. Ganzinger, V. Sofronie-Stokkermans, and U. Waldmann. Modular proof systems for partial functions with weak equality. In D. Basin and M. Rusinowitch, editors, *International Joint Conference on Automated Reasoning, IJCAR'04*, volume 3097 of *Lecture Notes in Artificial Intelligence*, pages 168–182. Springer, 2004.

[GSSW06] H. Ganzinger, V. Sofronie-Stokkermans, and U. Waldmann. Modular proof systems for partial functions with Evans equality. *Information and Computation*, 204(10):1453–1492, October 2006.

[Häh03] R. Hähnle. Complexity of many-valued logics. In M. Fitting and E. Orlowska, editors, *Beyond Two: Theory and Applications of Multiple Valued Logic*, volume 114 of *Studies in Fuzziness and Soft Computing*, chapter 3, pages 211–233. Springer, Berlin, 2003.

[Hil04] T. Hillenbrand. A superposition view on Nelson-Oppen. In U. Sattler, editor, *Contributions to the Doctoral Programme of the Second International Joint Conference on Automated Reasoning*, volume 106 of *CEUR Workshop Proceedings*, pages 16–20, 2004.

[Hod93] W. Hodges. *Model Theory*. Cambridge University Press, 1993.

[Hod97] W. Hodges. *A Shorter Model Theory*. Cambridge University Press, 1997.

[IJSS08] C. Ihlemann, S. Jacobs, and V. Sofronie-Stokkermans. On local reasoning in verification. In C. R. Ramakrishnan and J. Rehof, editors, *Tools and Algorithms for the Construction and Analysis of Systems, TACAS'08*, volume 4963 of *Lecture Notes in Computer Science*, pages 265–281. Springer, 2008.

[ISS09] C. Ihlemann and V. Sofronie-Stokkermans. System description: H-PILoT. In R. A. Schmidt, editor, *Conference on Automated Deduction, CADE-22*, volume 5663 of *Lecture Notes in Artificial Intelligence*, pages 131–139. Springer, 2009.

[ISS10a] C. Ihlemann and V. Sofronie-Stokkermans. On hierarchical reasoning in combinations of theories. In J. Giesl and R. Hähnle, editors, *International Joint Conference on Automated Reasoning, IJCAR'10*. Springer, 2010. To appear.

[ISS10b] C. Ihlemann and V. Sofronie-Stokkermans. On hierarchical reasoning in combinations of theories. AVACS Technical Report No 60, 2010. SFB/TR 14 AVACS.

[ISS10c] C. Ihlemann and V. Sofronie-Stokkermans. System description: H-PILoT. AVACS Technical Report No 61, 2010. SFB/TR 14 AVACS.

[JSS07] S. Jacobs and V. Sofronie-Stokkermans. Applications of hierarchical reasoning in the verification of complex systems. *Electronic Notes in Theoretical Computer Science*, 174(8):39–54, 2007.

[Mac77] A. Macintyre. Model completeness. In J. Barwise, editor, *Handbook of Mathematical Logic*, pages 139–180. North-Holland, Amsterdam, 1977.

[Mal71]   A. I. Mal'cev. Axiomatizable classes of locally free algebras of various types. In Wells B. F. III, editor, *The Metamathematics of Algebraic Systems. Collected Papers: 1936-1967*, volume 66 of *Studies in Logic and the Foundation of Mathematics*, chapter 23. North-Holland, Amsterdam, 1971.

[McA93]   D. A. McAllester. Automatic recognition of tractability in inference relations. *Journal of the ACM*, 40(2):284–303, 1993.

[McK43]   J. C. C. McKinsey. The decision problem for some classes of sentences without quantifiers. *The Journal of Symbolic Logic*, 8(3):61–76, 1943.

[MN05]   S. McPeak and G. C. Necula. Data structure specifications via local equality axioms. In K. Etessami and S. K. Rajamani, editors, *Computer Aided Verification, CAV'05*, volume 3576 of *Lecture Notes in Computer Science*, pages 476–490. Springer, 2005.

[NO79]   G. Nelson and D. C. Oppen. Simplification by cooperating decision procedures. *ACM Transactions on Programming Languages and Systems*, 1(2):245–257, 1979.

[NW01]   A. Nonnengart and C. Weidenbach. Computing small clause normal forms. In A. Robinson and A. Voronkov, editors, *Handbook of Automated Reasoning*, chapter 6, pages 335 – 367. Elsevier, Amsterdam, 2001.

[Opp80a]   D. C. Oppen. Complexity, convexity and combinations of theories. *Theoretical Computer Science*, 12:291–302, 1980.

[Opp80b]   D. C. Oppen. Reasoning about recursively defined data structures. *Journal of the ACM*, 27(3):403–411, 1980.

[PG86]   D. A. Plaisted and S. Greenbaum. A structure-preserving clause form translation. *Journal of Symbolic Computation*, 2(3):293–304, 1986.

[Pre29]   M. Presburger. Über die Vollständigkeit eines gewissen Systems der Arithmetik ganzer Zahlen, in welchem die Addition als einzige Operation hervortritt. *Comptes Rendu du Premier Congrès des Mathématicienes des Pays Slaves*, pages 92–101, 1929.

[RRZ05]   S. Ranise, C. Ringeissen, and C. G. Zarba. Combining data structures with nonstably infinite theories using many-sorted logic. In B. Gramlich, editor, *Frontiers of Combining Systems, FroCoS'05*, volume 3717 of *Lecture Notes in Computer Science*, pages 48–64. Springer, 2005.

[Sko20]   T. Skolem. Logisch-kombinatorische Untersuchungen über die Erfüllbarkeit und Beweisbarkeit mathematischer Sätze nebst einem Theorem über dichte Mengen. In *Skrifter utgit av Videnskabsselskapet i Kristiania, I. Matematisk-naturvidenskabelig klasse*, volume 4, pages 1–36. 1920. Reprinted as 1920a in T. Skolem, Selected Works in Logic (J. E. Fendstad, ed.), Scandinavian University Books, Universitetsforlaget, Oslo 1970, pp. 103-136.

[SS02]   V. Sofronie-Stokkermans. On uniform word problems involving bridging operators on distributive lattices. In U. Egly and C. Fermüller, editors, *Automated Reasoning with Analytic Tableaux and Related Methods, TABLEAUX'02*, volume 2381 of *Lecture Notes in Artificial Intelligence*, pages 235–250. Springer, 2002.

[SS03]   V. Sofronie-Stokkermans. Resolution-based decision procedures for the universal theory of some classes of distributive lattices with operators. *Journal of Symbolic Computation*, 36(6):891–924, 2003.

[SS05]   V. Sofronie-Stokkermans. Hierarchic reasoning in local theory extensions. In R. Nieuwenhuis, editor, *Conference on Automated Deduction, CADE-20*, volume 3632 of *Lecture Notes in Artificial Intelligence*, pages 219–234. Springer, 2005.

[SS06a]   V. Sofronie-Stokkermans. Interpolation in local theory extensions. In U. Furbach and N. Shankar, editors, *International Joint Conference on Automated Reasoning, IJCAR'06*, volume 4130 of *Lecture Notes in Artificial Intelligence*, pages 235–250. Springer, 2006.

[SS06b]   V. Sofronie-Stokkermans. Local reasoning in verification. In S. Autexier and H. Mantel, editors, *Verification Workshop, VERIFY'06*, 2006.

[SS07]   V. Sofronie-Stokkermans. Hierarchical and modular reasoning in complex theories: The case of local theory extensions. In B. Konev and F. Wolter, editors, *Frontiers of Combining Systems, FroCos'07*, volume 4720 of *Lecture Notes in Computer Science*, pages 47–71. Springer, 2007.

[SS08]   V. Sofronie-Stokkermans. Efficient hierarchical reasoning about functions over numerical domains. In A. Dengel, K. Berns, T. M. Breuel, F. Bomarius, and T. Roth-Berghofer, editors, *Advances in Artificial Intelligence, 31st Annual German Conference on AI, KI'08*, volume 5243 of *Lecture Notes in Computer Science*, pages 135–143. Springer, 2008.

[SS10]   V. Sofronie-Stokkermans. On combinations of local theory extensions. In *Workshop on Programming Logics in memory of Harald Ganzinger, WPLHG'05*. To appear, 2010.

[SSI07a]   V. Sofronie-Stokkermans and C. Ihlemann. Automated reasoning in some local extensions of ordered structures. *Journal of Multiple-Valued Logics and Soft Computing*, 13(4-6):397–414, 2007.

[SSI07b]   V. Sofronie-Stokkermans and C. Ihlemann. Automated reasoning in some local extensions of ordered structures. In *International Symposium on Multiple-Valued Logic, ISMVL'07*. IEEE Computer Society, 2007.

[Tin03]   C. Tinelli. Cooperation of background reasoners in theory reasoning by residue sharing. *Journal of Automated Reasoning*, 30(1):1–31, 2003.

[Tin07]　C. Tinelli. The impact of Craig's Interpolation Theorem in computer science. Invited talk at *Interpolations: A conference in honor of William Craig*, 2007. Slides available at http://www.cs.uiowa.edu/~tinelli/html/talks.html.

[TR03]　C. Tinelli and C. Ringeissen. Unions of non-disjoint theories and combinations of satisfiability procedures. *Theoretical Computer Science*, 290(1):291–353, 2003.

[TZ05]　C. Tinelli and C. G. Zarba. Combining nonstably infinite theories. *Journal of Automated Reasoning*, 34(3):209–238, 2005.

[WDF+09]　C. Weidenbach, D. Dimova, A. Fietzke, R. Kumar, M. Suda, and P. Wischnewski. SPASS version 3.5. In R. A. Schmidt, editor, *Conference on Automated Deduction, CADE-22*, volume 5663 of *Lecture Notes in Artificial Intelligence*, pages 140–145. Springer, 2009.

[Wei88]　V. Weispfenning. The complexity of linear problems in fields. *Journal of Symbolic Computation*, 5(1/2):3–27, 1988.

[Whe76]　W. H. Wheeler. Model-companions and definability in existentially complete structures. *Israel Journal of Mathematics*, 25:305–330, 1976.

[ZSM05]　T. Zhang, H. B. Sipma, and Z. Manna. The decidability of the first-order theory of Knuth-Bendix order. In R. Nieuwenhuis, editor, *Conference on Automated Deduction, CADE-20*, volume 3632 of *Lecture Notes in Artificial Intelligence*, pages 131–148, 2005.

[ZSM06]　T. Zhang, H. B. Sipma, and Z. Manna. Decision procedures for term algebras with integer constraints. *Information and Computation*, 204(10):1526–1574, 2006.

Index

$\mathcal{A} \preccurlyeq \mathcal{B}$, 13
$\mathcal{A} \equiv \mathcal{B}$, 15
$\mathcal{A}_\Theta$, 64
(Comp_s), 26
(Comp_w), 26
(Comp_w^Ψ), 65
(EEmb_w^Ψ), 65
(ELoc^Ψ), 67
(Emb_s), 26
(Emb_w), 26
$(\mathsf{Emb}_w^{\mathsf{fd}})$, 26
(Emb_w^Ψ), 65
$\mathcal{K}[G]$, 32
$\mathcal{K}[\Psi]$, 64
$\mathcal{K}[\Theta]$, 64
$\mathcal{K}^{[G]}$, 35
$\mathcal{K}{<}\Theta{>}$, 50
(Loc), 32
(Loc^Ψ), 67
$\mathsf{PMod}_s(\Sigma_1, T_1)$, 26
$\mathsf{PMod}_w(\Sigma_1, T_1)$, 26
$\mathsf{PMod}_w^\Psi(\Sigma_1, T_1)$, 65
$\Phi^{[P]}$, 72
Ψ-
    completability, 65
    embeddability, 65
    locality, 67
Σ_1-flat, 28
Σ_1-linear, 28
Σ_1-quasiflat, 28
$\mathsf{est}(\mathcal{K}, \Gamma)$, 63
$\forall\exists$-formula, 10
$\forall$-
    elimination, 15
    introduction, 15
$\forall\exists$-fragment
    of a theory, 38
κ-categorical, 86

amalgamate, 78
amalgamation property (AP), 78
array property, 52
array property fragment, 51, 52
Λ-, 59
atom, 9
augmented clause, 27
    universal, 27
bound variables, 10

carrier, 11
clausal word problem, 31
clause, 10
compatible (theory), 80
completability
    of partial models, 26
completion
    of a poset, 43
conjunctive normal form, 10
cotheories, 77
Craig's Interpolation Theorem, 15

Dedekind-MacNeille completion
    of a poset, 43
deductive closure, 10
definitional extension, 102
dense, 42
depth
    of a term, 9
description logics, 43
diagram, 14
    partial, 26
domain
    of a partial function, 17

elementarily equivalent, 15
elementary
    diagram, 14
    embedding, 13
    extension, 13
    substructure, 13
embeddability
    of partial models, 26
embedding, 13
equivalent, 12
existential formula, 10
expansion
    of a structure, 13
extended pointer clause, 72
extension
    of a structure, 13

finitely local, 32
finitely stably local, 36
first-order language, 9
formula, 9
    closed, 10
    open, 10
    preserved under map, 12
    quantifier-free, 10
    true in a structure, 11
free variables, 10
fresh constants, 13

ground
    formula, 10
    term, 10

homomorphism, 12

image
    of a partial function, 17
index guard, 52
    with Λ, 58
interpolation, 4
isomorphism, 13

join, 42
join-dense, 42
joint embedding property (JEP), 77

lattice, 42
    complete, 42
Lemma
    on Constants, 15
    on Constants for partial algebras, 22
    on diagrams, 14
linear order, 41
literal, 10
local extension, 32
    stable, 35
local instances, 32

maximal element
    of a poset, 41
meet, 42
meet-dense, 42
minimal
    embeddability, 50
    locality, 50
    model, 50
minimal element
    of a poset, 41
model, 11
    companion, 78
    completion, 78
model complete theory, 16, 75
monotone function, 41
monotonicity
    of semantic consequence, 12

negation normal form, 10
    not enough to ensure locality, 34
nullable, 71

open, 10

partial function, 17
partial model, 19
partial order, 40
partial semantics, 18
pointer fragment, 72
poset, 40
positive diagram, 14
Presburger arithmetic, 51

preserved in union of chains
    formula, 16
projection, 53
    with additional constant, 59
quantifier elimination
    theory admitting, 16
read set, 50
reduct
    of a structure, 13
root
    of a term, 9
satisfiable
    formula, 12
    set of formulas, 12
semantic consequence, 12
semilattice, 42
sentence, 10
shielded
    variable, 38
signature, 9
stably local instances, 35
strong partial model of a theory, 26
structure, 11
submodel completeness, 79
substitution, 10
Substitution lemma, 13
    for partial algebras, 20
substructure, 13
    generated by a set, 13
subterm, 9

table of a partial algebra, 65
taut operator, 63
term, 9
term closure operator, 63
theorem
    Chang-Łos-Susko, 16
    compactness, 12
    elementary chain, 16
    interpolation, 15
    Löwenheim-Skolem, 15

theory, 10
    complete, 15
    of arrays, 51
theory of acyclic lists, 77
total order, 41
types, 12

union of chain, 16
    of partial models, 89
universal
    clause, 10
    formula, 10
universal closure
    of a formula, 10
universal fragment
    of a theory, 38
universally closed
    clause, 10
unsatisfiable
    formula, 12
    set of formulas, 12

valuation, 11
variable abstraction, 24
variables, 9

weak
    Π-embedding, 22
    Π-homomorphism, 22
    partial model of a theory, 25
    substructure, 22

Die VDM Verlagsservicegesellschaft sucht für wissenschaftliche Verlage abgeschlossene und herausragende

Dissertationen, Habilitationen, Diplomarbeiten, Master Theses, Magisterarbeiten usw.

für die kostenlose Publikation als Fachbuch.

Sie verfügen über eine Arbeit, die hohen inhaltlichen und formalen Ansprüchen genügt, und haben Interesse an einer honorarvergüteten Publikation?

Dann senden Sie bitte erste Informationen über sich und Ihre Arbeit per Email an *info@vdm-vsg.de*.

Sie erhalten kurzfristig unser Feedback!

VDM Verlagsservicegesellschaft mbH
Dudweiler Landstr. 99
D - 66123 Saarbrücken
www.vdm-vsg.de

Telefon +49 681 3720 174
Fax   +49 681 3720 1749

Die VDM Verlagsservicegesellschaft mbH vertritt

Printed by Books on Demand GmbH, Norderstedt / Germany